D1171845

WATERGATE
AND THE
CONSTITUTION

THE WILLIAM R. KENAN, JR.
INAUGURAL LECTURES
The College
The University of Chicago

WATERGATE AND THE CONSTITUTION

Philip B. Kurland

The University of Chicago Press

Chicago and London

The University of Chicago Press, Chicago 60637
The University of Chicago Press, Ltd., London

Published 1978
Printed in the United States of America

82 81 80 79 78 6 5 4 3 2 1

Library of Congress Cataloging in Publication Data

Kurland, Philip B
Watergate and the Constitution.

(The William R. Kenan, Jr., inaugural lectures)
Includes bibliographical references and index.
1. Separation of powers—United States.
2. United States—Constitutional law. 3. Watergate Affair, 1972– I. Title. II. Series.
KF4565.K87 342′.73′062 77–18338
ISBN 0–226–46393–1

To Mary Jane
and
Julie, Martha, and Ellen
My fair lady and
our fair ladies

Contents

Great critics have taught us one essential rule. . . . It is this, that if ever we should find ourselves disposed not to admire those writers or artists, Livy and Virgil for instance, Raphael or Michelangelo, whom all the learned had admired, not to follow our own fancies, but to study them until we know how and what we ought to admire; and if we cannot arrive at this combination of admiration with knowledge, rather to believe that we are dull, than that the rest of the world has been imposed on. It is as good a rule, at least, with regard to this admired constitution. We ought to understand it according to our measure; and to venerate where we are not able presently to comprehend.

—Edmund Burke

Gloucester, 'tis true that we are in great danger;
The greater therefore should our courage be.

. . . .

There is some soul of goodness in things evil,
Would men observingly distil it out;

—William Shakespeare, *Henry V*

You remember in The Cloister on the Hearth, *in tight moments how Gerard's companion used to say*: "Courage, mon ami, le diable est mort." *No, my friends, the devil isn't dead; but take heart of grace; we shall get him yet!*

—Learned Hand, *The Spirit of Liberty*

Preface

This is neither a text nor a treatise on either Watergate or the Constitution. It is rather a series of essays meant for nonlawyers on the theme perhaps best described as the constitution and reconstitution of the Constitution. I have chosen the essay form here, as I have done before, because as Felix Frankfurter once said, "the essay is tentative, reflective, suggestive, contradictory and incomplete. It mirrors the perversities and complexities of life." It also allows for repetition of the same themes in different contexts, which I have indulged here. The tone is frequently, I admit, acerbic, ironic, sardonic, iconoclastic, for which I offer no apologies, because I think this tone appropriate to the subject matter. And, as La Rochefoucauld would have it: "No one merits praise for his kindness if he does not have the strength to be mean."

Once again, I am indebted to my secretary, Mrs. Artie Scott, for the conversion of my manuscript into readable text. This is the umpteenth of the books I have written or edited that she has made ready for publication through prodigious efforts under unfair pressures. I am obligated, too, to Mr. Burt Rublin for suggestions about content and for eliminating many, if not all, errors of reference, grammar, and syntax. And to my students in The College of the University of Chicago, to whom the material herein was presented in the form of lectures for their questioning and criticism, I would express my thanks both for their tolerance and their intolerance of opinions that were often so distant from their own.

Mr. Edward I. Rothschild and Professor Daniel D. Polsby read the manuscript with care. They pointed out errors of fact and errors of judgment. I have corrected the errors of fact. I am grateful to them.

The William R. Kenan, Jr., Foundation, whose chair I occupy at the University of Chicago, has supported heterodoxy in undergraduate teaching and has afforded an example of beneficence to universities that other foundations might do well to emulate. The inaugural lectures which were derived from the contents of this volume were proudly delivered on this Foundation, without seeking its permission to do so. I can only hope that the trustees will be tolerant of my presumption and that the lectures may prove worthy of their unknowing sponsors.

In the spring of 1974 I had the honor to deliver the inaugural Law Memorial Lectures at the University of Mississippi School of Law. It was a happy and intellectually profitable occasion for me. Much of chapter 6 is borrowed from those lectures, for which I am under additional obligation to my gracious hosts on that occasion.

I

By Way of Introduction

Still one more book on the subject of Watergate certainly requires an excuse. My excuse is that I really do not propose to dwell on the events of Watergate. Those events only afford background. I shall speak, rather, about the constitutional questions that were implicitly or explicitly raised by those events.

Certainly I shall not try to tell the "inside story" of Watergate. I could not, if I would. I was never on the "inside": not of the Senate Select Committee; not of the special prosecutor's office; not of the judicial proceedings; nor yet of the House Judiciary Committee. I was once called upon by the chairman of the Select Committee, along with Alexander M. Bickel, to offer advice on the invocation of the judicial process by the committee. Our advice was not followed. It would have made no difference if it had been. But that is the only direct knowledge of Watergate activity that has come within my ken. Thus, I know nothing of the events of Watergate, except that which has appeared in public print.

Those interested in the "inside story" of Watergate will find that it is more than a "twice-told tale." It has been told many times, if seldom without the author's sense of self-importance getting in the way of the objectivity of the story. Leon Jaworski, the special prosecutor who succeeded Archibald Cox after the "Saturday night massacre," has told his "inside story" in a book entitled *The Right and the Power*. The Senate Select Committee's chief counsel, Samuel Dash, has also told his "inside story," with the title *Chief Counsel* and the subtitle, "Inside the Ervin Committee—The Untold Story of Watergate." These two tellings are essentially in controversy only over the question who is the greater hero. The White House staff has also told the "inside story" several times. Examples are John Dean's *Blind Ambition*; Jeb Magruder's *An American Life: One Man's Road to Watergate*; John Ehrlichman's *The Company*. Only the last is avowedly in the form of fiction. These stories are essentially in controversy only over the question who is the greatest villain. The Ehrlichman novel would place the blame on the CIA, thus joining a growing number of Americans in the belief that the CIA is the root cause of all our problems of political immorality.

The press, too, has had its say. Particularly noteworthy, certainly particularly remunerative, were Woodward and Bernstein's *All the President's Men* and *The Final Days.* Close behind on both counts was T. R. White's *Breach of Faith,* expressing a feeling of personal betrayal at President Nixon's behavior. For me, the best of the lot of these journalists' stories was Elizabeth Drew's *Washington Journal,* perhaps because it claimed no insider's knowledge. Drew's is an outsider's picture, well drawn, and the more objective because the first person singular was only the teller of the tale and not a participant either in the plot or the uncovering of it.

I refer you to these volumes and many others like them for explication of the facts of Watergate. Their concern is with personalities and drama and the assignment of culpability for distressing events. That is the stuff for novels and muckrakers—and the never-ending processes of the courts of criminal justice.

Many have treated Watergate as Lady Macbeth would have done her "damned spot."[1] Some with more success. All they asked was to put the memory of the evil behind us: not to forgive but only to forget. Still others have spent their time affixing personal blame. These have usually been concerned with the delineation of the warped personalities of President Nixon and his White House henchmen. An eminent psychiatrist, David Abrahamsen, brought out a psychiatric study with a legal title, *Nixon v. Nixon.* But this approach tends to reject the relevance of institutional failures. For many of these, as for many other Americans, the substitution in government of the righteous for the iniquitous will assure a cure of all our governmental ills.

The lust for personal power may, indeed, be the root of all evil. And, certainly, it cannot be gainsaid that acquisition of power may itself turn the righteous into the iniquitous. David Kipnis, for example, speaks of the metamorphosis of a powerholder. And he invokes the analogy of Greek tragedy, as did so many Watergate commentators, especially after the Nixon resignation. Kipnis, a psychologist, wrote:[2]

> The existence of metamorphic effects has been recognized from almost the earliest writings of man concerning the use of power. The Greek dramatists were particularly sensitive to the fate of persons who were at the high tide of their power and status. In the plays of Sophocles, for instance, the viewer is confronted with the image of great and powerful rulers transformed by their prior successes so that they are filled with a sense of their own worth and importance—with

> "hubris"—impatient of the advice of others and unwilling to listen to opinions that disagree with their own. Yet, in the end they are destroyed by events, which they discover, to their own anguish, that they cannot control. . . . Too often arrogance, bred of power, finally causes its own defeat and unhappy ending.

To treat Watergate as personal tragedy, however, is to ignore its fundamental dangers. That attitude speaks to the fall of Oedipus and Creon, but not to the consequences to the people of Corinth and Thebes. Surely one of the issues posed by Watergate was how to bring down the powerful leader who abused his authority and, at the same time, preserve the state from revolution that could spawn anarchy or totalitarianism. More important, I venture, is the question, How does one prevent the accession to such power by the just and unjust alike?

Some of our wiser Supreme Court Justices have reminded us: "Evil men are rarely given power; they take it over from better men to whom it had been entrusted."[3] One of these judges has also pointed out what we know to be true: "The accretion of dangerous power does not come in a day. It does come, however slowly, from the generative force of unchecked disregard of the restrictions that fence in even the most disinterested assertion of authority."[4]

There are some wise men who find no danger to liberty in power itself but only in its abuse, which is not, for them, a necessary corollary. Even these, however, would concede a reasoned basis for apprehension. And their suggestion is to take the path that the American constitution writers took in 1787. Thus, Lord Radcliffe wrote:[5]

> One attitude is to be afraid of power. That is not a poor or cowardly attitude in face of the reckless use that men have made of their authority over other men. But if mistrust is the dominant note, then it may be best expressed by such constitutional devices as those of the American Constitution. Power is placed under restraint; it is deliberately shared out so that it cannot all be grasped in the same hand.

The remarkable men who framed our government almost two hundred years ago were indeed convinced of the need to protect against concentration of governmental power. None can read the basic document without becoming quickly cognizant that the new governmental authority was limited by division and hedged by restraints. However much and however often we are told that sovereignty is indivisible, it remains clear that the writers of the Constitution sought to divide it, first, between the nation and the states; second, within the national government, by allocation of powers among three branches; third, within the national government, by providing checks and balances of each branch on the others; and, finally, by providing a Bill of Rights which forbade the national government to act at all on certain aspects of the lives of Americans.

As Justice Brandeis once wrote:[6]

> The doctrine of the separation of powers was adopted by the Convention of 1787, not to promote efficiency but to preclude the exercise of arbitrary power. The purpose was, not to avoid friction, but, by means of the inevitable friction incident to the distribution of the governmental powers among three departments, to save the people from autocracy.

The crisis of Watergate was a crisis of cumulated power. The *Oxford English Dictionary* defines crisis as "the point in the progress of a disease when an important development or change takes place which is decisive of recovery or death." In this instance, death was avoided. And many have pronounced us cured. The distinguished historian Henry Steele Commager, in a postscript to his book, *The Defeat of America: Presidential Power and the National Character*, withdrew from the pessimism of the title and wrote:[7]

> Confronted, for the first time in our long history, with a chief magistrate who betrayed his oath of office, we have resorted to that "magistracy of the law" and vindicated once again the wisdom of the Founding Fathers. Thus, we have demonstrated to the world and, let us hope, to future generations that the Constitution is alive and well, that it can be adapted to the exigencies of governance and that in an emergency an enlightened and determined democracy can protect and defend its principles, its honor and its heritage.

The notion that because we have come through one critical period we have been restored to health is more wish than reality. Perhaps we have removed a cancerous growth that could have killed us. We have not rid the system of the disease. And we shan't do so simply by saying that people are going to be different.

The constitutional limitations on power have been eaten away slowly but surely. There is no longer a division of sovereignty between the nation and the states; the sovereign power is entirely in the nation. There are only tenuous remnants of the concepts of separation of powers and checks and balances within the national government. Power has accumulated in the executive branch and, at least through the Watergate period and probably beyond, in the White House Office. The only countervailing force to the White House within the executive is the bureaucracy, which acknowledges no superior; it stays on to watch White House staffs and Presidents and cabinet officers come and go. (Anyone who reads of the English bureaucracy in Richard Crossman's

Diaries of a Cabinet Minister and Iris Murdoch's *A Word Child* will understand the awesome power and the equally awesome waste of bureaucratic government.) Congress has become a decaying House of Lords. Meanwhile the courts have carved out a duchy of their own, free of both legislative and executive constraints and even free of the judicial restraints that were once found in an obligation to adhere to precedent. A dukedom to which sovereigns pay homage.

The constitutional crisis of Watergate was that anticipated in the youthful Shelley's lines from *Queen Mab*:[8]

> Power, like a desolating pestilence,
> Pollutes whate'er it touches.

Still more appropriate, I would suggest, are William Hazlitt's cynical observations:[9]

> Man is a toad-eating animal. The admiration of power in others is as common to man as the love of it in himself; the one makes him a tyrant, the other a slave.

The constitutional crisis of Watergate was the result of a long buildup of concentrated governmental power. It was the result of the failure to adhere to the limitations on authority that are explicit and implicit in the Constitution. It was the result of long denial of institutional values in favor of temporary political expediency. The tragedy of Watergate lies not in the pitiful character of the man exiled from the White House; it lies rather in the continued failure of the nation to take steps first to cabin and then to dissipate that accumulated power, the failure to revive our constitutional notions of limitations on authority. The flow to the government of power over the lives of Americans has been at flood tide for generations. There is still no sign of ebbing.

Faith in those chosen to succeed the fallen Nixon will not suffice. Tolstoi told us: "In order to gain possession of power, and to retain it, one must have a love for it, and the love of power is incompatible with goodness; it accords with the opposite qualities of pride, duplicity, and cruelty."[10] It is this same understanding of the nature of man that underlay the writing of the Constitution of the United States. Thus, Benjamin Fletcher Wright, in his introduction to the John Harvard Library edition of *The Federalist*, wrote:[11]

> . . . the conception of human nature stated, reiterated, and depended upon in *The Federalist* is pessimistic or, in the most usual sense of the word, realistic. Men are not to be trusted with power, because they are selfish, passionate, full of whims, caprices, and prejudices. Men are not fully rational, calm, or dispassionate. Moreover, the nature of man is a constant; it has had these characteristics

> throughout recorded history. To assume that it will alter for the better would be a betrayal of generations unborn.

Madison made the point clearly in *The Federalist* No. 51, in words that may be overfamiliar to you:

> If men were angels, no government would be necessary. If angels were to govern men, neither external nor internal controls on government would be necessary. In framing a government which is to be administered by men over men, the great difficulty lies in this: you must first enable the government to control the governed; and in the next place oblige it to control itself. A dependence on the people is, no doubt, the primary control on the government, but experience has taught mankind the necessity of auxiliary precautions.

The failure to utilize "auxiliary precautions," the institutional limitations set out in the Constitution, was the cause of Watergate and remains the danger of its repetition with, perhaps, even more ominous effects.

This is not merely ancient learning. Benjamin V. Cohen, who shared some of the White House power of Franklin Delano Roosevelt, said in May of 1953:[12]

> The experience of the last quarter of a century would suggest that in a society where total power resides in a single organ under the effective control of a dominating personality or a small and united group of men, the law, as we know it, is likely to have little influence on the exercise of total power. Totalitarianism, no matter to what purposes or objectives it may be dedicated, tends to become total tyranny. It probably is no accident that communism and naziism, starting from opposed premises, become strikingly alike in practice. It is no accident that under totalitarian government procedural safeguards of individual rights do not exist or have little significance.
>
> Freedom depends not merely upon the letter of the law but upon the way power is organized, distributed, and controlled.

I shall not dwell further here on the basic element of the constitutional crisis of Watergate. This theme runs throughout the book. I shall also treat lesser, but by no means small, constitutional questions thrown up by the events of Watergate. Before I get to these specific questions, however, it is necessary to say something about the Constitution, to which we must resort for the answers to constitutional questions. For there is question not only about what the Constitution means but also about what the Constitution is.

We are all more or less familiar with the document that was written in 1787 called the Constitution of the United States and that has been amended formally some twenty-six times. The concept of a written constitution marked both the American and the French Revolutions and many revisions of national governments that have occurred since. The concept of the written constitution is that it defines the authority of government and its limits, that government is the creature of the constitution and cannot do what it does not authorize and must not do what it forbids. *A priori*, such a constitution could have only a fixed and unchanging meaning, if it were to fulfill its function. For changed conditions, the instrument itself made provision for amendment which, in accordance with the concept of a written constitution, was expected to be the only form of change and, therefore, as Madison put it, "guards equally against that extreme facility, which would render the Constitution too mutable; and that extreme difficulty, which might perpetuate its discovered faults."[13]

Of more immediate interest is Madison's explanation why the Convention rejected the Jeffersonian notion that the written constitution should be subjected to continual revision and interpretation by the people themselves. Jefferson's *Notes on Virginia* had suggested that conventions be called both to alter the Constitution and for "correcting breaches of it,"[14] at the behest of two of the three branches.

Madison put the argument for such references to the people with some cogency, but his rejection of the master's position was not persuasive. It was clearly antidemocratic in tone, as had been so much of Madison's work at the Convention. The argument for resort to the people went like this:[15]

> As the people are the only legitimate fountain of power, and it is from them that the constitutional charter, under which the several branches of government hold their power, is derived, it seems strictly consonant to the republican theory, to recur to the same original authority, not only whenever it may be necessary to enlarge, diminish, or new-model the powers of the government, but also whenever any one of the departments may commit encroachments on the chartered authorities of the others. The several departments being perfectly coordinate by the terms of their common commission, none of them, it is evident, can pretend to an exclusive or superior right of settling the boundaries between their respective powers; and how are the encroachments of the stronger to be prevented, or the wrongs of the weaker to be redressed, without an appeal to the people themselves, who, as the grantors of the commission, can alone declare its true meaning, and enforce its observance?

The notion of the judicial branch as the ultimate arbiter of separation of powers or of the meaning of the Constitution was obviously not in Madison's mind when he was busy defending and selling the Constitution in *The Federalist*. His opposition to resort to the people rested on several grounds. One of these was that "frequent appeals" to the people for interpretation would[16]

> deprive the government of that veneration which time bestows on every thing, and without which perhaps the wisest and freest governments would not possess the requisite stability. . . . A reverence for the laws would be sufficiently inculcated by the voice of an enlightened reason. But a nation of philosophers is as little to be expected as the philosophical race of kings wished for by Plato. And in every other nation, the most rational government will not find it a superfluous advantage to have the prejudices of the community on its side.
>
> The danger of disturbing the public tranquility by interesting too strongly the public passions, is a still more serious objection against a frequent reference of constitutional questions to the decision of the whole society. Notwithstanding the success which has attended the revisions of our established forms of government, and which does so much honor to the virtue and intelligence of the people of America, it must be confessed that the experiments are of too ticklish a nature to be unnecessarily multiplied.

He concluded that "the greatest objection of all" is that "such appeals would not answer the purpose of maintaining the constitutional equilibrium of the government." This, he said, because "the tendency of republican governments is to an aggrandizement of the legislative at the expense of the other departments" and in an appeal to the people, the legislative branch would likely have the greatest sway over them. Clearly, Madison was not always prescient, for in our government, at least, it has been the aggrandizement of the executive and judicial branches that has put us in our contemporary difficulties.

In *The Federalist* No. 50 Madison devoted his time to rejecting the proposition "that instead of *occasional* appeals to the people, which are liable to the objections urged against them, *periodical* appeals are the proper and adequate means of *preventing and correcting infractions of the Constitution.*" Here he afforded no new arguments. Instead, he resorted to the Pennsylvania experience with a board of censors to resolve constitutional questions, which he found unsatisfactory because the membership was not apolitical, because it lacked the necessary talents, and because the legislature refused to abide by its judgment. In *The Federalist* No. 51, from which I have already quoted, Madison defended the system of checks and balances of each branch on the other as the proper means for avoiding constitutional violations and self-aggrandizement by any of the three branches.

The process of amending the Constitution has not been confined to the formal amendment processes set forth in Article V. Instead, other means have grown up and become dominant. Most amendments have come about because the document has been called on to function in a vastly changed and quickly changing world. The same words cannot mean the same thing for a Jeffersonian agricultural society and for a twentieth-century urban, industrial complex. The human political condition cannot remain constant when the human social condition has radically altered. Over the course of history, our country has moved from an "indestructible union of indestructible states" to a nation. This came about not by reason of laws but by reason of events, not least of which were the startling innovations in communication and transportation which have shrunk not only the nation but the world as well, with necessary effects on the constitutional allocations of authority. It is not that the Constitution's original language no longer has anything to say about the interstate commerce power, or the war power, or the foreign affairs power. What it has to say is necessarily different, however, from what it said when it was written and there were not yet steamships or mass-produced goods or revolvers, no less jet and rocket propulsion and atomic explosives. Changed societal conditions, in short, have provided one additional, extraordinarily important form of amendment of the Constitution.

A similar, but not the same, form of constitutional change is effected through the recognition of long-standing custom. When a power that is neither expressly conferred nor expressly forbidden by the Constitution is exercised by one branch of government over an extended period of time, it frequently comes to be accepted as legitimate. Of course, one cannot define the moment when such exercise or usurpation of power becomes valid. It is in this regard that the American and English constitutions, the one written and the other customary, reveal their similarities. But their difference in this matter is also of great interest. The ultimate arbiter of the amended status of the English constitution is its legislature; in the United States it is the judiciary.

The constitutional changes effected by changed conditions and custom do not write themselves into the Constitution. They have to be pronounced by an appropriate agency of government. It is, I think, the Secretary of State who certifies the legitimacy of a formal amendment to the Constitution. It is the Supreme Court that validates change by custom or altered social conditions or by simple fiat. Thus, the primary force for constitutional amendment in this country has become the judiciary. This is, itself, a constitutional amendment that has come about through custom and, in part at least, necessity.[17] Certainly the Constitution did not specifically provide for judicial review, no less for the Supreme Court's role as the final voice on the meaning of the Constitution. The two are not the same, although we no longer recognize the difference. Judicial review could provide for the supremacy of the Court as interpreter of the Constitution in the realm of the judiciary, *i.e.*, where the courts were called upon to resolve a case or controversy, leaving the other branches supreme in their own constitutionally delegated areas. Since, however, there are few issues that are no longer subject to the judicial process, judicial review has come to mean ultimate control over the Constitution's current meaning. The courts are no longer merely courts, *i.e.*, resolvers of disputes, but legislative bodies announcing fundamental principles and policies of government.

Although the concept of judicial review was more ignored than supported in *The Federalist*, with the exception of Hamilton's No. 78, there is little to dispute the expected supremacy of the Constitution in any controversy in which the Constitution weighs on one side and a state legislative or executive act or a state judicial act on the other. The controversy has raged, instead, over the capacity of the federal courts to render invalid national legislative or executive action that is not plainly inconsistent with constitutional language. To what degree, in other words, are the courts free to rewrite the Constitution, to decide that it proscribes or prescribes legislative or executive action?

Controversy over the proper role of the judiciary as architect rather than engineer of the Constitution has been a long-drawn-out one. One may mark four points on the one hundred and eighty degree arc that delineates the conception of judicial review, with recognition that every point on the arc has been marked out by one or more constitutionalists. To begin with there is the most simple of descriptions of the proper role of the Court. It is to be found in Justice Owen J. Roberts's opinion in *United States* v. *Butler*:[18]

> When an act of Congress is appropriately challenged in the courts as not conforming to the constitutional mandate the judicial branch of the Government has only one duty,—to lay the article of the Constitution which is invoked beside the statute which is challenged and to decide whether the latter squares with the former. All the court does, or can do, is to announce its considered judgment upon the question. The only power it has, if such it may be called, is the power of judgment. This court neither approves nor condemns any legislative policy. Its delicate and difficult office is to ascertain and declare whether the legislation is in accordance with, or in contravention of, the provisions of the Constitution; and, having done that, its duty ends.

This statement has been mocked as either jejune or sophistical, and it probably is both. The Constitution is not a T-square that even the most sophisticated carpenter can use to call forth a determination of constitutional congruity or incongruity. Nevertheless, it would behoove those whose disdain is invoked to compare Roberts's statement in *Butler* with Alexander Hamilton's description in *The Federalist* No. 78, or Chief Justice John Marshall's landmark opinion in *Marbury* v. *Madi-*

son.[19] The former assures us that the Court has neither force nor will but only judgment. The latter makes clear that only patent constitutional violations would incur judicial rejection by a declaration of unconstitutionality.

The next attitude would not rely solely on the words of the Constitution, as Roberts's opinion suggested, but on the true meaning of the words derived from the language plus history. It will appear strange to some that the foremost spokesman for this proposition is the late Justice Hugo L. Black, who contributed so much to the changing of the Constitution. Here is some of his language:[20]

> Our written Constitution means to me that where a power is not in terms granted or not necessary and proper to exercise a power that is granted, no such power exists in any branch of the government—executive, legislative, or judicial. Thus, it is language and history that are the crucial factors which influence me in interpreting the Constitution—not reasonableness or desirability as determined by justices of the Supreme Court.

Justice Black's views may be considered cynical, if we take his modification of the words of the Constitution to include implied powers that are, in the language of the Constitution, "necessary and proper." For long ago, Chief Justice Marshall, in strong reliance on earlier pronouncements by Hamilton, had declared "necessary and proper" to mean convenient and appropriate. The Marshall opinion affords an interesting example of adherence to the letter of the Constitution in its interpretation. For it turns out that the phrase "necessary and proper," after proper parsing, boils down to one of the most expansive rather than most restrictive means of reading the Constitution. "Let the end be legitimate, let it be within the scope of the constitution, and all means which are appropriate, which are plainly adapted to that end, which are not prohibited, but consist with the letter and spirit of the constitution, are constitutional."[21]

It should be noted here, what many have chosen to forget, that the Necessary and Proper Clause describes a congressional power and only a congressional power: it affords no additional authority to either the judicial or executive branch. And it should be noted that *McCulloch* v. *Maryland* was an exercise of judicial review that sustained national legislation even as it struck down state law.

Nevertheless, Justice Black made it clear that he did not mean to duck the application of the words of the Constitution by distorting them, as perhaps was done in *McCulloch*. And the example he adduces makes this more than clear:[22]

> Similarly, in the case this term of *Katz* v. *United States*, 389 U.S. 347, 364 (1967), I simply could not find that the words of the

> Fourth Amendment prohibiting unreasonable searches and seizures also prohibit eavesdropping. Fully realizing that an argument based on the meaning of words lacks the scope, and no doubt the appeal, of broad policy discussions and philosophical discourses on such nebulous subjects as privacy, I just cannot say that a conversation may be "searched" or "seized" within the ordinary and generally accepted meanings of those words. When this is reinforced by the historical evidence that the Framers were aware of the practice of eavesdropping, which is mentioned even in Blackstone's *Commentaries*, I cannot help but believe that if they had desired to outlaw or restrict the use of evidence obtained by such a practice, they would have used the appropriate language in the Fourth Amendment to do so.

It is a little surprising that the good Justice did not state that the language of the Fourth Amendment contains no exclusionary rule at all, nor did he note that what was involved in *Katz* was a telephone wiretap and that the language of the Constitution fails to inhibit because it makes no reference to telephonic wiretaps. But Justice Black was never one to read the Fourth Amendment broadly and was always one to pick a historical text that supported his position, rather than to rely on historical text to create his position. And since history is no more an objective science than law, Justice Black was not extraordinarily limited in the expression of his will by espousing the measure of constitutional language as defined by history.

Both the Roberts and Black positions may—in the context of this volume—be labeled as "strict constructionist" theory. But, as you see, "strict construction" is not a term to be strictly construed.

We come next to a school of construction of judicial power that I would call "the Constitution clearly means exactly what it says, at least when it says something, but there are many places in which its words are obscure and we must give them meaning" school. I expect this approach is best attributed to Justice Felix Frankfurter.

In a contemporary comment on the *Butler* case, which included the Roberts dictum that I have already quoted, Frankfurter said:[23]

> The Constitution contains a few provisions that are defined either by the technical nature of the terms used or canalized by their history. About such provisions, there is relatively little controversy. But there are other provisions, with vague phrases like "due process" or undefined concepts like "commerce among the States," or still broader assumptions underlying the whole document like the doctrine of the separation of powers and the whole conception of our federalism. It is when such vague or purposely ambiguous or large dynamic conceptions appear for arbitrament before the Court, that questions of more-or-less, of matters of degree and appraisals of policy necessarily come into play and control the controversy. Usually the precedents

are sufficiently open or sufficiently conflicting to permit the Court to choose either one series or the other as the starting point. And the choice of premise usually predetermines the conclusion.

Given such an open-ended conception of the judicial power of interpretation of the Constitution, Frankfurter and those like him were always called upon to explain how the judges' tasks consisted of anything but the expression in their opinions and judgments of their personal predilections. And the answer frequently forthcoming usually left the skeptic unconvinced that, under the Frankfurter view, the written constitution was anything more than a starting point for rationalization of those personal preferences.

After fifteen years of experience on the Supreme Court, Frankfurter said this to the American Philosophical Society in 1954:[24]

> A judge whose preoccupation is with such matters should be compounded of the faculties that are demanded of the historian and the philosopher and the prophet. The last demand upon him—to make some forecast of the consequences of his action—is perhaps the heaviest. To pierce the curtain of the future, to give shape and visage to mysteries still in the womb of time, is the gift of imagination. It requires poetic sensibilities with which judges are rarely endowed and which their education does not normally develop. These judges, you will infer, must have something of the creative artist in them; they must have antennae registering feeling and judgment beyond logical, let alone quantitative, proof.
>
> The decisions in the cases that really give trouble rest on judgment, and judgment derives from the totality of a man's nature and experience. Such judgment will be exercised by two types of men, broadly speaking, but of course with varying emphasis—those who express their private views or revelations, deeming them, if not *vox dei*, at least *vox populi*; or those who feel strongly that they have no authority to promulgate law by their merely personal view and whose whole training and proved performance substantially insure that their conclusions reflect understanding of, and due regard for, law as the expression of the views and feelings that may fairly be deemed representative of the community as a continuing society.

It was, of course, this second group that Frankfurter thought worthy of the judicial power. This was due, in part, to Frankfurter's extraordinary faith in democracy, which persistently and adversely affected his image as a "liberal." But such freedom of judgment was denounced by Justice Black as a new form of "natural law," which forms no part of our Constitution.[25]

Two strings to Frankfurter's bow may be seen in the quotations. First, there are two different kinds of provisions in the Constitution, those that are fixed and were intended to be fixed, and those that are open and dependent for their meaning on the circumstances that give rise to their application. The second is concerned with the behavior of the judge presumably both in defining which provisions are open and which are closed and then in determining the proper application of the open provisions. Some constitutional provisions are open because they defy definition, even with the aid of history; some are open because there is no original history, *i.e.*, no gloss from the quills of the Founding Fathers; some are open because there is an overabundance of gloss from the pens of the authors; but then some are open only because original meaning is inconsistent with present judicial notions of necessity or desirability. While it is clear that the debates at the Convention in 1787 or in the later ratifying conventions do not give meaning to the words of the Constitution as a dictionary would, yet they do afford possibilities for resolving ambiguities—where the difficulty is ambiguity—and for affording understanding where the provisions were written to be defined in terms of future events. Here the obligation to "original meaning" parallels the obligation to *stare decisis*. But this is not the place to explore the meaning of meaning.[26]

It is readily to be seen that the adherents of each of the schools of constitutional interpretation to which I have alluded regard each of the others as pretending to do what they do not in fact do, or attempting to delude the public into a belief of the propriety of their own behavior and the impropriety of others'. The difficulty, of course, is that almost no one really believes it is possible to interpret the Constitution solely through its words, even when those words are placed in historical context. And few believe that a judge can, as Frankfurter suggests, persistently "pursue disinterestedness." If not in the words of a written constitution, and its history, if not in a disinterested search for "law as the expression of the views and feelings of the community," where does the meaning of the Constitution in fact lie?

Charles Evans Hughes once told us: "We are under a Constitution, but the Constitution is what the judges say it is, and the judiciary is the safeguard of our liberty and of our property under the Constitution."[27] That was spoken at the turn of the century. In 1967, the late A. A. Berle, one of the original Roosevelt Brain Trust, suggested an even more powerful role for the Justices. He said:[28]

> This is a report on a revolution. The unique fact is that the revolutionary committee is the Supreme Court of the United States. . . . Use of the word "revolution" implies no criticism of the Court. . . . Yet the situation does impose on the federal government problems of power which must be solved if the Supreme Court is not to endanger or lose its mandate through tides of political action. Revolutionary

progress does fuse judicial and legislative power, and possibly a degree of executive power as well. . . .

The suggestion here, as in Hughes's remark, is that the written constitution is nothing more nor less than a license to the nine persons who sit in the marble palace in Washington to make of it what they will. This is the most generally held view of how the Supreme Court behaves. More of its judgments are explicable in these terms than in any other. On the other hand, whether through pretense or otherwise, the language of the Court's opinions is not consistent with this notion. Only rarely does a Justice say, "This is the result in this case because I think this is the most desirable result in this case." Apparently the mystique must be maintained or the power that it protects will disintegrate. For surely we should agree with Judge Hand that the Supreme Court was not contemplated as this country's Platonic Guardians by the framers of the Constitution, nor do the Justices have the talents that would qualify them for that role.

Yet, it is not to be denied that Berle spoke closer to the facts of the day. There has been a fundamental shift in judicial function since about 1954. And this is particularly true in the area of constitutional law. I do not mean merely that the scope of the Constitution has been enormously enlarged, although that is certainly true. I mean that there has been a shift from the judicial role of deciding a particular case and giving reasons therefor, to pronouncing legislative principles that will govern not only the case before the Court but the action of everyone who comes within its terms. The courts have not been totally successful in this aspect of their legislative role, because they so regularly discount their own precedents that the pronouncements remain to be tested anew when the real issues actually arise. But the opinions nevertheless tend to deal in generalities rather than with the particulars of a case.

There has also been a shift from what was essentially a negative voice to an affirmative one. At one time, the Court used the Constitution to stop or to limit government behavior. It remained for the other branches to make the policy choice; the judiciary could only say no. Now the judiciary, as much as the other branches, indulges in affirmative decision-making. It no longer merely says that the legislative or executive policy is not valid; it now frames for itself what it regards as appropriate affirmative governmental policy. And its concerns have shifted from what was primarily a duty to resolve disputes between conflicting parties to the framing and enforcement of what it regards as appropriate remedies against all societal evils, whether they be legal, moral, economic, or social. To use Berle's words again: "Ultimate legislative power in the United States has come to rest in the Supreme Court of the United States."[29]

It is not easy, therefore, to speak with certainty about any constitutional rules. The problem is only in part the one stated by then-Justice Harlan Fiske Stone:[30]

> . . . the experience of the past one hundred and fifty years has revealed the danger that, through judicial interpretation, the constitutional device for the protection of minorities from oppressive majority action, may be made the means by which the majority is subjected to the tyranny of the minority. It was the lasting contribution of Justice Holmes that he saw clearly that the danger arose, not from the want of appropriate guiding formulas for the exercise of the judicial function, but from the judicial distrust of the democratic process, and from the innate tendency of the human mind to apply subjective rather than objective tests to the reasonableness of legislative action.

In commenting on a Supreme Court opinion, Stone wrote: "the Court's setting aside the plain command of Congress, without reference to any identifiable prohibition of the Constitution, and with only the support of platitudinous irrelevancies, is a matter of transcendent importance."[31] "Platitudinous irrelevancies" have come more and more to be the stuff of which Supreme Court opinions are composed. Nevertheless, whether or not the Court gets better about justifying its constitutional adjudications, judicial decisions, custom, and conditions, as well as the language of the Constitution itself, must be utilized in seeking answers to the constitutional questions of the Watergate period.

I would close this chapter with an admonition to the reader from my former professor and mentor, Thomas Reed Powell, about the peculiar ways of lawyers, judges, and law professors. He said, "lawyers should still be humble when they realize how many of their craft pronounce pontifical conclusions with all too little sign of mastery of the elements of the problems that the conclusions seek to solve."[32] In Platonic language that reads: "[B]efore they have discovered any means of effecting their wishes—that is a matter which never troubles them—they would rather not tire themselves by thinking about possibilities; but assuming that what they desire is already granted to them, they proceed with their plan, and delight in detailing what they mean to do when their wish has come true."[33]

2

The Congressional Power of Inquiry

The role of Congress as grand inquisitor is almost as old as the nation. It has had a long and checkered career. One will look in vain in the text of the Constitution, however detailed Article I may seem to be, for the source of this power and function. Like Topsy, the inquisitorial power of Congress "never was born. It just growed like cabbage and corn." Yet even those most insistent on the impropriety of constitutionally implied powers, such as Raoul Berger,[1] have no doubts whatsoever about the constitutional legitimacy of this implied congressional function.

Senator Sam Ervin, who also subscribes to a strict interpretation of presidential powers, described the congressional power:[2]

> Congress can probe into every matter where there is legitimate federal interest. In the modern age, where government is involved in multifaceted aspects of our daily lives, there are increasingly few areas where Congress may not delve. . . .
>
> The Constitution [he does not say where] and statutes give Congress a solemn duty to oversee the activities of the executive branch. . . .
>
> Congress also has the duty and the right to publicize its findings on corruption and maladministration. Indeed, fulfilling its responsibility to inform the public about the state of government is one of Congress's most significant functions. . . .
>
> But as great as Congress's powers are, they are subject to weighty limitations. Congress must act with valid legislative purpose. It cannot probe purely private affairs nor expose private activity solely for the sake of exposure. It cannot usurp the functions of the executive and judicial branches and prosecute, try, and convict for criminal offenses. The legislative trials of the loyalty investigations era are a black mark on the history of congressional inquiries. . . .
>
> A congressional committee cannot venture beyond the responsibilities given it by its parent House through authorizing or enabling resolutions.

As will be noted again and again in this volume, the constitutional authority at issue—here the power of legislative inquiry—cannot be evoked from the words of the Constitution itself. We cannot impose paternity on the Founding Fathers. Necessity was probably its mother. But its legitimacy is long past question.

It is true—to shift the metaphor—that there are straws to be found in parliamentary, colonial, Convention, and post-Convention history to support the notion that the constitution makers might have assumed the existence of such legislative power, although they did not mention it. But, if bricks cannot be made without straw, neither can they be made of straw alone. And there is some difficulty in relying on such history to justify Senate inquiry into malversations of executive branch officials.

There can be no doubt that there was a history of parliamentary investigation before the American states separated from Great Britain and established their national constitution. As George Keeton remarks: "Committees of Inquiry into allegations of misconduct, whether of public servants or others, have been a part of the ordinary machinery of the two Houses of Parliament, and particularly of the House of Commons, at least since the Restoration of Charles II in 1660."[3]

The difficulty with this pre-Revolutionary history is that the work of parliamentary committees of inquiry was, in almost every instance, the machination of newly installed ministries to impose blame for the deficiencies of government on the ministries that had just been ousted from office. In 1667, the House of Commons, following the fall of Clarendon, appointed a committee to investigate the expenditures of taxes by the king and his ministers.[4] And, in 1679, after the dissolution of the Restoration Parliament, and the consequent exile of the Duke of York, the House of Commons established a committee of inquiry into the state of the navy, an attack directed at Samuel Pepys, who is known to us as a diarist but who was then the loyal supporter and henchman of the Duke of York.[5] Although Pepys suffered incarceration pending the outcome of the investigation, the inquiry, like many that were to follow, petered out with no conclusion. Thus, as Keeton put it: "The Committee of Inquiry, therefore, appears in its first use as a tribunal of investigation after the Restoration as a party instrument making no claim to impartiality."[6]

This remained the characteristic mode for parliamentary inquiries throughout the pre–American Revolution period. Sir Robert Walpole's life affords demonstration enough. In 1715, at the beginning of his career, Walpole was instrumental in creating a committee for the investigation of the alleged wrongdoings of Lord Bolingbroke, particularly with reference to the negotiations that led to the Peace of Utrecht. Bolingbroke was already out of office; indeed, in anticipation of Walpole's actions, Bolingbroke had left the country for France. (Since it was in France that Bolingbroke turned to philosophy and history and friendship with Voltaire and Montesquieu, we indirectly owe to Walpole the important political and historical analyses that Bolingbroke wrote which had such important effect on the thinking of American revolutionaries.)[7] It was Walpole's committee report that resulted in the impeachment of Bolingbroke and started Walpole's star on its rise.[8]

When the South Sea Bubble burst in 1720, the ministry of which Walpole was a part became endangered by a parliamentary inquiry of both Houses into the relationships between the members of the ministry—and the Crown—and the corporate directors of the ill-fated venture.[9] The ministry barely survived this highly partisan probe, largely as a result of the timely death of one villain who could be made the scapegoat. In 1742, when Walpole was driven from the premiership, after twenty-two years of rule of highly dubious ethical standards, parliamentary inquiry was again invoked. This time Walpole was slated for the role that he had once assigned Bolingbroke. He, however, escaped impeachment by the narrowest of margins.

While it is clear that the writers of the Constitution were familiar with the facts of parliamentary inquiry, it is less than clear that this was the kind of behavior that they wished the American Congress to emulate. There is almost nothing in the reported debates at the Convention or the ratifying conventions that followed to suggest that this power was intended to be included by implication among the extensive list of powers specifically stated. As the great protagonist of congressional authority, Professor Berger, has pointed out,[10] there is one place at the Constitutional Convention where the House of Representatives was referred to as the "grand inquest of the Nation";[11] and the phrase was twice repeated at the ratifying conventions;[12] and still again by James Wilson in his constitutional lectures of 1791.[13] But when one examines the context of these remarks, they do not seem to mean what Berger would read into them.

The reference in the records of the Convention indicates that the phrase was meant to refer to the impeachment process. The exact quotation is: "The House of Representatives shall be the grand Inquest of this Nation; and all Impeachments shall be made by them." And when Wilson used the phrase in his lectures, he seemed to be talking more of the legislative function than the inquisitorial power. What he said was:[14]

> A difference in the posts assigned to the two houses, and in the number and duration of their members, will produce a difference in their sense of the duties required and expected of them. The house of representatives, for instance, form the grand inquest of the state. They will diligently inquire into grievances, arising both from men and things. Their commissions will commence or be renewed at short distances of time. Their sentiments, and views, and wishes, and even

their passions, will have received a deep and recent tincture from the sentiments, and views, and wishes, and passions of their constituents. Into their counsels, and resolutions, and measures, this tincture will be strongly transfused. They will know the evils which exist, and the means of removing them: they will know the advantages already discovered, and the means of increasing them. As the term of their commission and trust will soon expire, they will be desirous, while it lasts, of seeing the publick business put, at least, in a train of accomplishment. From all these causes, a sufficient number of overtures and propositions will originate in the house of representatives. These overtures and propositions will come, in their proper course, before the senate.

Even if these authorities were to be read as justifying legislative inquiry, it is clear that they referred only to the House of Representatives and not to the Senate. But a real doubt about such implied adoption of English procedure derives from the fact that the parliamentary precedents were essentially revelations of the expression of political faction rather than searches for information or truth. And it was the purpose of the constitution makers to frame a government that would restrain faction rather than endorse it.[15] It must be remembered that the American party system was subsequent to, not antecedent to or contemporary with, the framing of the Constitution.[16]

When the English parliamentary system was to be followed, or adapted—as with impeachment—the framers let it be known in the words of the Constitution. When the English parliamentary system was to be rejected—as with bills of attainder and ex post facto laws—the framers let that be known in the same way. The parliamentary system of committees of inquiry falls somewhere in between. The problem is to determine the meaning of silence. And the answer, therefore, cannot be found in what was said; it has been found in what was done after the Constitution became a reality.

By 1885, the congressional power of inquiry could be extolled by no less a figure than the future President Woodrow Wilson. In his book *Congressional Government*, Wilson wrote the often-quoted proposition:[17]

> It is the proper duty of a representative body to look diligently into every affair of government and to talk much about what it sees. It is meant to be the eyes and the voice, and to embody the wisdom and will of its constituents. Unless Congress have and use every means of acquainting itself with the acts and the disposition of the administrative agents of the government, the country must be helpless to learn how it is being served; and unless Congress both scrutinize these things and sift them by every form of discussion, the country must remain in embarrassing, crippling ignorance of the very affairs which it is most important that it should understand and di-

> rect. The informing function of Congress should be preferred even to its legislative function. The argument is not only that discussed and interrogated administration is the only pure and efficient administration, but, more than that, that the only really self-governing people is that people which discusses and interrogates its administration.

While this passage is frequently quoted, it is usually not noted that Wilson was speaking here in normative rather than descriptive terms. Diligent oversight by Congress was what he believed necessary. But he recognized that the need was not reflected in actuality:[18]

> Congress stands almost helplessly outside of the departments. Even the special, irksome, ungracious investigations which it from time to time institutes in its spasmodic endeavors to dispel or confirm suspicions of malfeasance or of wanton corruption do not afford it more than a glimpse of the inside of a small province of federal administration. Hostile or designing officials can always hold it at arm's length by dexterous evasions and concealments. It can violently disturb, but it cannot often fathom, the waters of the sea in which the bigger fish of the civil service swim and feed. Its dragnet stirs without cleansing the bottom. Unless it have at the head of the departments capable, fearless men, altogether in its confidence and entirely in sympathy with its designs, it is clearly helpless to do more than affright those officials whose consciences are their accusers.

Wilson had a hundred years of history behind his judgments. We now have almost two hundred. But when Congress first entered the arena of legislative inquisition, it was writing on a blank slate.

The legislative power of inquiry came into the Constitution in 1792, when the House of Representatives, with some trepidation, undertook to investigate the smashing defeat of the American army under General St. Clair at the hands of the Indians at the headwaters of the Wabash River on 4 November 1791. Washington was informed of this catastrophe by messenger, and he in turn reported the event to Congress through his personal secretary. Things being no different then than now, the story leaked to the press, causing some furor, and the Secretary of War disingenuously reported to Congress that the cause of the defeat was "a deficient number of good troops."[19] It was too simple an answer either to satisfy the country or to satisfy the Congress.

St. Clair himself was asking for a court of inquiry to absolve him from liability. President Washington declined. In February a motion to investigate the defeat was offered in the House, without effect. On March 27, Congressman Giles of Virginia introduced a motion to ask Washington to conduct an investigation. Congressman Vining of Delaware, urging that the request to Washington would only embarrass the President without securing an investigation, suggested that the House itself undertake the investigation. He asserted that the House had that power because it had the impeaching power and investigation was certainly a precondition to impeachment.

There was opposition from Smith of South Carolina, who urged that the Congress had no authority. The execution of the laws was entrusted to the President and it was his responsibility to determine why the failures occurred. He thought that there was no wisdom in the House acting as the "grand inquest of the nation," and that the ludicrous behavior of the French National Assembly in this regard should not be repeated here:[20]

> Most members of the House were aware of the precedent-setting aspects of the proposal, but they also believed the virtual destruction of the nation's military force and the huge expenditure of funds demanded a public accounting. The motion [to establish a committee of inquiry] passed on a vote of 44 to 10.

The House passed a resolution asking the President to have the proper officers "lay before this House such papers of a public nature" as might afford it a basis for investigating the causes of St. Clair's defeat. Washington, who had seldom called a cabinet, did so on this occasion, meeting with his four departmental chiefs, Jefferson at State, Hamilton at Treasury, Knox at War, and the Attorney General, Edmund Randolph. (There was then no department for the Attorney General; the Department of Justice did not come into existence until 1870.) The cabinet was called with knowledge that this was the first exercise of legislative inquisition authority and the precedent of the response would be important. The meeting was adjourned without conclusion on the Saturday on which it was called and resumed on the following Monday. The ultimate response, which made the requested papers available to the House, also created the beginnings of the text on what we have come to call "executive privilege":[21]

> Jefferson noted that the group reached unanimity on the essential points: the House could conduct an inquest, institute inquiries, and call for papers. The President, however, could release such papers as the "public good would permit and ought to refuse those the disclosure of which would injure the public." Jefferson wrote that neither the House nor the committee had a right to call on department heads to release records. Requests for Executive records were to be made directly to the President.

The problem of "executive privilege" was the primary constitutional issue framed by the Select Committee's investigations and will be treated in following chapters. But the President did, in the St. Clair affair, afford all the documents to the House that it requested.

The House proceeded to prepare a report, at which the Secretary of War and General Hodgdon took umbrage. It pointed out the faults that led to the disaster but declined to recommend censure for any civil officials or courts-martial for any military officials.

The precedent-setting House investigation found its authority either in the Impeachment Clause or in its duty to inform the public of the conduct of government by the executive branch. It clearly did not rest on the need to secure information for the purpose of passing legislation. But with the precedent established, problems of constitutional authority disappeared, as legislative committee after legislative committee undertook investigations without further worry about the propriety of their doing so under the terms of the Constitution. (In 1798, in implementation of this inquiry power, Congress passed a statute authorizing both houses to put witnesses under oath.)[22]

As with much of our constitutional history, Congress performed its duties as it conceived them to be until the courts were brought in to tell it what it could and could not do. The Supreme Court was, at first, less than sympathetic to the notion that the House of Representatives could act as the grand inquest of the nation. When the House undertook an investigation into the events that led to the bankruptcy of Jay Cooke & Co., one of whose creditors was the United States, it ordered the attendance by subpoena of Hallett Kilbourn. Kilbourn appeared but refused to answer certain questions and refused to produce certain documents called for by the subpoena. The committee reported this recalcitrance to the whole House and asked that Kilbourn be held in contempt of Congress. Citations for contempt of Congress, then as now, had to be voted by the entire House or Senate as the case might be.[23] Kilbourn was arrested on the Speaker's warrant, but still refused to answer, and was charged with contempt and incarcerated in the congressional jail. Kilbourn brought the issue to the courts by petition for a writ of habeas corpus. Justice Miller wrote the opinion for the unanimous Court granting Kilbourn his freedom from congressional restraint.[24] Miller's reasons were not quite so clear as his conclusion, but that has been true of most Supreme Court opinions, both great and petty, both late and soon.

Miller examined the Constitution and found no basis therein for a congressional authority to impose any sanctions, except with regard to impeachment and discipline of its own members. If he did not find the power explicit in the Constitution, neither was it implicit in either of the grounds offered by Congress: first, that it was a power exercised by Parliament and inherited by Congress; second, that it was a power necessary to the performance of its legislative functions. It was, said Miller on highly dubious historical grounds,[25] because Parliament was not only a legislature but a "court of judicature" that it could assert the power of inquiry and punishment. Congress is only a legislative body and has no such authority. Moreover, in a not untypical judicial construction of the constitutional doctrine of separation of powers, the Court held that the function being exercised by the Congress here rightfully belonged to the judicial branch. Inquiry into private business transactions had no function except to establish wrongdoing by individuals and that was a judicial task. The inquiry could not be considered in aid of the legislative function since it "could result in no valid legislation on the subject to which the inquiry referred."[26] It must be remembered with reference to the last proposition that all government power had not yet been transferred to the national government by the Supreme Court. There were then, as there are not now, subjects that did not fall within the national ken.

Kilbourn was a strong restraint on the congressional power of investigation, but even if it had not been revised, it could not have seriously affected the Senate Select Committee in the Watergate affair. First, one of that committee's avowed purposes was the collection of data on which to base legislation. Second, the subject matter of the investigation was behavior of government employees rather than of individuals engaged in private affairs. On the other hand, *Kilbourn* would suggest the invalidity of the Ervin probe insofar as its goal was the exercise of what has come to be known as the informing function. And, insofar as it was engaged in unearthing evidence also sought in criminal proceedings, as it was, *Kilbourn* might be read as a bar. Just as the Court found the pending bankruptcy proceedings of Jay Cooke & Co. preemptive of the subject matter, so, too, might the special prosecutor's activities have been thought to be a similar barrier.

It will be recalled that in Watergate, Special Prosecutor Archibald Cox requested that the Senate hearings be stayed lest they interfere with his criminal law processes. He was turned down both by the Select Committee and by Chief Judge Sirica of the United States District Court of the District of Columbia, whom he asked to enjoin the televising of the Senate proceedings. And these judgments were surely correct, especially in light of the earlier retreat by the Supreme Court from such rigid restraints on congressional investigations as would have been imposed by *Kilbourn*.

In Supreme Court adjudication, the first judgment is not likely to be the last; nor is the second, the third, the fourth. And while *Kilbourn* has never been specifically overruled, it is of limited authority today. This is not the place to canvass all the Court's opinions on the subject, but reference to a few is called for. Two cases derived from the Teapot Dome investigation.[27] Both *McGrain* v. *Daugherty*[28] and *Sinclair* v. *United States*,[29] like *Kilbourn* v. *Thompson*, were concerned with the power of a congressional committee to compel the testimony of witnesses who were not government employees.

In *McGrain* v. *Daugherty*, the Court found a very different historical base from that stated in *Kilbourn*. And the conclusion was a very different one. After reviewing "legislative practice, congressional enactments and court decisions" the Court, in an opinion by Justice Van Devanter, stated:[30]

> We are of opinion that the power of inquiry—with process to enforce it—is an essential and appropriate auxiliary to the legislative function. It was so regarded and employed in American legislatures before the Constitution was framed and ratified. Both houses of Congress took this view of it early in their history—the House of Representatives with the approving votes of Mr. Madison and other members whose service in the convention which framed the Constitution gives special significance to their action—and both houses have employed the power accordingly up to the present time. The acts of 1798 and 1857, judged by their comprehensive terms, were intended to recognize the existence of this power in both houses and to enable them to employ it "more effectually" than before. So, when their practice in the matter is appraised according to the circumstances in which it was begun and to those in which it has been continued, it falls nothing short of a practical construction, long continued, of the constitutional provisions respecting their powers, and therefore should be taken as fixing the meaning of those provisions, if otherwise doubtful.

It did not matter that the resolution establishing the Teapot Dome committee did not speak of the potential of legislation. The subject matter was the administration of the Department of Justice. "The only legitimate object the Senate could have in ordering the investigation was to aid it in legislating; and we think the subject-matter was such that the presumption should be indulged that this was the real object. An express avowal of the object would have been better; but in view of the particular subject-matter was not indispensable."[31] Such a presumption of validity negated the charge that the investigation was for the purpose of "attempting or intending to try the Attorney General at its bar or before its committee for any crime or wrongdoing. Nor do we think it a valid objection to the investigation that it might possibly disclose crime or wrongdoing on his part."[32]

Sinclair reiterated the essence of *McGrain* v. *Daugherty*. The power of investigation was a necessary auxiliary to the legislative function. But it also established two conditions on congressional inquiry that have remained controlling:[33]

> . . . while the power of inquiry is an essential and appropriate auxiliary to the legislative function, it must be exerted with due regard for the rights of witnesses, and . . . a witness rightfully may refuse to answer where the bounds of the power are exceeded or where the questions asked are not pertinent to the matter under inquiry.

> It has always been recognized in this country, and it is well to remember, that few if any of the rights of the people guarded by fundamental law are of greater importance to their happiness and safety than the right to be exempt from all unauthorized, arbitrary or unreasonable inquiries and disclosures in respect of their personal and private affairs.

Thus is the Constitution slowly but effectively amended so that it may be read to fill the lacunae. Foresighted as the forefathers were, they could not have anticipated all the conditions which would require answers to questions that did not exist when they wrote. What the Court has told us here, as it has elsewhere about all branches of the government, is that the assumption and exercise of power over a long period of time will eventually be legitimated by the Supreme Court, which has constituted itself a continuing constitutional convention. The problems of such constitutional amendments tend to derive not so much from the legitimation of power as from the inadequate rationalizations for that legitimation.

The tools used in the congressional inquiry cases were familiar ones. One is called the legal fiction by which the Court indulges a presumption that something is true that it knows is not necessarily true. The presumption that congressional inquiry is addressed to gathering facts on which to base legislation is such a fiction. The investigation of the Attorney General's department and its behavior surely did not have legislation as its objective any more than did the St. Clair inquiry heretofore noted. The St. Clair inquiry, however, could have been considered an adjunct of the impeachment power, since it was conducted by the House of Representatives. The Senate inquiry in *McGrain* v. *Daugherty* could not have relied on that provision.

The other tool utilized by the Court to amend the Constitution in the congressional inquiry cases was what the late Alfred Kelly appropriately labeled "law office history." The opening paragraph of Kelly's article, in reliance on Mark Howe, makes the point:[34]

> In a recent review article, Mark DeWolfe Howe delivered himself of a few trenchant comments upon the increasing tendency which certain Justices of the United States Supreme Court have exhibited to resort to the "historical method of adjudication." Admittedly, he said, "tension between the complexities of confused reality and the simplicities of sure conviction has very probably always marked the divisions within the Court." But "only within recent years," he continued, "have the justices who have discovered and embraced the solacing simplicities [of historical adjudication] endeavored to persuade us that a careful reading of history confirms their confidence." And if the Justices "have not always succeeded in this effort," he added, "they have at least taught us that a selective interpretation of

history can provide much satisfaction to the interpreter." In short, in Professor Howe's opinion, the Court's recent historical "scholarship" is both simplistic and naïve.

Howe was certainly right about the modes of judicial historicism. But he was wrong about the proposition that these deficiencies are of only recent origin. Chief Justice Marshall, in *Martin* v. *Hunter's Lessee*[35] and elsewhere, certainly indulged in rewriting history to serve his cause.[36] Chief Justice Taney in the *Dred Scott* case was taken to task by the dissents of Justices McLean and Curtis for the same reason.[37] And the congressional inquiry cases reveal the same deficiencies.

Certainly, as Justice Miller said in *Kilbourn*, the British Parliament had judicial as well as legislative functions. But there is no evidence that they believed themselves to be undertaking judicial functions when they engaged in committees of inquiry. The previous references to the Walpole and Pepys inquiries are evidence enough that it was a parliamentary and not a judicial function in which they were engaged.

Nor were the later cases of *McGrain* v. *Daugherty* and *Sinclair* any better in this regard. Surely there were a multitude of congressional investigations on which the legitimacy of the power of Congress was rested in its lawmaking function. But these cannot accurately be said to be confined to exercises in the collection of data for the purpose of enacting legislation. The St. Clair investigation;[38] the investigation of James Wilkinson in 1810;[39] the investigation of the burning of Washington in 1814;[40] the investigation of Andrew Jackson's invasion of Florida in 1818;[41] the Calhoun investigation of 1826;[42] the investigation of the Second Bank of the United States in 1832;[43] the investigation of Sam Houston's misbehavior in 1832;[44] the investigation into the assault on Charles Sumner in 1856;[45] the Harper's Ferry inquiry of 1859;[46] the Covode inquiry into the misconduct of the Buchanan administration in 1860;[47] the investigation of the conduct of the war in 1861;[48] the investigation of the Joint Committee on Reconstruction in 1865;[49] the investigation of the Crédit Mobilier scandal in 1873;[50] the Ballinger-Pinchot inquiry of 1910;[51] the Clapp Committee investigation of 1912;[52] and the Pujo Committee of the same year;[53] in short, almost every major congressional inquiry that preceded the decisions in *McGrain* v. *Daugherty* and *Sinclair* indicates that Congress was not limited in the exercise of its inquiry power to the preparation of legislation.

The justification by the Court of congressional inquiries as an adjunct of the lawmaking function is not an unreasonable one. Surely, collection of information is a necessary prerequisite to framing legislation. But the presumption that all congressional investigations are in fact in aid of the lawmaking function is an indulgence in "law office history."

The history of congressional investigations reveals not that they are necessary to the lawmaking process, but rather that there is more to the job of the legislature than legislating. Oversight of government behavior, within the legislative as well as the executive and judicial branches, and the need to inform the public about such behavior and misbehavior—in short, the things that Woodrow Wilson was talking about—are also legitimate legislative functions. Surely the constitutional language provides that only the Congress may legislate; it does not demonstrate that the Congress may only legislate. The Court may have misled itself by an erroneous conception that the Constitution affords a strict separation of powers, when in fact it provides rather for an intricate system of checks and balances. And, indeed, checks and balances is what the Watergate inquiry was all about. The imperial presidency is not a question solely of the accumulation of power in the executive branch of government; the greater problem is that the accumulated power is exercised without being subjected to the oversight and scrutiny necessary to assure that the fiduciary obligations of the President are being met.

Thus, as Martin Shapiro has written:[54]

> By subsuming administrative investigations under the heading of investigations for legislative purposes, the Supreme Court has obscured two factors that lie at the heart of its own demands for a lawmaking and only a lawmaking purpose. First, a category of investigation that does not have as its sole or principal purpose the making of laws has from the very beginning of our government been recognized as legitimate. Second, exposure of individual misconduct discovered in the pursuit of information, not necessarily for making laws but for its own sake, has always been an integral and essential part of this category of investigation. . . .
>
> It is true that the gathering of information for the purpose of making law is often an element in the "problem" investigation, and indeed sometimes the problem is identified by the amount of proposed legislation on a given subject. But only the most opaque pair of legalistic dark glasses can blot out the obvious exposing or general informing function of many such investigations. . . .
>
> Congressional investigations are then multipurpose tools. Those purposes—lawmaking, administrative, educational, judicial, and self-preservative—closely parallel the general functions of Congress. The parallel suggests that in practice Congress has conceived of the investigation not simply as a scoop for gathering the raw materials of legislation but also as a flexible political device that can be utilized to implement any or all of its aims.

By the time of Watergate, these facts of life seem to have been implicitly, if not explicitly, accepted by the Supreme Court. The more recent restraints on Congress by the Court have not derived from the limits of the lawmaking function. Instead, they have been demands that specified constitutional inhibitions on government also be imposed on the legislative branch. Lawmaking is still spoken of by the Court as the pin for the investigating process.[55] But it has been recognized that the legislative function is broader than lawmaking, though subject to the restraints of the Bill of Rights. In *Watkins* v. *United States*,[56] the Court, speaking through Chief Justice Warren, said:

> The power of the Congress to conduct investigations is inherent in the legislative process. That power is broad. It encompasses inquiries concerning the administration of existing laws as well as proposed or possibly needed statutes. It includes surveys of defects in our social, economic or political system for the purpose of enabling the Congress to remedy them. It comprehends probes into departments of the Federal Government to expose corruption, inefficiency or waste. But broad as is this power of inquiry, it is not unlimited. There is no general authority to expose the private affairs of individuals without justification in terms of the functions of the Congress. . . . Nor is the Congress a law enforcement or trial agency. These are functions of the executive and judicial departments of government. No inquiry is an end in itself; it must be related to, and in furtherance of, a legitimate task of the Congress. Investigations conducted solely for the personal aggrandizement of the investigators or to "punish" those investigated are indefensible.
>
> It is unquestionably the duty of all citizens to cooperate with the Congress in its efforts to obtain the facts needed for intelligent legislative action. . . . This, of course, assumes that the constitutional rights of witnesses will be respected by the Congress as they are in a court of justice. The Bill of Rights is applicable to investigations as to all forms of governmental action. Witnesses cannot be compelled to give evidence against themselves. They cannot be subjected to unreasonable search and seizure. Nor can the First Amendment freedoms of speech, press, religion, or political belief and association be abridged.

In the *Watkins* case itself, a conviction for contempt of Congress was reversed essentially on procedural due process grounds. It was found that the committee's charter from the House and the chairman's definition of the committee's scope of inquiry were too vague to permit the witness to determine whether the questions put to him were in fact pertinent to the authorized inquiry. The Court suggested that Congress would have to be more careful in stating its charges to its committees of investigation:[57]

> It is the responsibility of the Congress, in the first instance, to insure that compulsory process is used only in furtherance of a legislative purpose. That requires that the instructions to an investigating committee spell out that group's jurisdiction and purpose with sufficient

particularity. Those instructions are embodied in the authorizing resolution. That document is the committee's charter. Broadly drafted and loosely worded, however, such resolutions can leave tremendous latitude to the discretion of the investigators. The more vague the committee's charter is, the greater becomes the possibility that the committee's specific actions are not in conformity with the will of the parent House of Congress.

When the Senate came to draw the "charter" under which the Select Committee was to operate,[58] it was fully cognizant of the constitutional restraints under which it must operate. And the chairman also drafted rules of procedure and guidelines for the conduct of the hearings.[59] The result was that few if any of the constitutional limitations placed on legislative inquiries by the Supreme Court became issues in the conduct of the Select Committee's Watergate hearings.

The general power of subpoena has consistently been treated by the courts as an inherent power of Congress.[60] Chief Justice Warren's opinion in *Watkins*, which makes clear the citizen's duty to respond to such subpoenas, is typical.[61] All standing committees of both Houses now have such authority either under law[62] or under Standing Rules.[63] Special or select committees may be given that power by the resolution that creates them, as it was given to the Senate Watergate committee by its charter.[64] Senate Resolution 60 included authorization to subpoena "any . . . officer . . . of the executive branch of the United States Government."[65] The White House argued that the language of the Resolution did not authorize a subpoena to the President. But that was settled to the contrary both by further Resolution of the Senate[66] and by judicial opinion.[67]

The means for enforcing a legislative subpoena are cumbersome. There are two, neither of which is very efficacious. The first is self-help. The second is by means of judicial contempt proceedings. Self-help is more of a threat than a reality. But it was threatened at least twice in the committee hearings. Thus, immediately after Alexander Butterfield had told the Select Committee's staff of the existence of the White House tapes, he proposed to take off for Russia on Federal Aviation Administration business. When he was told that his testimony was wanted immediately before the committee in full session, he replied that he could not come because of this previous engagement. Thereupon Senator Ervin sent him a message: "Tell Mr. Butterfield that if he is not here this afternoon I will send the sergeant at arms to fetch him."[68] Wherefore Butterfield was voluntarily present to tell the world the story of the existence of the White House tapes, a story that ultimately led to the first resignation of an American president.

Senator Ervin had earlier responded in a similar tone when President Nixon told his White House staff that they should not attend the hearings at the behest of the committee. Then, too, the putative witnesses backed down when Ervin announced he would cause them to be arrested by the sergeant at arms, if necessary. Fortunately, it was not necessary. The self-help of a Senate sergeant at arms is a puny force against executive branch soldiery. As Senator Baker was said to have observed, the sergeant at arms couldn't get beyond the White House gates if he had to.

The contempt process is one that has afforded a repeated testing ground for the power of legislative subpoena. It, too, is a dubious weapon. Like self-help, it is used more as a threat than a reality. It could result in the punishment of a recalcitrant witness including incarceration for the duration of a Congress under the common-law authority of Congress.[69] Since 1857, the process has been rather a judicial one than a legislative one.[70] Upon proper vote of the offended House, a criminal case may be brought against the offender, which requires both a grand jury indictment and the approval of the United States Attorney. There are obvious difficulties with this process. There are always doubts about how effectively a United States Attorney would proceed before the grand jury against other officials of the executive branch. Indeed, that was the reason that the Watergate cases were removed from the jurisdiction of the United States Attorney in the District of Columbia and given to the special prosecutor. Moreover, while the contempt process is a threat to a recalcitrant witness, it is not necessarily a good means of evoking testimony, simply because the course of a criminal contempt case is likely to take more time than the life span of the investigation. The process was never invoked by the Watergate committee. When G. Gordon Liddy, a self-styled "007," refused to testify, the committee simply ignored him. When Nixon refused to produce documents commanded by committee subpoena, the committee eschewed the contempt process in recognition that it was not likely to succeed against a President of the United States, even if, as was doubtful, a sitting President is subject to criminal contempt processes.[71]

The Fifth Amendment's privilege against self-incrimination is a recognized barrier to compelled testimony before Congress as well as the courts.[72] The Ervin Committee, unlike its predecessor committees in the Kefauver and McCarthy investigations,[73] did not provide the unedifying and cruel process of commanding the public appearance of those who would refuse to testify on grounds of the privilege against self-incrimination. Several potential witnesses took or threatened to take the Fifth Amendment in executive session, at one time or another, including McCord, Sloan, Magruder, Dean, and Colson. In each instance, the committee excused the witness from making his claim in public hearings, except insofar as it was a prerequisite to a grant of immunity. The policy of the committee was stated by Samuel Dash in his book:[74]

By excusing Colson we were implementing a policy Ervin and I had succeeded in getting the committee to adopt: no witness asserting his Fifth Amendment privilege would be forced to appear publicly before television cameras to repeat his refusal to answer questions on constitutional grounds. Other committees had engaged in the practice of exhibiting "Fifth Amendment" witnesses—some notoriously. But we concluded that public display of such witnesses could serve only an improper purpose of showmanship and did not perform any legislative or public-informing function.

The committee did, however, make use of its capacity to compel evidence by the use of the immunity laws. In 1857, the Congress had passed a law that permitted it to compel testimony even against a plea of the Fifth Amendment, provided that the witness was immunized from prosecution relating to the transaction about which the testimony was given.[75] This proved too great a boon to witnesses who "spilled everything" on the stand, thus buying wide protection against criminal prosecutions. In 1862, the Congress contracted the immunity, so that it extended protection only against use of the testimony, not against prosecution for the transaction with regard to which the testimony was given.[76] In 1892, the Supreme Court declared that immunity must extend not only to the use of the testimony but to the leads given to other evidence—the "fruits." The Court, in *Counselman* v. *Hitchcock*,[77] said: "In view of the constitutional provision, a statutory enactment, to be valid, must afford absolute immunity against future prosecution for the offense to which the question relates." This was read to mean that transactional immunity was required by the Fifth Amendment. But in 1964, the Supreme Court took another turn, suggesting that an immunity law would be adequate if it protected only against the use of the testimony and its fruits.[78] And the Nixon administration secured the passage of the Omnibus Crime Control Act, which contained provisions for use and fruits immunity only.[79] And this time, the Supreme Court upheld the statute as adequate protection under the Fifth Amendment for those who would be compelled to testify.[80]

The Ervin Committee did make use of this statute with regard to two of its most important witnesses: Magruder and Dean. Both were granted the use immunity provided by the statute and became willing witnesses before the committee. Indeed, it was the compelled Dean testimony that broke the case against the President. It might be noted that Senators Baker and Gurney opposed the grant of immunity to Dean, whom they regarded as the principal culprit defaming the President.[81] Had they succeeded, history might have been afforded a different view of the Watergate affair, although Dean did negotiate a similar immunity from the prosecutor. Whether that would have occurred in the absence of the Senate immunity, we do not know.

To my mind, the immunity laws rest on thin grounds. The standard for their validity is the requirement that they afford the witness all the protection he would have had if the Fifth Amendment privilege had been invoked. The fact of the matter is that the immunity grant can never be as broad as the right to silence.

There were several times when the question was raised whether the Watergate committee's investigation poached on the province of the criminal prosecutorial process. Suffice it here to note that in no instance did a court find that the committee exceeded its proper function in this regard.

The Senate Watergate committee was meticulous in affording witnesses the protections that the law was intended to give and in adhering to the Constitution, statutes, and Senate rules, with one important exception. As Senator Baker is reported to have stated: "The Ervin Committee did not invent the leak, but we elevated it to its highest art form."[82] It is not quite clear what he meant by "we." Certainly, the leaks were not from Ervin or his chief counsel, for whom they were extraordinarily "counterproductive." It was the view of at least one senator that the leaks could not be blamed primarily on the staff. "It's the damnedest thing I've ever seen," said Senator Talmadge. "I've been in the Senate seventeen and a half years and never has anything leaked from my staff. The Select Committee was like a sieve. My opinion is that Senators more than staff were guilty."[83]

Certainly the leaks were in direct violation of the rules of the committee and the rules of the Senate. They might even have been criminally prosecutable.[84] But the leak is a way of life in Washington. The press condemned the officials who engaged in leaking, at the same time extorting information from the officials who sought good relations with the media which they regarded as the makers and breakers of Washington officialdom. No effort was made to affix responsibility for the practice with regard to the Watergate committee. One day the legislative branch as well as the executive and even the judicial branch is going to have to undertake an enforceable, self-imposed discipline.

3

Executive Privilege to Deny Information to Congress

Raoul Berger, perhaps the most celebrated of the academic commentators on Watergate, in part because of the timely publication of his two books on executive privilege and impeachment,[1] declared that there is no such thing as executive privilege:[2]

> "Executive privilege"—the President's claim of constitutional authority to withhold information from Congress—is a myth. Unlike most myths, the origins of which are lost in the mists of antiquity, "executive privilege" is a product of the nineteenth century, fashioned by a succession of presidents who created "precedents" to suit the occasion. The very words "executive privilege" were conjoined only yesterday, in 1958.

If for Berger executive privilege was a myth and not a reality, for the Supreme Court of the United States, executive privilege was very much a reality, even if it had to be created by the Court itself: "The privilege is fundamental to the operation of Government and inextricably rooted in the separation of powers under the Constitution."[3]

It is possible that both Berger and the Supreme Court were right. It is possible that both Berger and the Supreme Court were wrong, except that when the Court speaks *ex cathedra*, the faithful are required to accept. But, as with all dogmas, there are heresies. And, for dogmatists, truth with a small "t" may also be a heresy.

It is possible that both the Court and Berger were right because, in fact, they were talking about two different things, even if the Court did not adequately acknowledge the difference. Berger was talking, as he said, of the power of the executive branch to refuse information to Congress and used "executive privilege" in that sense when he asserted that it was a myth. The Court, on the other hand, was not concerned with the authority of Congress vis-à-vis the President. Indeed, it said as much in a footnote:[4]

> We are not here concerned with the balance between the President's generalized interest in confidentiality and the need for relevant evidence in civil litigation, *nor with that between the confidentiality interest and congressional demands for information*, nor with the President's interest in preserving state secrets. We address only the conflict between the President's assertion of a generalized privilege of confidentiality and the constitutional need for relevant evidence in criminal trials.

It is unfortunate that, despite this disclaimer, the Court throughout its opinion spoke of "the confidentiality of Presidential communications" in terms general enough to suggest that its proclamations related to a constitutional privilege of broader dimensions than the limited evidentiary privilege with which it was actually concerned.

There are, however, myths of a different order that should be recognized as relevant to the issues under discussion. The myths derive from historical facts long since dissipated by the growth of government. One myth is that the laws are faithfully executed under the direct control and supervision of the President and his departmental chiefs in the Cabinet. The fact is that the laws are somewhat less than faithfully executed by large numbers of bureaus over most of which the President and his ministry exercise little control.

There is also a myth that the legislative functions are performed by the 100 senators and 435 congressmen elected to their offices for the performance of those functions. The fact, once again, is that there is a semipermanent bureaucracy on Capitol Hill that performs most of the legislative functions for most of the legislators.

There is a third myth that the members of the judiciary, and particularly the Justices of the Supreme Court, perform the judicial functions of passing judgment and furnishing the rationalizations for those judgments in the form of judicial opinions. Once again, the voting power is probably still in the judges and Justices of the national courts. But the writing of opinions and the reasons offered for them are more often than not left to a growing army of law clerks creating still a third bureaucracy in the federal system. The staff of the Supreme Court has multiplied at a far greater rate than those of the executive branch or the legislative branch. The problems of a faceless, semiautonomous bureaucracy are as deleterious to the performance of judicial functions as to the performance of legislative and executive functions.

These myths—historical but not contemporaneous truths—are the premises on which the constitutional concepts of separation of powers and checks and balances are assumed to operate. The result is that fictions are again dispositive of difficult questions of constitutional government. That the facts contradict constitutional principles seems to trouble few, if any, of us.

Those who justify the power of congressional inquiry as an appropriate inference from the constitutional grant of legislative power may, strangely enough, deny the validity of executive privilege on the ground that there is no specific provision for it in the language of the Constitution. Somehow, for them, the grant of executive power to the President cannot contain such implications. For, they observe, where the framers intended to create a privilege, they knew how to do so, as in the case of the congressional privilege in Article I and the privilege against self-incrimination in the Fifth Amendment.

Executive privilege is a multifaceted term. Here it means the right of the executive branch to deny access to information in its possession although the Congress has requested or commanded it to produce such information. But this definition needs breaking down to reflect the different reasons that might be given in support of such a privilege. By my count, there are essentially five of them. (I speak here only of the privilege of the executive against congressional inquest, not of the privilege that concerned the Court in *United States* v. *Nixon,* the privilege to reject judicial subpoena.)

The first—one that was involved in the decision rendered by the Supreme Court against Nixon's right to keep the tapes from judicial subpoena—is that confidential communications between the President and his advisers, or indeed similar communications among lesser mortals, must be protected; otherwise advice will not be as forthright and candid as is necessary to the functioning of the office. (George Reedy, who was President Johnson's press secretary, suggests that Presidents never get told anything except what they want to hear, which would make the privilege a meaningless one.)[5]

A second category refers to what may be called military secrets, the divulgence of which could lead to endangering the defense posture of the nation. A third category would be diplomatically important data that must be kept unpublished lest we suffer loss of strength in dealing with foreign nations. The fourth is data about individuals who have been the subject of criminal or civil investigations, information which is often of highly dubious veracity, but which, true or false, would, if published, seriously harm an individual's reputation, livelihood, or general rights of privacy. This was the basis for the executive's denying information to the McCarthy inquiries, and it is one aspect of executive privilege that is generally applauded, even by those who would eliminate all the other categories.

The fifth defense for the refusal to supply data to Congress, the one most frequently invoked, explicitly or implicitly, is that it is administratively inconvenient to supply what is asked for. No bureaucracy willingly submits its behavior to surveillance; no bureaucracy willingly surrenders its monopoly over the information on which its power depends. There is clearly no constitutional or statutory basis for this denial of access.

In addition to these five situations for which the invocation of executive privilege might be indulged, there is a totally different notion of the privilege that is also relevant to the Watergate affair. This position assumes, entirely without justification I think, that the privilege attaches not to the inquiry but to the person. On this theory, the President and the White House staff—and perhaps all those within the Executive Office of the President, a goodly number indeed—are immune from scrutiny of their behavior, their communications, and their work product. Thus, while cabinet officers may be called to account to Congress, those physically located in the White House or its numerous extensions may not. Henry Kissinger as Secretary of State was subject to congressional oversight; Henry Kissinger as presidential adviser on foreign policy was not. The privilege in this form derives from the proposition that some persons' communications, whatever their content, must be regarded as confidential.

This last notion finds its analogue in the constitutional congressional privilege that relieves congressmen from being called to account for their official behavior, especially speech, anywhere except in the proper house of Congress. But the congressional privilege is anything but a confidential communications privilege. It is rather a publication privilege. It attaches to the person or office, not the subject matter. This congressional privilege does not extend to criminal acts,[6] nor presumably would the parallel executive privilege. But to read executive privilege as equivalent to congressional privilege would be inconsistent with the history of congressional inquisitions, already recited, and still more inconsistent with the notion of impeachment which makes executive officials up to the President himself responsible directly to Congress for "high Crimes and Misdemeanors" committed in office.

The problem of executive privilege is not a growth that commenced with the Watergate affair, however prominent it became at that time. Until Watergate, however, there was no judicial determination of the constitutional nature of executive privilege. If the distinction between the privilege against the claims of Congress and the privilege against the claims of the judiciary is valid, we still do not have any judicial determination of the scope of executive privilege.

If the courts hadn't been concerned with the issue, Congress had. In 1971, the Subcommittee on Separation of Powers of the Senate Committee on the Judiciary held hearings on "Executive Privilege: The Withholding of Information by the Executive."[7] That subcommittee was chaired by Senator Sam Ervin of North Carolina and the subject was one with which he had a long familiarity. The issue was raised by a bill introduced by Senator J. William Fulbright, and the witness list, in addition to Fulbright, included Dean Acheson, Raoul Berger, William Bundy, J. Fred Buzhardt, Norman Dorsen, George Reedy, William H. Rehnquist, Dean Rusk, and a representative of William P. Rogers, who —if you can't remember him—was Nixon's Secretary of State when Henry Kissinger was only the presidential adviser on foreign affairs. Their views of executive privilege are of interest in determining the issues.

Senator Fulbright, then chairman of the Senate Foreign Relations Committee, was tired of, and upset by, the failure of the Nixon administration to keep Congress informed about its various machinations, whether in Southeast Asia, in South America, or in the Middle East. Fulbright was particularly distressed by the claimed exemption from legislative scrutiny of the work of Henry Kissinger and his staff, who were, in fact, in control of American foreign relations.[8] The argument was the one that I have already described: Kissinger and company were exempt from congressional scrutiny because their offices were located in the White House itself and not in the State Department.

The bill, in effect, called for the executive agencies to produce all data demanded by Congress, "unless executive privilege is invoked." But executive privilege could be invoked only by the President, *and* in writing, *and* accompanied by a statement of reasons why the privilege was being invoked. If information was denied without such an invocation of privilege, the recalcitrant executive office would have its financing automatically terminated.

The proposition that only the President could invoke executive privilege was not a novel one. Such a provision would in fact only codify written commitments to the same effect by Presidents Nixon, Johnson, and Kennedy.[9] Nor, it should be noted, did the bill deny the existence of executive privilege; it attempted to corral it pursuant to Congress's power "To make all Laws which shall be necessary and proper for carrying into Execution the foregoing Powers, and all other Powers vested by this Constitution in the Government of the United States, or in any Department or Officer thereof."

As Fulbright pointed out, the written commitments of the three Presidents had proved empty words:[10]

> . . . tactics of delay and evasion, permit the executive to exercise executive privilege without actually invoking it and without honoring the commitment of three Presidents that only the President would invoke executive privilege. As matters now stand, that commitment has been reduced to a meaningless technicality: Only the President may invoke executive privilege but just about any of his subordinates may exercise it—they simply do not employ the forbidden words. . . .
>
> In his memorandum to agency heads of March 24, 1969, outlining a procedure for compliance—or noncompliance—with Congressional

requests for information, President Nixon refers in passing—as if it were axiomatic—to the executive branch's responsibility of withholding certain information the disclosure of which would be incompatible with the public interest. Until and unless legislation is adopted by Congress to restrict executive privilege both as it applies to information and as it has been extended to shield individuals in high policy positions, the executive will continue to be the sole judge of that amorphous category called the public interest and of what is compatible or incompatible with it. It will still retain the power to decide for itself whether and to what extent it will be investigated. It will still be the judge and jury in cases of its own malfeasance and failures of judgment, of which there have been a great many in recent years.

The historical bases for sustaining or refuting the presence of a constitutionally implied executive privilege are, to be sure, certainly less convincing than the customs on which the constitutionality of the congressional investigatory power is based. History reveals essentially that Congress has frequently asserted the right to secure information from the executive branch. For the most part, these requests have been satisfied. On the other hand, and usually where critical societal questions were in issue, the executive frequently declined to make available the requested data to Congress. In these cases, sometimes Congress and sometimes the executive prevailed. It was a question of political power and the degree to which the President or the Congress was dominant at the time.

Alan Swan, in his testimony, encapsulated the history of these executive-legislative conflicts and, like the Supreme Court in *United States* v. *Nixon*, broke down the problem into three parts: investigative reports; foreign and military affairs; and internal deliberations of the executive branch. As to the history of secrecy with regard to investigative reports, he said:[11]

> [The precedents] are entirely equivocal. At most they show ambiguous action accompanied by brave words in which the Congress never acquiesced. . . . At the same time it cannot be denied that the progress of the Executive on this matter has been aided, perhaps decisively, by the occasional abuses of the investigative power.

The references to abuses of the investigative power are surely underlined by the history of gross misbehavior of both the House Committee on Un-American Activities, in the post–World War II era, and the investigations by Senator McCarthy during that same period. The high cost of this demagoguery and witch-hunting to the nation and to individuals is of public record and has left a deep and perhaps irremovable blot on the congressional escutcheon. The incapacity of Congress to keep secret what is told to them in secret in order to protect personal interests of nongovernmental employees is the major argument against the submission of such secrets to the scrutiny of the legislature. I am not here speaking of deliberate decisions by a committee or House vote that the materials labeled secret by the executive branch are not, in fact, entitled to secrecy, but rather of the Washington disease, of which I have already spoken, suffered both by Congress and the executive, of "leaking" the data for publication in the absence of proper authorization to do so.

In the foreign affairs category, the history as elucidated by Professor Swan was somewhat different:[12]

> [T]hroughout our history up to the first decade of this century, President and Congress alike recognized that the latter, particularly the Senate, had right to all information, without qualification, necessary to the discharge of its responsibilities concerning the Nation's foreign relations and that the Congress was free to make its own independent determination of what confidential information might be made public. At the same time, in recognition of the sensitivity of these matters and of the great weight to be attached to the President's judgment, the practice developed of extending to the President the courtesy of a discretion to withhold information. So long had this practice persisted, that toward the end of the period some partisans of the President, including some Senators, began attributing to it a mandatory character; a courtesy which had matured into a right upon which the President could insist. Such a view, however, was certainly contrary to the precedents and the theoretical foundations of the practice and appears never to have commanded a majority in the Congress.
>
> In the recent years since, the record becomes much less clear. Further systematic investigation is needed. Yet it does seem that calls to the President by resolution of the Senate or House appear with less frequency. The increased reliance upon committees, although essential, has bred a tendency to equate disclosures to and consultations with committee leaders as disclosure to the Congress. And while this has at times been a very effective way of imposing congressional views upon the Executive, it most surely has made it more difficult to preserve Congress in its historic role of guardian against excessive executive secrecy. Nor should we lose sight of the fact that in the intervening period the Executive has with increasing vigor asserted its claim to a plenary power to direct the Nation's foreign affairs. Under these circumstances, the Executive has been able without great difficulty to convert a historic courtesy into an unqualified claim of right, and to go largely unchallenged by Congress.

If the McCarthy era was evidence of the abuses committed on individuals by failure to keep secret investigative information secured from the executive branch, the evils of the power of the President to keep from Congress the facts about our foreign relations are revealed by the

Vietnam era. Starting with President Kennedy, exacerbated by President Johnson, and brought to the ultimate by President Nixon, the executive branch not only successfully refused Congress knowledge of what was actually going on, but did not cavil at telling downright lies both to the Congress and to the American public. The Bay of Pigs, the Cuban missile crisis, and the events revealed in the "Pentagon Papers," are sufficient evidence of this form of immorality by President Kennedy. The Gulf of Tonkin affair, the bombings of North Vietnam, and the excursions in Laos reveal the Johnson period deceptions. The five years of the conduct of the war and peace negotiations by the Nixon administration, including the bombings in Cambodia, certainly demonstrate the problems of excluding Congress from its rightful participation in making policy for the nation.

Dean Acheson, before the subcommittee, could testify from his own experience that the State Department and the Senate Foreign Relations Committee dealt with each other openly and constructively.[13] He conceded that things were different now because, he seemed to suggest, Kissinger was not a Stimson, a Marshall, an Acheson, a Dulles, and because Fulbright was not a Senator George or a Senator Vandenberg or a Senator Connally. But he was not prepared to suggest that a deterioration of the quality of personnel involved warranted congressional command to the executive to tell it what was going on in our foreign relations. And again, he insisted that secrets could not be communicated to Congress because "secrecy hardly outlasts the hearing hour itself, before everything said or produced is given to the press."[14]

The history in Swan's third category, internal executive communications, is even less decisive:[15]

> Finally, a word concerning the most difficult and perhaps most deceptive grounds asserted for the privilege: the protection of the internal deliberative processes of the executive branch. In theory it can be readily defended. It is not difficult to perceive that the power of Congress to scrutinize the opinions, the recommendations, the thinking processes, of the executive could inhibit the giving of candid and unpopular advice and the exercise of independent judgment, and in so doing render the Executive wholly subservient to Congress. Not surprisingly, therefore, the precedents for this privilege go back at least to 1833 when Andrew Jackson irately refused the Senate's request for a document purportedly read by him to the Cabinet regarding the removal of deposits from the Bank of the United States.
>
> Yet, this is potentially a most mischievous privilege. Virtually every scrap written in the executive branch can, if desired, be labeled an internal working paper. Rarely are matters neatly labeled "facts," "opinions," "advice." It can be used as readily to shield opinion corrupted by graft and disloyalty as to protect candor and honest judgment.

It was in this last category that most of the issues of executive privilege in the Watergate matter arose. And the history of Watergate is certainly sufficient to justify Professor Swan's concern about the abuse of the confidential communications privilege.

The hearings in 1971 developed consensus on some issues and conflicts on others. But it did not result in legislation. Congress, as usual, was too pusillanimous to engage the executive branch in direct confrontation over their respective powers. Congress, in fact, has the tools available, if it wishes to use them, to secure data that is refused it. Perhaps Congress is craven because it recognizes that Congress is less highly regarded by the public than is the President, any President. But then, perhaps, it is less highly regarded because of its docility and refusal to perform its constitutional functions. Certainly the Senate was never more esteemed than when it was conducting the Watergate hearings in full view of the public. Certainly the House proved its right to public trust in its Nixon impeachment inquiry, and not least when it was under the lights of the television cameras.

Most congressional committee operations do not get extensive news coverage. The 1971 hearings were among the many nonevents of congressional behavior so far as the news media were concerned. Had there been coverage, the public would have learned that Congress was in fact being denied a vast amount of information that it sought from the executive branch. Few if any of the denials came pursuant to the assertion of executive privilege by the President. Most were based on simple determinations by some one down the bureaucratic line that he preferred not to gather or deliver the information to the national legislature.

It was generally agreed at the 1971 hearings, however, that, whatever the scope of executive privilege, which none could adequately determine, it was a privilege personal to the President and could be asserted only by him. The concept of the privilege of those who contended for its existence was the necessity for keeping diplomatic and military secrets and for protecting confidential communications within the executive branch. Most of the argument about protection of secrets went not to the question of accessibility by Congress but rather to the dangers of general publication. For the most part, the senators testified that there never had been a leak from their committees and the executive officials spoke, as Acheson did, as if everything that was communicated was published. Obviously the truth was to be found somewhere in between.

Strangely, perhaps, the proponents of congressional prerogative spoke to the desirability of judicial review to resolve irreconcilable conflict between legislative right and executive privilege. Mr. Acheson, however, in his typically acerbic style, said of judicial review:[16] "Justice Frankfurter used to quote all the time, from Alexis de Tocqueville who said: 'In the United States every political question sooner or later is turned into a judicial question.' This is true, and it has been a disaster."

During the course of the Watergate investigation by the Senate, a series of satellite Senate "Watergate" hearings occurred. Included among these were the Judiciary Committee hearings on the nominations of Patrick Gray to be chief of the FBI[17] and of Elliot Richardson to be Attorney General.[18] There were also inquiries conducted under the mantle of the Judiciary Committee joined by the Government Operations Committee on the broad subject of secrecy, including the question of executive privilege.[19] The testimony here, particularly of two Attorneys General, Kleindienst and Richardson, is revealing of the problem in the Watergate context.

Kleindienst was arrogant, self-righteous, derogatory, cynical: typical of what we have come to think of as the Nixon administration posture—that it was subordinate only to the deity. A reading of his entire testimony would be informative. It is possible here to give only excerpts. He contended that executive privilege protected the President's staff from inquiry by Congress even with regard to criminal activities:[20]

SENATOR MUSKIE. . . .

> . . . As I think you are quite familiar, the Congress does, in connection with its investigative activities, often get into extensive investigations relating to crime, alleged crime for the purposes of developing legislative interests with regard to your department, the Department of Justice.
>
> If in connection with those inquiries the extent of which I assume you would agree is to be determined by the Congress, Congress comes to believe members of the President's staff have knowledge relating to the commission of crime, whether or not they themselves are the persons involved; is it your view that in connection with that legitimate process that the doctrine of executive privilege as you have defined it would make it possible for the President to withhold their testimony from the Congress?

MR. KLEINDIENST. That is my opinion, Senator Muskie.

Kleindienst also told the committee, in response to a question from Senator Kennedy based on Kleindienst's testimony, that the Attorney General was the final arbiter of what materials the Congress could secure from the Department of Justice:[21]

SENATOR KENNEDY. . . .

> So that I can understand somewhat more clearly, Mr. Kleindienst, your response and explanation to Senator Mathias, do I understand you to say that you are going to be the final arbiter as to what material will be made available to the Congress under these rather general outlines that you have given?

Mr. Kleindienst. Within the scope of my responsibilities as Attorney General and with respect to the investigative reports of the FBI, I think I would say I would be the arbiter on that.

In fact, Kleindienst had already bowed to the pressures of the Watergate committee but not to those of the Judiciary Committee, thus creating some intra-Senate jealousies, as revealed in Senator Kennedy's exchange:[22]

Mr. Kleindienst. On the Watergate situation, we worked out a procedure with Senator Ervin and Senator Baker and Senator Eastland and Senator Hruska so that the Senators and their counsel could have a complete, unrestricted access to the files of the FBI to aid in their investigation. I think I am the first Attorney General in 50 years who has ever done that.

Senator Kennedy. To certain Senators. And you were part of an agreement to let staff members view materials but not all representatives.

Mr. Kleindienst. That is right. . . .

Senator Kennedy. This was not the particular committee that had the question of jurisdiction over considering the nominee for the FBI?

Mr. Kleindienst. No. . . .

Senator Eastland and Senator Hruska were informed that I would apply the same procedure to the subsequent Judiciary Committee proceeding and they both acceded to that.

It was probably this agreement that caused Senator Ervin's gracious introduction of Kleindienst to the committee: "I would like to testify that the Attorney General has been most cooperative with the Senate Committee in its present activities and I think he deserves praise for so doing."[23]

However cooperative about the Senate Select Committee's access to the Department of Justice files, before the 1973 committee on executive privilege, Kleindienst was engaged in a favorite sport of the Nixon administration: "stonewalling." When asked whether executive privilege would extend to impeachment hearings, he surprisingly asserted that it would:[24]

Senator Roth. When I was on the House side there was an effort to bring about impeachment proceedings for a member of the Supreme Court. [The reference was to Congressman Gerald Ford's attempt to impeach Justice William O. Douglas.] Would the House have the right in such a case to procure evidence or information with respect to charges affecting a man's right to continue to hold office?

Mr. Kleindienst. In an impeachment proceeding?

Senator Roth. Yes.

MR. KLEINDIENST [showing what was occupying his thoughts]. Where they are impeaching the President of the United States—

SENATOR ROTH. Not necessarily the President, an officeholder, a judge for example.

MR. KLEINDIENST. If you are conducting an impeachment proceeding based upon high crimes and misdemeanors and you want to subpoena someone from the President's staff to give you information, I believe that, based upon the doctrine of separation of powers, the President would have the power to invoke executive privilege with respect to that information.

Mr. Kleindienst's understanding of the impeachment process also revealed the executive branch's deprecation of the possibility of an impeachment in the Watergate affair. Time after time he adverted to the possibility of presidential impeachment. Two exchanges with Senator Ervin are revealing:[25]

SENATOR ERVIN. If you will pardon the interjection. I think under your interpretation there would be no danger of the President's being impeached because he could forbid any witnesses to testify before the Senate or court.

MR. KLEINDIENST. I think you put a nice question, Senator Ervin, but you carried my hypothetical argument out to its logical extreme. If the only evidence necessary to impeach the President was contained in the bosom of his confidential adviser, I think his impeachment proceeding might not be predicated upon evidence. You do not need facts to impeach the President, because the Congress, if it has the votes, is the sole judge. The House passes a resolution, the Senate tries it, he is impeached, and there is no court of appeal. That is the end, with or without facts.

. . . .

SENATOR ERVIN. Your position is the President has implied power under the Constitution to deny to the Congress the testimony of any person working for the executive branch of the Government or any document in the possession of anybody working for the Government?

MR. KLEINDIENST. Yes, sir, and you have a remedy, all kinds of remedies, cut off appropriations, impeach the President . . .

SENATOR ERVIN. I understand that the main duty of the President under the Constitution and the main thing he ought to do under his oath of office is to "take care that the laws be faithfully executed," and I do not believe the President has the power to make sure the laws are not used.

MR. KLEINDIENST. If you ever found a President who abused his office you have your remedy and it is very carefully set forth, and if the new President abuses it you can get another one. . . .

You do not need evidence to impeach a President. You get the resolution passed by the House and the trial by the Senate and if the Senate votes on that trial, and if the Senate agrees, he is impeached. That is the end of it.

SENATOR ERVIN. You cannot try cases without evidence, even impeachment trials.

When the issue was made that congressional inquiry into violations of the criminal law by executive officials was not only proper but necessary, Kleindienst stuck to his guns. One more example. This time the colloquy was with Senator Muskie:[26]

SENATOR MUSKIE. . . .

You are certainly taking privilege as a protection of safeguards against allegations of crime for aides to the President. Well, now, why should they have a special safeguard that is not given to ordinary citizens, a special safeguard of this kind? Frankly, in all of my reading on executive privilege I have not previously encountered the assertion that executive privilege exists for the President to protect his aides against allegations of crime.

MR. KLEINDIENST. In terms of investigations it is an academic question whether he may invoke the privilege. No President has invoked the privilege regarding grand jury proceedings. President Nixon has stated he will not invoke it with respect to anybody on his staff. I do not believe any President would.

SENATOR MUSKIE. But if you say a criminal conspiracy involved the administration, its aides, the same administration appoints the Attorney General, the attorneys under it, determines what evidence will go before grand juries, what cases will be tried, and you say executive privilege exists in part to protect administrations against that kind of inquiry.

MR. KLEINDIENST. Yes, sir, but only if invoked by the President, under the doctrine of separation of powers. That is to say, criminal acts of our citizens whether by a Senator or anybody else should be very carefully looked into under constitutional safeguards our system has evolved. No President has ever kept anybody on his staff away from the criminal justice system. But Presidents in the past have directed their staff not to appear before the Congress, and the privilege could go into something like that. In many instances they said go down there and talk about your criminal conduct.

Attorney General Kleindienst did acknowledge the validity of some of the propositions put forth by the committee. He disqualified himself from participation in any of the Watergate prosecutions, even before the special prosecutor had been appointed. Later he worked out a deal with the special prosecutor. There is some irony in the fact that he pleaded guilty to violating 2 U.S.C. § 192, refusal to answer pertinent questions before a Senate committee. He was sentenced to thirty days in jail and a fine of $100. But his sentence was suspended.[27]

Attorney General Richardson did not come to the 1973 hearings until June 26. It was not an auspicious moment for the defense of executive privilege. The Watergate hearings were in full swing, and so Senator Kennedy could open the subcommittee hearings in this manner:[28]

> If yesterday's testimony at the caucus room teaches us anything, it demonstrates beyond debate that Government secrecy breeds Government deceit, that executive privilege nurtures executive arrogance, that national security is frequently the cover for political embarrassment, and that the best antidote to official malfeasance, misfeasance, and nonfeasance is the sunshine and fresh air of full public disclosure of official activities.
>
> High Government officials sat around in the Attorney General's office calmly discussing the commission of bugging and mugging and kidnapping and blackmail. How could they do this? They all thought that they would always be able to plead that any disclosure of their deliberations would intrude upon executive decisionmaking, and thus inhibit Federal employees in the future from giving free and frank advice to people like the Attorney General.

The Attorney General of whom Kennedy was speaking was, of course, John Mitchell and not Elliot Richardson. Richardson provided a sharp contrast to Mitchell's minion, Kleindienst. He is a Boston brahmin with sufficient credentials to appear both as scholar and dispassionate civil servant. The combativeness that had been present during the Kleindienst questioning did not arise between the senators and Richardson. Besides, Nixon had by then retreated from the position that his White House staff would not be permitted to testify before the Select Committee. But, if Nixon was in retreat, Richardson wasn't. Executive privilege was still to be defended as a necessary corollary of executive power.

Richardson was the epitome of the reasonable man in his testimony. His thesis was that comity between the two political branches of government was called for, that it had worked in the past and could work in the future if both branches were to perform their appropriate functions. In his book—almost everyone who left the administration because of the Watergate affair, even those who left with their reputations intact, or even enhanced as was the case with Richardson, wrote a book—Richardson summarized his position:[29]

> Significant constitutional issues, to be sure, remain undecided. *United States* v. *Nixon* involved a criminal proceeding, not a congressional inquiry; on the other hand, the evidence demanded did not concern national secrets. Considerations of comity and common

> sense, in any case, make it important still to rely, in executive-legislative relationships, upon practical considerations. What are these considerations? A sensible place to start is with two hierarchical lists: one ranking the purposes for which information is needed, from most urgent to least urgent; the second ranking the sensitivity of the information, from most to least seriously damaging if publicly disclosed. Other variables that may have a bearing include the comparative difficulty of preventing the leakage of information originally disclosed on a restrictive basis and, perhaps, the circumstance that a particular situation involves an inherent element of conflict as between the White House and the Congress. The separation of powers, after all, presupposes that the relationship among the branches of government will to a degree be adversarial.
>
> Even separate powers should try to get along—and this is all the more true when their common responsibility is the general welfare of the same citizenry. In international relations the spirit of mutual accommodation is called "comity." In June 1973, "comity" was the theme that I kept hammering on during nearly four and one-half hours of Senate testimony on freedom of information, executive privilege, and secrecy in government. I was determined not to let myself get trapped in the kind of theoretical exercise which led Attorney General Richard G. Kleindienst . . . to assert that executive privilege was so broad that the President could withhold from the Congress all papers or information held by any of the 2.5 million employees of the executive branch.

But, if the exchange was more civil, it was no more productive for the subcommittee's objectives. Had Ervin been there, he would probably have summarized the Richardson testimony in the biblical admonition: "Come now, and let us reason together."[30] Or perhaps, the exchange between Shakespeare's Hotspur and Glendower in *1 Henry IV* would have been a more accurate precis:[31]

GLENDOWER
  I can call spirits from the vasty deep.
HOTSPUR
  Why, so can I, or so can any man;
  But will they come when you do call for them?
GLENDOWER
  Why, I can teach you, cousin, to command the devil.
HOTSPUR
  And I can teach thee, coz, to shame the devil
  By telling truth. "Tell truth, and shame the devil."
  If thou have power to raise him, bring him hither,
  And I'll be sworn I have power to shame him hence.
  O, while you live, tell truth and shame the devil!

MORTIMER

Come, come, no more of this unprofitable chat.

The most profitable "chat" to come from the hearings was a workable definition of "executive privilege." I resort again to a colloquy in the 1973 hearings between Ervin and Kleindienst:[32]

SENATOR ERVIN. I concede that while there is no statement in the Constitution on executive privilege, I believe there is room for it in a very limited area, and if I were to define it myself, I would define executive privilege in these words: "Executive privilege is the power of the President to keep secret confidential communications between the President and an adviser or even among the advisers of the President which are made for the purpose of enabling the President, of assisting the President, to exercise in a lawful manner some constitutional or legal obligation resting upon him in his official capacity." . . .

MR. KLEINDIENST. That is a well-thought-out statement, as is customary for you.

I think it is too narrow and I am also inclined to say I think it is academic because I think the separation-of-powers doctrine confers that duty and responsibility, if you will, to the President of the United States.

SENATOR ERVIN. I would say that is a statement of the principle, and that all other things are merely an application of the principle; for example, the keeping of secrecy in military operations to assist the President in carrying out his powers as Commander in Chief. The secrets with respect to diplomatic negotiations are to assist the President in carrying out his obligations in negotiations with foreign countries and his powers as a speaking voice in foreign relations.

The definition of the principle was one thing. The application of the principle was another. For the principle cannot answer the question who is to be the arbiter of the propriety of its application. All the opponents of presidential power, whether Raoul Berger or the ACLU or Clark Clifford,[33] who testified at length, would make the courts that authority, although how the questions could properly be framed for speedy adjudication was never made clear. Arthur S. Miller, a consultant to the Ervin subcommittee, argued that the way to do it was to pass a statute defining the procedures and processes for the invocation of executive privilege so that a judicial test of the statute could resolve the general problem rather than leave its development to *ad hoc* decisions such as eventuated in *United States* v. *Nixon*. But, as usual, the Senate was given more to talk than to action, and the various statutory proposals that the 1973 hearings were supposedly considering died in the 93d Congress, as they had in the 92d, as they would in the 95th, and as they are likely to do each time the Congress seeks to assert its power against the executive branch.

Prior to the decision in *United States* v. *Nixon*, the ghost of executive privilege haunted the Select Committee's investigations. At the outset, Nixon asserted that he would invoke executive privilege to prevent all members of the White House staff from testifying before the Select Committee. Later, under the pressure of public opinion, he withdrew from that position. First, however, he sought to negotiate the matter—without success—with the committee. The reason for the attempt to make a deal with the committee was stated by Leonard Garment, White House counsel, to Samuel Dash, chief counsel of the Select Committee:[34]

> . . . it's very awkward for the President to have his counsel assert executive privilege and prevent his assistants from answering questions from your committee on Watergate matters on live TV before the whole public. Many people don't understand the legal concept of executive privilege, and will assume that it is the same thing as asserting the Fifth Amendment right against self-incrimination. They will draw all kinds of terrible inferences against the President or the White House staff member.

Certainly the evaluation was correct, unless when executive privilege was invoked an adequate reason for its invocation were also to be given. And this the President was unwilling to supply.

The problem of executive privilege arose again in connection with the testimony of John Dean. Dean was negotiating with the committee for the grant of use immunity, all that he could get under the existing statute.[35] At that time, Dean's lawyer, Charles Shaffer, stated:[36]

> The President has ordered Dean not to disclose any matters relating to national security on pain of criminal prosecution. That's one problem. Also, Dean's position was counsel to the President, and he may be prohibited from disclosing presidential conversations to which he was a party by reason of attorney-client privilege or executive privilege.

Dean acknowledged that none of his proposed testimony related in any way to matters of national security and further agreed that none of it properly fell within either privilege. The lawyer-client privilege did not protect criminal conspiracies between lawyer and client; nor, it was believed, did executive privilege permit the concealment of criminal acts.

As we all know now, Dean talked before the committee and the television cameras and made a devastating case against the President, if he could be believed. It was still true at that time, however, that in a contest between Dean's credibility and the President's—even the credibility of the President's silence—Dean was not likely to be the victor. Corroboration of Dean's testimony was to be found only in the White House tapes, and it was with regard to these that the stiffest defense of executive privilege was made. When that defense was ultimately broken by the Supreme Court in *United States* v. *Nixon*, the end of the Nixon presidency was quickly at hand.

It should be made clear, however, that it was not the committee's subpoena to the President for the tapes—Congress had never subpoenaed a President before—that brought forth the judicial command for production. For one reason or another, the courts steadfastly declined to enforce the committee's subpoena. The usual alliance between the second and third branches of government against the first branch, the Congress, held fast. It was in a conflict between the President and the judicial branch over a judicial subpoena for the tapes that the Supreme Court ruled in favor of its own power and ordered the production of the tapes.

If the Watergate processes contributed to an elucidation of the legal doctrine of executive privilege, they also afforded unfortunate proof of the validity of the executive worry that submission of the data to Congress is the equivalent of news media publication. I have already quoted Senator Baker's remark: "The Ervin Committee did not invent the leak, but we elevated it to its highest art form." It's not clear whether he was bragging or complaining. James Hamilton's more objective statement cannot be denied:[37]

> The Watergate game was played for high stakes. The Machiavellianism abounding during the investigations should not be underestimated. Leaks seeming to come from the committee may well have emerged from those under scrutiny or other sources. A well-placed leak could discredit the committee's endeavors by making it appear negligent or reckless in protecting its confidences. Or a leak could injure upcoming witnesses, publicize an aspect of a witness's testimony favorable to him, or divert attention from major issues. Because leakers do not as a rule tout their improper activities, and newsmen —the usual recipients of leaks—do not broadcast their confidential contacts, it was often impossible to pinpoint whether a particular leak came from committee or outside sources. Nevertheless, it can be said with assurance that senators and staff were the funnels for much of the confidential information that mysteriously appeared in the public domain during the committee's probes.

The likelihood of publication is certainly a factor in determining the legitimacy of the executive's assertion that information with some claim to confidentiality should not be transmitted to a body at least some of whose members may wish to make individual judgments as to the necessity for secrecy. When persons given access to the material include not only committee members but the entire Congress, and when the materials are available for publication, not only by the entire Congress, but by a very substantial part of its bureaucracy, confidentiality is not easily maintained.

On the other hand, it must be clear that the executive branch does not come to this question with clean hands. Despite Senator Baker's remark, the executive branch rather than the legislative is the master of the leak. Many of the confidential stories uncovered by so-called "investigative reporting" that appear in our daily and weekly press are mere handouts by executive branch officials, as Woodward and Bernstein's fascinating books, *All the President's Men* and *The Final Days*, demonstrate so fully. Confidentiality is a problem that goes far beyond executive privilege. For, as James Hamilton put it, "the principal protection against leaking [is] individual integrity, a commodity often sorely lacking."[38]

4

Judicial Arbiter

The courts were involved in the Watergate affair from the beginning. Indeed, if one takes a narrow view of the appropriate time period, it may be said that the Watergate episode was opened by the trial of the burglars accused of the break-in at the Democratic headquarters in the Watergate complex and that it was effectively closed by the Supreme Court decision in *United States* v. *Nixon*,[1] which commanded the production of the tapes even as the House Judiciary Committee met under the glaring lights of the television cameras.[2] In fact, the judicial processes wound on for many months after Nixon left the White House, particularly with the trial and appeals of those to whom the new President refused to grant mercy, as he had done to his predecessor. The Supreme Court declined to review the convictions in the last days of the 1976 term.[3]

The primary constitutional question addressed by the courts was that of "executive privilege." Two sets of cases were involved here. The first by the special prosecutor's office, the second by the Select Committee. The special prosecutor got almost all he asked; the Select Committee got nothing.

Let me trace first the failure of the Senate Committee to secure aid and comfort from the judiciary. As soon as Alexander Butterfield had publicly spilled the beans about the existence of the White House tapes, the committee issued subpoenas to the President for their production. He declined to honor them and thereby put the members of the Select Committee in a procedural box. They could, of course, have sought a presidential contempt citation from the entire Senate. But they knew that this was not likely to be forthcoming. Nor was it clear that a contempt of Congress citation would be enforceable against the President of the United States. Surely they could not seize him, as they had Kilbourn, and bring him before the bar of the Senate. Nor was it likely that they could get the United States Attorney to bring criminal contempt proceedings against the President. Still more dubious was the question whether a President of the United States is subject to criminal prosecutions while he holds office.

A conference was called with Senators Ervin and Baker, the chief counsel, chief minority counsel, and several other staff lawyers. Senator Ervin had invited two consultants from his Subcommittee on Separation of Powers to help canvass the possibilities for enforcement of the subpoenas through civil actions in the courts. These consultants informed the group that, in their opinion, jurisdiction for civil suit was highly uncertain, unless the trial court was anxious to rule in the committee's favor. They recommended the passage of legislation that would create jurisdiction.[4] Only Senator Ervin wanted to follow this course. Baker said a statute could not be secured under existing conditions. The staff and Senator Baker preferred to take their chances on various tenuous arguments for jurisdiction. The committee therefore went to court without the statute. (As it turned out, the statute would not have been of any help.)

When the committee filed its action, a subpoena sought by the special prosecutor had already been granted.[5] The committee could see no reason why it should not be equally successful. But Judge Sirica could. Emulating Marshall's judicial modesty in *Marbury* v. *Madison*,[6] Sirica found an absence of judicial power to enforce the congressional subpoena.[7]

It was refreshing, if frustrating, to read of the limited capacities of federal courts, especially in light of their theretofore—and thereafter—persistent grasp for power:[8]

> For the federal courts, jurisdiction is not automatic and cannot be presumed. Thus, the presumption in each instance is that a federal court lacks jurisdiction until it can be shown that a specific grant of jurisdiction applies. Federal courts may exercise only that judicial power provided by the Constitution in Article III and conferred by Congress. All other judicial power or jurisdiction is reserved to the states. And although plaintiffs may urge otherwise, it seems settled that federal courts may assume only that portion of the Article III judicial power which Congress, by statute, entrusts to them. Simply stated, Congress may impart as much or as little of the judicial power as it deems appropriate and the Judiciary may not thereafter on its own motion recur to the Article III storehouse for additional jurisdiction. When it comes to jurisdiction of the federal courts, truly, to paraphrase the scripture, the Congress giveth, and the Congress taketh away.

No doubt, Judge Sirica, like the devil, enjoyed quoting scripture, especially to Sam Ervin. As Sirica held, the Senate committee could not sue in the name of the United States: only "the Department of Justice, under direction of the Attorney General" can bring such a suit. Since it was necessary to reject all possible grounds for jurisdiction, Sirica also rested on a weaker reed, the need to satisfy the jurisdictional amount requirement for a case that "arises under the . . . laws . . . of the United States."[9] The difficulty with this basis for jurisdiction was explained by Sirica:[10]

> Unlike the statutes heretofore discussed, this provision includes a monetary sum or value as an incident of jurisdiction, the $10,000 jurisdictional amount. Although the amount has varied over the years, defendant is correct in his assertion that whatever the sum, it is a jurisdictional prerequisite. The satisfaction of a minimum amount-in-controversy is not a technicality; *it is a requirement imposed by Congress which the courts may not dispense with at their pleasure.*

The issue in controversy here, access of the Senate committee to the tapes, the court said, could not be valued at more than $10,000.

It is true that this irrational jurisdictional requirement exists. But there were cases that the court could have invoked to find that the issue was in fact worth more than $10,000.[11] He rejected these cases, in order to defeat jurisdiction.

Since jurisdiction was Congress's to bestow, as Sirica stated, Congress then bestowed it by passage of a law authorizing jurisdiction over the committee's suit. But this, too, proved of no avail. This time the question came before Judge Gesell for resolution, and he at least was not embarrassed to set up the supremacy of the judiciary as the one ultimately to determine whether Congress displayed an adequate interest to secure the tapes.[12] It seemed that it did not:[13]

> It has not been demonstrated to the Court's satisfaction that the Committee has a pressing need for the subpoenaed tapes or that further public hearings before the Committee concerning the content of those tapes will at this time serve the public interest.

Some years ago it might have been thought that the people's elected representatives were the proper authority to determine what was in the public interest. That era has long since passed. Gesell would have it that the sole function of Congress was to legislate—and that the Senate would best leave it to the judiciary to take care of the more important Watergate issues. With a becoming immodesty, Judge Gesell declared:[14]

> The Committee's role as a "Grand Inquest" into governmental misconduct is limited, for it may only proceed in aid of Congress' legislative function. The Committee has, of course, ably served that function over the last several months, but surely the time has come to question whether it is in the public interest for the criminal inves-

> tigative aspects of its work to go forward in the blazing atmosphere of ex parte publicity directed to issues that are immediately and intimately related to pending criminal proceedings. The Committee itself must judge whether or not it should continue along these lines of inquiry, but the Court, when its equity jurisdiction is invoked, can and should exercise its discretion not to enforce a subpoena which would exacerbate the pretrial publicity in areas that are specifically identified with pending criminal charges.
>
> The Court recognizes that any effort to balance conflicting claims as to what is in the public interest can provide only an uncertain result, for ours is a country that thrives and benefits from factional disagreements as to what is best for everyone. In assigning priority to the integrity of criminal justice, the Court believes that it has given proper weight to what is a dominant and pervasive theme in our culture. To be sure, the truth can only emerge from full disclosure. A country's quality is best measured by the integrity of its judicial processes. Experience and tradition teach that facts surrounding allegations of criminal conduct should be developed in an orderly fashion during adversary proceedings before neutral fact finders, so that not only the truth but the whole truth emerges and the rights of those involved are fully protected.

This kind of tunnel vision is endemic in the federal judiciary. For it, the important aspect of Watergate was that those guilty of criminal acts should be punished after receiving due process of law. There is no doubt that, for the federal courts in the District of Columbia, it was more important to punish criminals than to reveal the institutional deficiencies that were the origins of the constitutional crisis. But this is only to say in one more way that the judicial function is more important than the legislative.

On appeal, the Court of Appeals for the District of Columbia affirmed the trial court on different, if no more persuasive, grounds.[15] It argued that it need not reject the existence of a legislative oversight power, as the trial court had done. But the House Judiciary Committee had already instituted its impeachment hearings and since the House hearings rested on specific constitutional authority, said the Court, it was sufficient expression of congressional power of inquiry to leave access to the tapes to the House Judiciary Committee:[16]

> . . . the Judiciary Committee now has in its possession copies of each of the tapes subpoenaed by the Select Committee. Thus, the Select Committee's immediate oversight need for the subpoenaed tapes is, from a congressional perspective, merely cumulative. Against the claim of privilege, the only oversight interest that the Select Committee can currently assert is that of having these particular conver-

> sations scrutinized simultaneously by two committees. We have been shown no evidence indicating that Congress itself attaches any particular value to this interest. In these circumstances, we think the need for the tapes premised solely on an asserted power to investigate and inform cannot justify enforcement of the Committee's subpoena.

One can only speculate whether subpoenas from two federal courts conducting separate criminal trials should also be regarded as "merely cumulative." The Court of Appeals then went on to dispose of the need for the materials in support of the committee's "legislative function":[17]

> The sufficiency of the Committee's showing of need has come to depend, therefore, entirely on whether the subpoenaed materials are critical to the performance of its legislative functions. There is a clear difference between Congress's legislative tasks and the responsibility of a grand jury, or any institution engaged in like functions. While fact-finding by a legislative committee is undeniably a part of its task, legislative judgments normally depend more on the predicted consequences of proposed legislative actions and their political acceptability, than on precise reconstruction of past events; Congress frequently legislates on the basis of conflicting information provided in its hearings.

Therefore, said the court in its opinion, these facts are not among those necessary to the congressional legislative function and we deny enforcement of the subpoena. It will readily be seen that the court here was relying on the existence of executive privilege as the barrier to access by the Select Committee. It was a balancing of the privilege against the need of the Select Committee that was indulged by the court. It had held previously, in *Nixon* v. *Sirica*,[18] that there was an executive privilege against which it measured the needs of the grand jury for the data, and found the grand jury's interest superior. The Court of Appeals, therefore, did here what the Supreme Court was later to refuse to do, treat executive privilege vis-à-vis judicial subpoena as equally applicable to congressional inquiries. As the Supreme Court was to do, however, the Court of Appeals here, as it had in *Nixon* v. *Sirica*, reasserted the supremacy of the judicial branch. The executive and the legislative branches were to be confined in their operations to the degree that the judicial branch determined, not what was constitutionally prescribed, but what was the better public policy. Who better equipped with the bases for judgment as to public policy than the federal judiciary, whose black robes, like those of Merlin, confer access to wisdom, truth, and justice unavailable to ordinary mortals. It was years ago that this attitude was attacked by a federal judge as the "cult of the robe," and forty years ago that it was attacked by a President: "The judicial branch also is asked by the people to do its part in making democracy successful."[19]

It is apparent that the federal courts, despite Sirica's notions that their jurisdiction and the substantive rules governing that jurisdiction were entirely in the hands of Congress, continually and successfully frustrated the Select Committee's demand for information against an assertion of executive privilege by the President. For it was not the courts that made available the data to the House Judiciary Committee, although they approved it, but an act of the special prosecutor's office.[20]

The story of the judiciary's own right of access to the tapes by way of subpoena is a very different one. From the beginning of that quest, the courts upheld their own authority to compel the President to produce the evidence that he claimed to be privileged. When Archibald Cox went to Sirica for enforcement of his grand jury subpoena, Sirica was forthcoming. At least, he was prepared to examine the tapes himself to determine whether they contained data appropriate for the eyes of the prosecutor and the members of the grand jury.[21]

Sirica started with the legislative history of the Constitution, which afforded him evidence that there is no basis in the Constitution for executive privilege. His quotation from Charles Pinckney set the tone:[22]

> No privilege of this kind was intended for your Executive, nor any except that which I have mentioned for your legislature. The Convention which formed the Constitution well knew that this was an important point, and no subject had been more abused than privilege. They therefore determined to set the example, in merely limiting privilege to what was necessary and no more.

Sirica did not read this as a ban on executive privilege but rather as a license to the courts to determine "what was necessary." From there, he went on to cite the Supreme Court decision in *United States* v. *Reynolds*,[23] which found, he said, "an executive privilege, evidentiary in nature, for military secrets."[24] From this he derived the notion that, despite the original premise, there is also "an evidentiary privilege based on the need to protect Presidential privacy."[25] He did not point out that the *Reynolds* case was decided in the context of a statute which provided for privilege for military secrets. But that could make no difference to him, since surely there was nothing that Congress could do that the courts could not. Thus immediately, once again, came the assertion of judicial supremacy:[26]

> The Court, however, cannot agree with Respondent that it is the Executive that finally determines whether its privilege is properly invoked. The availability of evidence including the validity and scope of privileges, is a judicial decision.

The mode for effectuating judicial supremacy required all that was called for by the subpoena to be submitted to the court *in camera* for its review:[27]

> If after judicial examination *in camera,* any portion of the tapes is ruled not subject to privilege, that portion will be forwarded to the grand jury at the appropriate time. To call for the tapes *in camera* is thus tantamount to fully enforcing the subpoena as to any unprivileged matter. Therefore, before the Court can call for production *in camera*, it must have concluded that it has authority to order a President to obey the command of a grand jury subpoena as it relates to unprivileged evidence in his possession.

The court answered this question by a not uncommon judicial technique of stating its conclusion in its premise:[28] "Analysis of the question must begin on the well established premises that the grand jury has a right to every man's evidence and that for purposes of gathering evidence, process may issue to anyone." The burden was, therefore, on the President to show that, by reason of his office, he is not "every man." That burden, the court found, the President could not carry.

The conclusion that the office of the presidency is entitled to no special treatment is followed by an encomium to the grand jury process:[29]

> The grand jury is well known to Anglo-American criminal justice as the people's guardian of fairness. Ever since the Earl of Shaftesbury relied upon its integrity, the grand jury has been promoted as a shield for the innocent and a sword against the guilty. . . . [W]hen that group, independent in its sphere, acts according to its mandate, the court cannot justifiably withhold its assistance, nor can anyone, regardless of his station, withhold from it evidence not privileged.

The judge saw in the grand jury the representatives of the people, a role he was not prepared to concede to the elected members of the Congress. This praise for the grand jury would be amusing if the matter were not so serious. Today, the grand jury, far from serving its original purpose, has become a mere tool of the prosecutor. It is more often an engine of oppression than a protector of liberty.[30] It has been abandoned in England, where it was born, and in many American states, as an anachronism. Today, a grand jury indictment differs little from a prosecutor's information. Both are the product of the prosecutor. There is little evidence of grand jury independence.

Given the problem of balancing the need of the grand jury for the evidence and the "need to favor the privacy of Presidential deliberations, to indulge a presumption in favor of the President"[31]—a strange presumption in light of the earlier portions of the opinion—the court would examine the documents in the case and, in its wisdom, reveal what should be revealed and conceal what, in its wisdom, should be concealed. In making such judgment, the court made it clear that "If the interest served by a privilege is abused or subverted, the claim of privilege fails."[32]

The President and the special prosecutor appealed the trial court judgment. The prosecutor sought a ruling that the materials were to be turned over to that palladium of justice, the grand jury, without prior judicial scrutiny. Again, there was doubt that the appellate court had jurisdiction to review such an interlocutory order. But the Court of Appeals for the District of Columbia Circuit, showing none of the qualms that Sirica demonstrated carefully to limit judicial authority to that which Congress specifically mandated, quickly resolved the question in favor of its own jurisdiction, at least as to the President's appeal.

The Court of Appeals found, what no one else has been able to discover, "the longstanding judicial recognition of Executive privilege,"[33] and the equally long-standing power of courts to override it.[34] In fact, the judicial opinions cited by the court as authorities do not deal with the immunities of Presidents and certainly not with the confidential communication privilege asserted in the case before it. And the reliance for the most part is on dicta rather than holdings. Be that as it may, the court had no difficulty in concluding that a grand jury has the right to every man's evidence—including the President's—unless it is privileged. Whether it is privileged is to be determined not by the President but by the judiciary, for no man is above the law and the judiciary is the law. In balancing the interests of the grand jury against those of executive privilege, the court thought the President hoist by his own petard, and those of former White House associates who had informed against him:[35]

> Our conclusion that the general confidentiality privilege must recede before the grand jury's showing of need, is established by the unique circumstances that made this showing possible. In his public statement of May 22, 1973, the President said: "Executive privilege will not be invoked as to any testimony concerning possible criminal conduct or discussions of possible criminal conduct, in the matters presently under investigation, including the Watergate affair and the alleged cover-up." We think that this statement and its consequences may properly be considered as at least one factor in striking the balance in this case. Indeed, it affects the weight we give to factors on both sides of the scale. On the one hand, the President's action presumably reflects a judgment by him that the interest in the confidentiality of White House discussions in general is outweighed by such matters as the public interest . . . in the integrity of the level of the Executive Branch closest to the President, and the public interest in the integrity of the electoral process. . . . Although this judgment in

> no way controls our decision, we think it supports our estimation of the great public interest that attaches to the effective functioning of the present grand jury. . . .
>
> At the same time, the public testimony given consequent to the President's decision substantially diminishes the interest in maintaining the confidentiality of conversations pertinent to Watergate. The simple fact is that the conversations are no longer confidential. . . . In short, we see no justification, on confidentiality grounds, for depriving the grand jury of the best evidence of the conversations available.

Why these arguments should not have been equally applicable to the Senate inquiry, we shall never know.

The Court of Appeals for the District of Columbia Circuit is made up not only of judges but of statesmen. It did not want to be overbearing; so, as it said:[36]

> Two days after oral argument, this Court issued a Memorandum calling on the parties and counsel to hold conversations toward the objective of avoiding a needless constitutional adjudication. Counsel reported that their sincere efforts had not been fruitful. It is our hope that our action in providing what has become an unavoidable constitutional ruling, and in approving, as modified, the order of the District Court, will be followed by maximum cooperation among the parties. Perhaps the President will find it possible to reach some agreement with the Special Prosecutor as to what portions of the subpoenaed evidence are necessary to the grand jury's task.

This was a license to negotiate a settlement that would deprive the trial court order of any force and effect. What was thought to be an act of statesmanship, however, turned out to be equivalent to throwing a lighted match into a tank of kerosene. Indeed, the decision of the Court of Appeals in *Nixon* v. *Sirica* was the decisive event of Watergate: not because of its constitutional ruling, but because the chain of events that followed clearly turned public opinion against the man in the White House. The role of the federal judiciary as mediator in problems of state—witness the mediation in the Hayes-Tilden election—is of dubious validity or worth. If its legitimacy turns on its success, there is no doubt that this mediation power, at least, was conceived on the wrong side of the blanket.

Nixon grasped the offer of the Court of Appeals to negotiate a settlement. He announced that he would not appeal the judgment to the Supreme Court because it was not in the best interests of the nation "to leave this matter unresolved for the period that might be required for a review by the highest court," although he was confident that his position would be sustained there.[37]

Nixon's notions about negotiating consisted of an attempt to dictate the compromise to be effected. His approach was more than devious; it was predicated on plain prevarication. His plan was to provide summaries of the relevant tape material—summaries that he prepared—to both the Senate Select Committee and the grand jury. The veracity of those summaries was to be tested by submitting the tapes themselves to Senator Stennis for comparison with the summaries. And, as part of this "negotiated" compromise, he said:[38]

> Accordingly, though I have not wished to intrude upon the independence of the special prosecutor, I have felt it necessary to direct him, as employee of the Executive Branch, to make no further attempts by judicial process to obtain tapes, notes, or memoranda of Presidential conversations. I believe that with the statement that will be provided to the court, any legitimate need of the special prosecutor is fully satisfied and that he can proceed to obtain indictments against those who may have committed any crimes.

The plan was totally rejected by Cox. Although it was announced that Ervin and Baker had agreed to the proposal, the fact was that the proposal they had agreed to was not the proposal announced by the President.[39]

The President's next step was to order the Attorney General, Elliot Richardson, to fire Cox as special prosecutor. Richardson declined and resigned. The Deputy Attorney General also declined and sought to resign but was fired for refusing to obey orders. The third in command, the Solicitor General, Robert Bork, a nonpolitical officer, was urged by both Richardson and Ruckelshaus to remain in office after doing what was certainly going to be done sooner or later.[40] Bork fired Cox. The consequence was a windstorm of criticism of Bork, who had made a hard choice if not the right one. Subsequent to his action, a trial court held, and later the Supreme Court implied, that Cox could not legally be fired so long as the executive order specifying his tenure remained in effect.[41] If, as some have suggested, Bork recognized the illegality of his act, he was, of course, not justified in his actions on the ground of "superior orders." But he did not have the benefit of hindsight now available to us. As Elliot Richardson has recorded it:[42]

> Bill Ruckelshaus had also sent over a letter of resignation. The President refused to accept it and directed General Haig to fire him instead. Who, then, would be left to fire Archibald Cox? The Solicitor General, Robert H. Bork, was next in line. He believed that the President had the right to order Cox fired and had no personal compunctions about wielding the axe. He felt, however, that if he went through with it he should then resign himself. "I don't want to stay on and be perceived as an *apparatchik*," he said. Bill and I persuaded

him that this should not in itself be a sufficient concern to justify the drastic loss of continuity at Justice that would result if he also resigned.

The result of the dismissal of Cox was what General Haig called a "firestorm." Almost immediately, two hundred and twenty thousand telegrams were sent to the President and Congress, an extraordinary portion of which condemned the action. All sorts of persons, from the president of the American Bar Association to George Meany, many of whom would be expected to be in the President's camp, chastised him publicly. The House of Representatives began to take seriously the notion of impeachment and took steps toward that end. The public reaction was so extreme that when Charles Alan Wright appeared before Judge Sirica on October 23, four days after the Cox firing, he announced that the President had decided to "comply in all respects" with the court order.[43]

General Alexander Haig told a news conference on the same day that "the President concluded after very painful and anguished discussions that the circumstances were sufficiently grave that he should abandon his very strongly and long held right to protect the prerogatives of his office not only for himself but for future Presidents."[44] Haig denied that the decision had been a consequence of the impeachment move, claiming that it derived rather from the "whole milieu of national concern" over the recent events.[45] (Parenthetically, it may be noted that the promise to deliver all the tapes subpoenaed was not fully met; some of them turned out to be nonexistent, and one contained an eighteen and one-half minute erasure. It was never explained by whom the erasure was made, but it was established that the deletion was intentional.)

One week later, the House Judiciary Committee began its impeachment inquiry. The investigations of presidential and White House misbehavior had now turned into a three-ring circus: the Senate committee was going forward; the criminal investigations were proceeding, soon under the new prosecutor, Leon Jaworski, to whom the President promised complete independence; and the impeachment inquiry was proceeding in the House of Representatives. Meanwhile it appeared that all government in Washington dependent on presidential direction had come to a grinding halt. Watergate overshadowed everything.

The appetite or needs of the grand jury—or its alter ego, the special prosecutor—for the tapes were not sated by what was delivered to them after screening by Sirica. After a period of negotiated deliveries, the President finally called a halt. Jaworski had to go to court again; again the court issued an order for production. This time, the President declined to obey. He quickly filed his appeal in the Court of Appeals, and thus opened the door for the prosecutor to ask for review by the

Supreme Court of the United States before judgment by the Court of Appeals. This was the route that had brought an earlier President's overreaching to grief in the *Steel Seizure Case*.[46] The same occurred this time. The Supreme Court just could not abstain from playing a role in this constitutional crisis of our time. If it did not act immediately, it might find that events had passed it by, and so it granted certiorari, had a special hearing, and came down with the decision under the unfortunately appropriate title *United States* v. *Nixon*.[47] Its decision came down on the very day that the impeachment hearings went public on national television. Its contribution to their outcome is not to be denied.

The Court quickly overcame doubts about its jurisdiction to review what was essentially an interlocutory order. It had equally little difficulty in determining that the issue was a justiciable one, although the President claimed that this was a controversy within the executive branch and not subject to resolution by the courts. The regulations under which the special prosecutor was acting had the force of law and removed his actions from control by the Attorney General or the President. There was a real case or controversy not resolvable by any authority within the executive branch. Moreover, the technical requirements of Rule 17 of the Federal Rules of Criminal Procedure, governing the issuance of subpoenas, had been met. Thus, the Court addressed the issue of executive privilege.

Once again, the Court starts out with an announcement of its own preeminence:[48]

> In the performance of assigned constitutional duties each branch of the Government must initially interpret the Constitution, and the interpretation of its powers by any branch is due great respect from the others. . . . Many decisions of this Court, however, have unequivocally reaffirmed the holding of *Marbury* v. *Madison*, 1 Cranch 137 (1803), that "[i]t is emphatically the province and duty of the judicial department to say what the law is." *Id.*, at 177.

The Court then went on to say that, while there was no direct precedent with regard to presidential privilege for confidential communications, "other exercises of power by the Executive Branch and the Legislative Branch have been found invalid as in conflict with the Constitution. . . . Since this Court has consistently exercised the power to construe and delineate claims arising under express powers, it must follow that the Court has authority to interpret claims with respect to powers alleged to derive from enumerated powers."[49] As if to convince itself rather than its audience, the Court repeated its precedents on its own authority. "We therefore reaffirm that it is the province and duty of this Court 'to say what the law is' with respect to the claim of privilege presented in this case."[50]

Recognizing its own interest in confidentiality—and it would indeed be interesting to discover what the Court's reaction would be to a subpoena to the Justices for their conference notes for use in a criminal trial—the Court didn't take long to find a confidential communication privilege for the President in the Constitution. Indeed, it was "too plain to require further discussion."[51] But the privilege was not an absolute one:[52]

> To read the Art. II powers of the President as providing an absolute privilege as against a subpoena essential to enforcement of criminal statutes on no more than a generalized claim of the public interest in confidentiality of nonmilitary and nondiplomatic discussions would upset the constitutional balance of "a workable government" and gravely impair the role of the courts under Art. III.

The confidential communication privilege is, nevertheless, a most important one:[53]

> The expectation of a President to the confidentiality of his conversations and correspondence, like the claim of confidentiality of judicial deliberations, for example, has all the values to which we accord deference for the privacy of all citizens and, added to those values, is the necessity for protection of the public interest in candid, objective, and even blunt or harsh opinions in Presidential decisionmaking.

For those who wondered where in the Constitution the privilege was to be found, the answer was: "The privilege is fundamental to the operation of Government and inextricably rooted in the separation of powers under the Constitution."[54] Nevertheless, fundamental as the privilege is, it must be abated when in conflict with the need of criminal courts for evidence:[55]

> In this case the President challenges a subpoena served on him as a third party requiring the production of materials for use in a criminal prosecution; he does so on the claim that he has a privilege against disclosure of confidential communications. He does not place his claim of privilege on the ground they are military or diplomatic secrets. As to these areas of Art. II duties the courts have traditionally shown the utmost deference to Presidential responsibilities. . . . No case of the Court, however, has extended this high degree of deference to a President's generalized interest in confidentiality. Nowhere in the Constitution, as we have noted earlier, is there any explicit reference to a privilege of confidentiality, yet to the extent this interest relates to the effective discharge of a President's powers, it is constitutionally based.

The last two sentences could as easily have read: "No case of the Court, however, has rejected this high degree of deference to a President's generalized interest in confidentiality. Nowhere in the Constitution is there any explicit reference to a privilege for diplomatic or military secrets," etc.

And so the opinion goes on, like the description of a tennis match. First the Court is on the side of the privilege and then on the side of the subpoena, over and over again, until ultimately it is game, set, and match—to the referee:[56]

> We conclude that when the ground for asserting privilege as to subpoenaed materials sought for use in a criminal trial is based only on the generalized interest in confidentiality, it cannot prevail over the fundamental demands of due process of law in the fair administration of criminal justice. The generalized assertion of privilege must yield to the demonstrated, specific need for evidence in a pending criminal trial.

"The generalized assertion of privilege must yield to the demonstrated, specific need for evidence in a pending criminal trial." Perhaps the same thing could not be said about the clearly constitutionally defined privilege against self-incrimination. But can it not be said about the confidential communication privileges that have no constitutional base at all, such as the lawyer-client privilege, the priest-penitent privilege, the spousal privilege? If not, why not? After all, it was so held, said the Court, with reference to the privilege of secrecy of grand jury proceedings.[57]

We are told that there is a constitutional basis for the executive privilege, which is divided, not into five parts, as I suggested earlier, but only into three parts: confidential communications, military secrets, and diplomatic secrets. It would appear that the first is outweighed by the need for evidence in criminal trials, while the other two may or may not be. We are also told that the discussion of executive privilege was confined so that it did not necessarily control claims for materials either in civil litigation or by Congress, or where—whether this is a fourth category is not revealed—"the President's interest [is] in preserving state secrets."[58]

The consequences of the decision are known. After toying with the idea of disobeying the Supreme Court's judgment, which was by a unanimous 8 to 0 vote, but recognizing that the failure to abide the decision would constitute a count in an almost certain impeachment by the House, the President agreed to surrender the tapes. Indeed, he went further and published them and thereby provided the House Judiciary Committee with "the smoking gun" demanded by those congressmen who had been dragging their heels on impeachment. The President tested the waters, found them boiling, and submitted his resignation.

United States v. *Nixon* was the penultimate judicial decision in the Watergate affair. The ultimate decision was in the criminal trial of Ehrlichman and company. The initial judicial participation was that of Judge Sirica in the case of the burglary defendants. Let me turn now to these and one or two other judicial Watergate escapades in constitutional law.

You will recall that one of the concerns of the federal courts about enforcing the Senate subpoenas was that publicizing the material thus secured could preclude the capacity of the criminal defendants to secure a fair trial, *i.e.*, it would be impossible to empanel a jury unbiased by knowledge of the events on which they were to sit in judgment. This question of the adverse effects of undue publicity arose again and again. But, outside the context of the Senate investigation, it weighed very lightly indeed on the judiciary.

The special prosecutor had determined to turn over to the House Judiciary Committee—not to the Senate Select Committee—the evidence he had secured from the tapes and other subpoenas, as well as an evaluation of the grand jury testimony. Two of the Watergate defendants, Haldeman and Strachan, took exception to that proposal on the ground that the publication of the data would prejudice their trials. The Court of Appeals denied them relief by sustaining the trial court's discretion in approving the delivery.[59]

There is no doubt that the law provides for preserving the secrecy of grand jury proceedings "except where there is a compelling necessity" to breach it.[60] But the Court found that the defendants' complaint about this breach of security was inadequate or, at least, premature:[61]

> We note, as did also the District Judge, that, if the disclosures to the public so feared by petitioners do in fact take place and have the consequences that petitioners predict, they will be free at trial to raise these claims in the light of what has actually happened, and to seek the traditional relief ranging from continuance through change of venue to dismissal of their indictments. It appears to be premature at the least to make their speculations about future prejudice the basis for present employment of our extraordinary writ power. With respect to the substance of those speculations, we cannot be unaware of the fact that the Special Prosecutor has concluded that his interests in successful prosecutions can be reconciled with this transmittal for consideration in the impeachment process—thereby suggesting that the dangers in his estimation are not great. The District Judge who received the indictment, perused the materials accompanying the report, and expressed his general interest in the fairness of the trial over which he will preside later this year, also concluded that it is unlikely that this transmittal will interfere with a fair trial.

By putting the burden on the defendants to show that their predilections should overcome the preferences of the special prosecutor and the trial judge, the court avoided determining whether there was a "compelling necessity" for the invasion of the confidentiality of the grand jury process. Not that such an issue would have proved troublesome. For, after all, the question of "compelling necessity" is only one aspect of what is the "public good," a question that the federal courts in the District of Columbia never had any difficulty in resolving.

Indeed, when the question here postponed as premature arose at the trial of the White House defendants, the courts were adequately satisfied that whatever publicity had occurred did not preclude the empanelment of a jury that would judge the defendants solely on the basis of the evidence produced in court and without bias or prejudice from the publicity.[62] The *voir dire*—the examination of potential jurors before they are chosen—indicated that of the 120 called, only 13 "indicated they had an unfavorable opinion about the defendants."[63] Of the jurors selected, "none had expressed an opinion about the defendants' guilt, although one had heard that there had been a break-in [the Fielding break-in, not the Democratic National Committee break-in] by someone and another had heard that Ehrlichman was 'involved' . . . [N]one expressed any particular interest in Watergate. . . . [The judge's] examination did not reveal a deep seated prejudice against defendants that would make the voir dire procedure suspect."[64]

One must conclude that if the jurors were as ignorant as the court made them out to be, they were far too ingenuous to comprehend or to analyze the evidence that was to be produced at the trial. On the other hand, apparently the presumption of innocence indulged for jurors far outweighs the presumption of innocence for defendants. And one cannot but wonder how a court that had been so concerned to keep the subpoenaed data from the Senate committee on the grounds that the undue publicity would adversely affect the criminal law processes must have felt about the inadequacy of its predictive capacities; for everything that the Senate committee had sought had been published before the Ehrlichman trial. Even for federal judges, however, hindsight proves more accurate than foresight.

There is still one more inconsistency—or what appears to be an inconsistency—between earlier decisions and the one in the *Ehrlichman* case. For the case again presented the question of executive privilege, this time for an ex-President. The question arose here on Ehrlichman's subpoenas for presidential records and for testimony by Nixon both at the trial and by way of interrogatories. Despite the duty of every man to appear to testify when called, despite the fact that the burdens of office no longer inhibited such appearance, the presumption of privilege was held not sufficiently overcome by a demonstration of Ehrlichman's need for either the answers to his specific interrogatories, the papers he sought from the files, or the appearance of the witness. The courts, trial and appellate, simply decided that the ex-President's data collection and his testimony would not be relevant. This evidence was not to be submitted to the petit jury. Whether an earlier request for the same materials by the prosecutor for the use of the grand jury would have met the same fate is highly doubtful in light of the judicial precedents.

The *Ehrlichman* case, and its companion cases in the Court of Appeals for the District of Columbia,[65] raised some interesting but still unanswered questions of constitutional law. Throughout the Watergate episode the primary defense offered for the misconduct of the Plumbers and their bosses had been that their actions were taken for purposes of "national security," under the direction of their superiors. These propositions were again offered in defense in the criminal trials.

Ehrlichman was charged, inter alia, with conspiring to violate the constitutional rights of Dr. Fielding, whose office was invaded and searched by the Plumbers under the direction of Ehrlichman. Ehrlichman's defense was twofold: First, that the break-in and search were legal because of the President's authority in the field of foreign affairs to order such entries. Second, that if the entry and search were not in fact legal, Ehrlichman lacked the requisite intent to commit the crime because he believed that they were in fact legal.

The appeals court, like the trial court, rejected both defenses. It held that good faith belief in the legality of his actions was not enough to afford Ehrlichman a defense. So long as he intended the actions which in fact deprived Fielding of his civil rights, Ehrlichman could be found guilty of the crime.[66] This conclusion required a rather tortuous reading of a tortuous opinion by the Supreme Court in an infamous case called *Screws* v. *United States*,[67] which has always been more or less of an enigma. This question, however, presented no constitutional problem.

On the second element of the defense, the legality of the entry, there was indeed an underlying constitutional question. And the Department of Justice, not a party to this prosecution, filed a brief amicus curiae in this case and companion cases asserting that a President has implied power to authorize "black bag" jobs without judicial warrant, where the entries and searches are related to foreign affairs rather than domestic concerns. The court's opinion did not reach the implied power of the presidency for such warrantless searches, because it found that there was no presidential authorization in this instance:[68]

> The defendant totally misapprehends the critical role played by the President and the Attorney General, when the "national security" exception is invoked. It is argued that this exception gives government officials the power surreptitiously to intrude on the privacy of citizens without the necessity of first justifying their action before an

> independent and detached member of the judiciary. Unless carefully circumscribed, such a power is easily subject to abuse. The danger of leaving delicate decisions of propriety and probable cause to those actually assigned to ferret out "national security" information is patent, and is indeed illustrated by the intrusion undertaken in this case, without any more specific Presidential direction than that ascribed to Henry II vexed with Becket.[69]
>
> As a constitutional matter, if Presidential approval is to replace judicial approval for foreign intelligence gathering, the personal authorization of the President—or his alter ego for these matters, the Attorney General—is necessary to fix accountability and centralize responsibility for insuring the least intrusive surveillance necessary and preventing zealous officials from misusing the President's prerogative.

The last quoted sentence was repeated in the opinion, as if to make up for the absence of even a shadow on the Constitution to support such details as to how the President's foreign affairs powers are to be managed, if indeed he has such powers as the court hypothesizes. It should be pointed out that two of the three judges, *i.e.*, a majority of the court, while conceding that the question was not present on the facts of the case, insisted on answering the question whether even the President or his Attorney General could authorize home or office invasion without judicial warrant. They found no such authority explicit or implicit in Article II.

When the Court of Appeals turned from Ehrlichman's case to that of Bernard Barker and Eugenio Martinez, two of the Watergate burglars who had also carried out the invasion of Dr. Fielding's office, it turned a more sympathetic ear to what was a dubious claim of "superior orders." If allowed to become law, it will exonerate the lower echelons, and perhaps all but the highest, for invasion of individual freedoms, on claims of reasonable reliance on superior orders. Thus, the Court of Appeals' majority, in separate opinions by Judges Wilkey and Merhige and over the dissent of Judge Leventhal, created a new defense of reasonable ignorance of the law.

Judge Wilkey rested in part on the decision by the Department of Justice not to prosecute Richard Helms, Director of the CIA, for a 1971 break-in in Virginia. Wilkey said:[70]

> Helms, like the present defendants, was involved in a 1971 break-in to conduct a visual search for evidence of national security violations. The positions of both Helms and the present appellants rest upon good faith belief that their warrantless physical intrusions were legally authorized. Helms' belief, which led the Justice Department to decline prosecution, was that a statute authorized him to ignore the commandments of the Fourth Amendment. Barker's and Martinez's

belief was that there was authorization within the White House for this intrusion relating to national security—a legal theory which, if valid, would be of constitutional rather than merely statutory dimensions. Though both were mistakes of law, appellants' view thus appears to be supported by sounder legal theory than that of Helms, who seems to assert that a statute can excuse constitutional compliance. Yet even in the case of Helms, the Attorney General concluded that any prosecution for the physical search would be inappropriate.

The court leaves it quite unclear why Ehrlichman was held to the strict letter of the law, while Barker and Martinez could rely on their reasonable belief of the law. The difference apparently related not to an understanding of the law, but whether the persons accused were executing orders or issuing them. And while this may distinguish Ehrlichman from the two Cubans, it does not distinguish Ehrlichman from Helms, on whose case that of Barker and Martinez was predicated. Surely the argument of the court as to the substantiality of the claims is the same for all four men:[71]

> As to the *reasonableness* of the legal theory on which Barker's and Martinez's actions rest, they thus have at least the position of the Attorney General behind them. This is not to hold here that the position is correct, but surely two laymen cannot be faulted for acting on a known and represented fact situation and in accordance with a legal theory espoused by this and all past Attorneys General for forty years.

When the legal question that the Court of Appeals declined to address gets to the Supreme Court, it will likely choose between two theories. It may rule against any implied presidential power of home and office invasion in foreign affairs cases, or it may assert that only a specific authorization from the President or the Attorney General will suffice as a substitute for a judicial warrant in this area. The effect of either decision on the *Barker* doctrine is far from clear.

Two other constitutional questions afforded by the Watergate affair are worthy of at least cursory notice. The first of these resulted from the fact that, even before the burglary trial, the *Los Angeles Times* published a story based on a taped interview with Alfred Baldwin in which he said he had a role in the burglary. Lawyers for one of the defendants sought a subpoena of the tape of the interview, which was in the hands of the Washington bureau chief of the *Times*. The court issued the subpoena but the newsman refused to produce the tape. He was held in jail until released pending resolution of the question whether he was entitled to keep the tape from the court because of a newsman's privilege to keep his sources confidential. The *Times* had pledged confidentiality to Baldwin for the taped interview. Before the issues could be ultimately resolved by the judicial process, however, Baldwin released the newspaper from its pledge of secrecy and the tape was turned over to the court.

At best, the newspaper's claim to privilege rested on weak grounds. Baldwin was named in the news stories as the source for the published material. The essence if not the totality of the interview was also published. There was little substance to the claim for secrecy. And, more important, the newsman's privilege to protect even anonymous informants was rejected by the Supreme Court in an opinion in *Branzburg* v. *Hayes* in 1972.[72] That opinion is an interesting precursor to the executive privilege cases, for in both the question was, To what degree is there implied in the Constitution a privilege to keep relevant data from revelation to the grand jury? The Court's opinion in *Branzburg* is instructive, as the following excerpts reveal:[73]

> The sole issue before us is the obligation of reporters to respond to grand jury subpoenas as other citizens do and to answer questions relevant to an investigation into the commission of crime. Citizens generally are not constitutionally immune from grand jury subpoenas; and neither the First Amendment nor any other constitutional provision protects the average citizen from disclosing to a grand jury information that he has received in confidence. The claim is, however, that reporters are exempt from these obligations because if forced to respond to subpoenas and identify their sources or disclose other confidences, their informants will refuse or be reluctant to furnish newsworthy information in the future. This asserted burden on news gathering is said to make compelled testimony from newsmen constitutionally suspect and to require a privileged position for them.
>
> . . . .
>
> Thus, we cannot seriously entertain the notion that the First Amendment protects a newsman's agreement to conceal the criminal conduct of his source, or evidence thereof, on the theory that it is better to write about crime than to do something about it. Insofar as any reporter in these cases undertook not to reveal or testify about the crime he witnessed, his claim of privilege under the First Amendment presents no substantial question. The crimes of news sources are no less reprehensible and threatening to the public interest when witnessed by a reporter than when they are not.
>
> . . . .
>
> Finally, as we have earlier indicated, news gathering is not without its First Amendment protections, and grand jury investigations if instituted or conducted other than in good faith, would pose wholly different issues for resolution under the First Amendment. Official harassment of the press undertaken not for purposes of law enforce-

> ment but to disrupt a reporter's relationship with his news sources would have no justification. Grand juries are subject to judicial control and subpoenas to motions to quash. We do not expect courts will forget that grand juries must operate within the limits of the First Amendment as well as the Fifth.

It is somewhat surprising, in light of this opinion and the efficacy of the investigative reporting that surrounded the Watergate affair, that reporters were not called on more often by the investigating authorities for proof that what they published was based on evidence. But when the Committee for the Reelection of the President (CREEP) subpoenaed the *New York Times*, the *Washington Post*, the *Washington Star News*, and *Time* magazine for their unpublished material on the Watergate affair, Judge Richey quashed the subpoenas. "This court," he said, "cannot blind itself to the possible chilling effect the enforcement of . . . these subpoenas would have on the press and the public."[74] On the other hand, it must not be assumed that reporters unwilling to testify formally were not more than willing suppliers of information. Leaks were not one-directional; they moved from the media as well as to it.

The last constitutional question I would address is more tenuous but not less troublesome. It is more tenuous because it has never received Supreme Court attention. Judge Sirica, it will be recalled, was anything but satisfied with the sufficiency or veracity of the testimony offered at the burglary trial. And so, when the time came for the sentencing of the Watergate burglars, he meted out conditional sentences of twenty to forty years, the maximum allowed by law. It must be admitted that these were extraordinary sentences for a burglary, even by Sirica, who had a reputation as a hanging judge. At the time of the sentencing, he made clear the reasons for their extraordinary length:[75]

> For these reasons I recommend your full cooperation with the Grand Jury and the Senate Select Committee. You must understand that I hold out no promises or hopes of any kind to you in this matter but I do say that should you decide to speak freely I would have to weigh that factor in appraising what sentence will be finally imposed in this case. Other factors will of course be considered but I mention this one because it is one over which you have control and I mean each one of the five of you.

The implications of the sentencing power had already resulted in James McCord's request for a private interview with Sirica, and McCord's sentencing had been postponed for that reason. McCord, in his request, had made it clear that he understood that if he were regarded as uncooperative he could "expect a much more severe sentence."[76]

Whether this form of judicial blackmail has constitutional authority is not yet decided by the Supreme Court. We do know that threats of increased sentences may not properly be used to deter appeals.[77] And we do know that increased or diminished sentences may not be used to promote pleas of guilty.[78] There is a question whether increased imprisonment may be a price imposed for a failure to be more forthcoming.[79] Certainly that is not the reason for imposing a sentence on a convicted felon or misdemeanant.

It is clear that the judiciary played a vital part in bringing the Watergate crisis to its denouement. Its judgments, some of highly innovative nature, forced the White House to the revelation of records of its misdeeds. The indirect results of its judgments, however, were more important. The public perceived its judgments to put the most popular and least political branch on the side of removal of the president. The judiciary made it possible for the House of Representatives to bring in a bill of impeachment and likely that the Senate would bring in a verdict of guilt. And they made it possible for Nixon to see that such impeachment and judgment were in the offing. In terms of its own proper function, the judicial branch brought to fruition criminal trials of the White House wrongdoers and subjected them to what most of the public regarded as appropriate punishment.

The judicial branch, in helping to resolve this constitutional crisis, enhanced its public image, but also moved one step forward to the next most imminent one. For in continuing to expand its own role in the government of the United States, the third branch again proved that we have arrived at the stage described by Raoul Berger in his new book *Government by Judiciary*. Sooner or later, this country must directly face the question whether it is prepared to entrust the judiciary with the mantles of Plato's guardians. The answer to that question will also determine the future of American democracy and, perhaps, even of American liberty.

5

The Powers of Appointment and Removal

In a confidential memorandum to Leon Jaworski, which Jaworski published in his book *The Right and the Power*, his aide, George Frampton, wrote:[1]

> Viewed broadly, the creation of a Special Prosecutor was a unique and extra-constitutional reaction by our constitutional system to preserve its integrity in the face of an emergency where those in control of the administration of justice were themselves charged with subverting it. It has always seemed to me that inherent in creation of this constitutionally precarious institution are unique risks of failure. To avoid these risks we have hewed to a very few fundamental principles. These are: that we will pursue charges of wrongdoing to a conclusion wherever they lead, without regard to political influence or considerations but with regard only to the truth; that we will do our utmost as lawyers and human beings to make "just" decisions, however unpopular or misunderstood they may be, while recognizing the infirmity of any one view (or even a majority view) of what is just; that we will be scrupulous in conduct of our investigations and trials; and that in every matter we will proceed upon well-settled and established precedent and principles of law and practice.
>
> This last—consistent adherence to precedent, to well-established legal and justice principles—has been especially critical because it has been the primary source of public credibility for an office that in its birth derived no credibility from the Constitution or history.

The self-righteousness of the statement may seem reminiscent of the public statements of the Nixon administration, engaged in "extra-constitutional" activities for the preservation of the Nation. But that is not the issue to be faced. The first issue here rather is the difference between "extra-constitutional" and unconstitutional. Can a power be constitutionally exercised by any branch of national government although it cannot credibly be justified by the authority of the Constitution? In what ways was the special prosecutor's role "extra-constitutional," as Frampton asserted?

The special prosecutor concept gained support when Kleindienst resigned as Attorney General and even before Richardson took office. On 1 May 1973, Senator Charles Percy, Republican of Illinois, moved a resolution in the Senate, sponsored by Senators Goldwater, Dole, and Buckley among others, calling on the President to appoint a special prosecutor, whose appointment would be subject to Senate confirmation.[2] On May 3, twenty-nine Democratic senators, led by Adlai Stevenson and joined by Mike Mansfield, memorialized Richardson to appoint a special prosecutor. On the same day, a resolution offered in the Senate by Republicans, moved by Senator Brooke and joined by Hugh Scott, Peter Dominick, John Tower, and Clifford Hansen, called on Elliot Richardson, Attorney General designate, to appoint a special prosecutor.[3] A similar resolution had been offered in the House on May 1, sponsored by the chairman of the House Republican Conference, John B. Anderson, and the chairman of the Republican Congressional Campaign Committee, Robert H. Michel.[4]

The Richardson confirmation hearings were pending and members of the Senate Judiciary Committee had made it clear that they would extract a promise to appoint a special prosecutor as a condition of approval of Richardson's appointment. The unfolding of the story may be told in the words of Richardson, who retrospectively gives himself credit for voluntarily moving the creation of a special prosecutor's office:[5]

> . . . seven days after the announcement of my nomination, I held a press conference . . . at which I announced my decision:
>
> > I have decided that I will, if confirmed, appoint a Special Prosecutor and give him all the independence, authority, and staff support needed to carry out the tasks entrusted to him. Although he will be in the Department of Justice and report to me—and only to me—he will be aware that his ultimate accountability is to the American people.
>
> . . . .
>
> The original terms of the Special Prosecutor's charter were my own; its final terms were worked out between Archibald Cox, members of the Senate Judiciary Committee, and myself. They provided that I, as Attorney General, would delegate to the Special Prosecutor "full authority" over the Watergate investigation, leaving to the Attorney General only his "statutory accountability for all matters falling within the jurisdiction of the Department of Justice." I had insisted on this clause because it seemed to me axiomatic that no one who delegates authority can thereby rid himself of all responsibility

for its exercise. For this reason the charter also reserved to the Attorney General the power to remove the Special Prosecutor, but only for "extraordinary improprieties on his part."

All these precautionary provisions were shattered when the President ordered Richardson to fire Cox for his insistence on using the judicial process to secure access to the tapes against the expressed wishes of the President. As Richardson acknowledged, when he was ordered to fire Cox he had no choice but to resign, for his commitment to the Senate had been breached.

It seems to me that on these facts and events to the date of the "Saturday night massacre," there is not much to Frampton's proposition about the "extra-constitutional" nature of the special prosecutor. If firing Cox was "extra-constitutional"—it could be illegal without being unconstitutional—the creation and conduct of that office certainly was not. The Department of Justice has frequently had special prosecutor forces in operation with regard to the peculiar evils of the day. Even Kennedy's "Get-Hoffa" group was not "extra-constitutional," except, perhaps, in the methods it used. Nor should the Jaworski succession to the Cox mandate in any way be considered "extra-constitutional." It should be remembered that the special prosecutor's office, as created, was an office within the Department of Justice.

During the Teapot Dome episode, in the Coolidge Administration, several nominations for a special prosecutor proved unsatisfactory. Thereupon Coolidge named two prosecutors, from outside the Department of Justice, Owen J. Roberts and Atlee Pomerene, under a congressional resolution calling for Senate approval of the nominees. Coolidge said that employment of outside counsel was "in accord with former precedents." Early in 1952, Truman named Newbold Morris, a New York lawyer, to act within the Department of Justice to direct a probe of government corruption. But he lasted only two months. Friction developed between Morris and Attorney General Howard McGrath. When McGrath discovered that Morris was circulating a questionnaire about outside sources of income of various federal officials, he fired Morris. Truman thereupon announced McGrath's resignation. But the probe died. Neither of these appointments was regarded as "extra-constitutional."

The constitutional problems arose not in the actual appointments and assignments of the Watergate prosecutors, but in the various alternatives for appointment and removal considered but never executed after the Cox dismissal. For example, on 22 May 1974, Senator Stevenson, anticipating the possibility that Jaworski would be fired for his efforts to secure the tapes, introduced legislation providing for emergency appointment of a special prosecutor by a panel of federal judges if the office should become vacant.[6]

The problems of the constitutional dimensions of the President's power to hire and fire go back, once again, to the very first Congress. Unlike the case of executive privilege or congressional power of inquiry, there is a specific provision of the Constitution that must be—or, at least, should be—the starting point.

Article II, § 2, cl. 2, says of the President:

> He shall have Power, by and with the Advice and Consent of the Senate, to make Treaties, provided two-thirds of the Senators present concur; and he shall nominate, and by and with the Advice and Consent of the Senate, shall appoint Ambassadors, other public Ministers and Consuls, Judges of the supreme Court, and all other Officers of the United States, whose Appointments are not herein otherwise provided for, and which shall be established by Law; but the Congress may by Law vest the Appointment of such inferior Officers, as they think proper, in the President alone, in the Courts of Law, or in the Heads of Departments.

The language speaks only to nominations and appointments and not at all to the question of removal from office. And it has been the removal issue that has wracked the country from time to time. The only presidential impeachment in our history was in large measure concerned with the question whether Congress could forestall the removal of cabinet officers by President Andrew Johnson without Senate consent.

If there is nothing in the language of the Constitution to help determine who was intended to have the power of removal, there is also nothing in the reported debates at the Constitutional Convention, or in the reported debates at the various ratifying conventions, to aid us.[7] From the usually helpful source, *The Federalist*, we do have Hamilton's statement in No. 77:

> It has been mentioned as one of the advantages to be expected from the cooperation of the Senate, in the business of appointments, that it would contribute to the stability of the administration. The consent of that body would be necessary to displace as well as to appoint. A change of the Chief Magistrate, therefore, would not occasion so violent or so general a revolution in the officers of the government as might be expected, if he were the sole disposer of offices. Where a man in any station had given satisfactory evidence of his fitness for it, a new President would be restrained from attempting a change in favor of a person more agreeable to him, by the apprehension that a discountenance of the Senate might frustrate the attempt, and bring some degree of discredit upon himself. Those who can best estimate the value of a steady administration, will be most disposed to prize a provision which connects the official existence of public men with the approbation or disapprobation of that body which,

from the greater permanence of its own composition, will in all probability be less subject to inconstancy than any other member of the government.

Despite the clarity of the Hamiltonian statement, it was not regarded as dispositive of the question. *The Federalist*, apparently, is authoritative only when it is congenial to the wishes of the decision-maker. The problem has since been treated on an ad hoc basis by the Congress, the President, and the courts. The question is still not fully resolved as a constitutional matter, however much Congress has tended to acquiesce in granting the President the power of removal. The distinction between constitutional mandate and legislative provision is important. The tendency to confuse the two, as if they were one, is the primary reason for the failure of resolution of the constitutional question.

The issue came before the very first Congress when a bill was proposed creating the office of foreign affairs—the Department of State—with a provision that the President should be free to discharge the occupant of the office of Secretary at his discretion. The question arose on the motion by the Madison forces simply to provide for the office, saying nothing about removal. The House broke into three camps. It was Madison's ultimate position that the removal power followed the appointment power, but with the advice and consent provision inapplicable. He stated this as a constitutional command, without offering evidence about the intent of the framers. He had two sets of opponents in the House; those who held that the removal authority must follow the appointment process by including the necessity for advice and consent of the Senate; and those who thought that, in the silence of the Constitution, the question of how removal was to be effected was a matter within congressional discretion to dispose.

The bill passed, on Madison's urging, without any provision for removal. It has been taken since by many to mean that the Madisonian constitutional position had been upheld. But Madison had, through parliamentary maneuver—by excision of the removal clause—secured not only the votes of those who were of his own constitutional persuasion but also the votes of those who took the stated Hamiltonian position that the Constitution commanded Senate acquiescence in removal. Moreover, those who thought provision for removal was within Congress's discretion need not have voted against excision of the provision, and at least two of them did not. As Thomas Tucker put it: "I am embarrassed on this question . . . because the vote is taken in such a manner as not to express the principles upon which I vote."[8] Tucker was one of those who believed the power of removal was within the congressional ken for determination.

Madison rested his argument on a conception of separation of powers that avoided the checks and balances for which the Constitution had made provision. In fact, at the Constitutional Convention, he had moved for exclusive power of appointment in the President.[9] This failed. What he could not achieve at the Convention he could seek to redress in the First Congress. His argument was that the provision for the advice and consent of the Senate was a constitutional imposition on what was clearly an executive function, but because of the specific words must be obeyed. The implied removal power, however, was inhibited by no such constitutional qualification and therefore remained an unconditioned executive function.

Madison was not a Jeffersonian democrat in principle. Like Hamilton, who may have regretted the language he had used in *The Federalist* to sell the Constitution to the people of New York, he was, at the Convention, an executive supremacist.[10] Excerpts from Madison's argument in the House state his constitutional position this way:[11]

> I agree that if nothing more was said in the constitution than that the President, by and with the advice and consent of the Senate, should appoint to office, there would be great force in saying that the power of removal resulted by a natural implication from the power of appointing. But there is another part of the constitution, no less explicit than the one on which the gentleman's doctrine is founded; it is that part which declares that the executive power shall be vested in a President of the United States. The association of the Senate with the President in exercising that particular function, is an exception to this general rule; and exceptions to general rules, I conceive, are ever to be taken strictly. [How quickly he assumed that the assignment of the executive power is "no less explicit" than the details of the appointing power.] But there is another part of the constitution which inclines, in my judgment, to favor the construction I put upon it; the President is required to take care that the laws be faithfully executed. If the duty to see the laws faithfully executed be required at the hands of the Executive Magistrate, it would seem that it was generally intended he should have that species of power which is necessary to accomplish that end. Now, if the officer when once appointed is not to depend upon the President for his official existence, but upon a distinct body, (for where there are two negatives required, either can prevent the removal,) I confess I do not see how the President can take care that the laws be faithfully executed. It is true, by a circuitous operation, he may obtain an impeachment, and even without this it is possible he may obtain the concurrence of the Senate for the purpose of displacing an officer; but would this give that species of control to the Executive Magistrate which seems to be required by the Constitution?

Obviously, Madison's argument depends on the premise that appointment of government officers is inherently—and therefore constitutionally—an executive function. There was little support for this position in the structure of state governments and certainly the debates at the Convention did not hesitate to suggest assigning the appointing function totally to the legislature.[12] The arguments on behalf of exclusive authority for the legislature or the executive were compromised in the advice and consent provision that was ultimately promulgated.

Despite the fact that the congressional vote on the bill was not necessarily—was indeed not likely to be—a majority approval of Madison's argument, and despite the weakness about definition of the executive power, the actions of this First Congress were, through the first half of the nineteenth century, usually taken to be a decision that the Constitution precluded legislative inhibition on the presidential removal power. There was a tendency not to take notice, for example, of the fact that the Act for the Government of the Northwest Territory, passed in 1789, among others, made provision for congressional removal of officers of government,[13] and that in creating the office of comptroller, the legislature, at Madison's behest, restricted the presidential removal power.[14] These acts hardly denote congressional acquiescence in Madison's original constitutional reading.

Moreover, it soon appeared that, if Congress could not condition removal on Senate participation, it could prescribe terms of office that the President would be expected to obey. In no less famous a case than *Marbury* v. *Madison*,[15] the great Chief Justice John Marshall announced:

> Where an officer is removable at the will of the executive, the circumstance which completes his appointment is of no concern; because the act is at any time revocable; and the commission may be arrested, if still in the office. But when the officer is not removable at the will of the executive, the appointment is not revocable, and cannot be annulled. It has conferred legal rights which cannot be resumed.
>
> The discretion of the executive is to be exercised until the appointment has been made. But having once made the appointment, his power over the office is terminated in all cases, where by law the officer is not removable by him. The right to the office is *then* in the person appointed, and he has the absolute, and unconditional power of accepting or rejecting it.
>
> Mr. Marbury, then, since his commission was signed by the president, and sealed by the secretary of state, was appointed; and as the law creating the office, gave the officer a right to hold for five years, independent of the executive, the appointment was not revocable, but vested in the officer legal rights, which are protected by the laws of his country.
>
> To withhold his commission, therefore, is an act deemed by the court not warranted by law, but violative of a vested legal right.

Marshall's political footwork in *Marbury*, however, was as adept as Madison's had been in the House of Representatives on the State Department bill, and so it is not clear whether this ruling was necessary to a decision and therefore an adjudication of the point by the Court, or merely dictum, because of the declaration that the Court was without authority to issue a writ of mandamus. There would be no need to talk about the power of the Court to issue mandamus if Marbury was not entitled by law to the commission. On the other hand, there was no need to talk about the right to office if the Court declared that it had no jurisdiction to do anything about it anyway.

In the latter half of the nineteenth century, events took a strange turn. The Congress, which was supposed to have established in 1789 the constitutional rule that it could not inhibit the presidential removal power, proceeded and continued to enact legislation that in fact imposed conditions on that power. The Supreme Court, on the other hand, which had declared in 1803 that Congress had the authority to prescribe terms for the exercise of presidential removal, tended to accept the Madisonian thesis that the power could not be qualified.

Thus, as examples of congressional behavior, laws were enacted providing that the President should have no power of removal; that the President could remove only with the advice and consent of the Senate; that the President could remove only for the causes specified in the statute; that the President could remove only for specified causes and after notice and hearing; that the President could not remove until a successor had been chosen and qualified; and that the President could remove only on communication to the Senate of the reasons for the removal.[16]

In 1833, following the removal of Secretary of the Treasury Duane by Andrew Jackson, because Duane refused to remove federal deposits from the Bank of the United States, and Duane's replacement by Roger B. Taney during a congressional recess, motions of censure were moved and passed in the Senate. Webster, Clay, and Calhoun all condemned the action in the kind of oratory that is no longer heard on the floor of the Senate. But during the Watergate affair there were certainly echoes of a choice paragraph uttered in 1835 by Senator Clay:[17]

> Inherent power! That is a new principle to enlarge the powers of the general Government. . . . The partisans of the Executive have discovered a third and more fruitful source of power. Inherent power! Whence is it derived? The constitution created the office of President, and made it just what it is. It had no powers prior to its existence. It can have none but those which are conferred upon it by the instrument which created it, or laws passed in pursuance of that instrument. Do gentlemen mean by inherent power, such power as is exercised by the monarchs or chief magistrates of other countries? If that be their meaning they should avow it.

The issue reached proportions of a constitutional crisis in 1867, as a result of the passage of the Tenure of Office Act.[18] The statute forbade the removal of certain civil officers, including cabinet officers, until their successors were appointed with the advice and consent of the Senate. President Johnson vetoed the legislation, but it was passed over his veto. He then purported to remove Secretary of War Stanton. This action was the basis for eight counts in a bill of impeachment brought in by the House of Representatives. And these were among the counts that almost brought the President down. On each of the counts put to a vote, thirty-five senators voted for conviction, nineteen against. Professor Michael Les Benedict has spelled out the case for Johnson's impeachment in a recently published monograph.[19] But, right or wrong, it is clear that by 1867, if not by 1833, Congress had abandoned its original view of the presidential removal power that purported to derive from the act of 1789.

If Congress had changed its mind, however, the Supreme Court had too, and tended to follow Madison rather than Marshall. The combination of the executive branch and the judicial branch against the congressional branch, as I have suggested before, is pervasive in our constitutional history, except on rare occasions, as when Marshall tried to make a Jeffersonian out of Jefferson and when the Supreme Court struck down Truman's seizure of the steel mills in 1952.[20]

The distinction between what is commanded by the Constitution with regard to the removal power and what may be commanded by the legislature was the major issue, but the early debates and decisions related only to the first category of appointments in the constitutional provision, those to be made only with the advice and consent of the Senate. A second category of appointments was provided by the Constitution: as to "inferior officers," "Congress may by Law vest the Appointment . . . as they think proper, in the President alone, in the Courts of Law, or in the Heads of Departments." The Supreme Court dealt with removal under both provisions. Despite the clear constitutional differences between appointments that did and those that did not require senatorial confirmation, the Court persistently utilized dicta in one kind of case to justify conclusions in the other species.[21]

The climax of the removal cases was to come in the Supreme Court's decision in *Myers* v. *United States*.[22] The judicial antagonists in that case were Chief Justice William Howard Taft and Justice Louis Brandeis. Each had an occasion to write an opinion for the Court on cognate issues prior to the *Myers* case. Brandeis, in an "inferior officers" case, repeated the proposition that: "The power to remove is, in the absence of statutory provision to the contrary, an incident of the power to appoint."[23] In *Wallace* v. *United States*,[24] Taft wrote the opinion for the Court in a case which involved the removal of a military officer:[25]

> Before the Civil War there was no restriction upon the President's power to remove an officer of the Army or Navy. The principle that

the power of removal was incident to the power of appointment was early determined by the Senate to involve the conclusion that, at least in absence of restrictive legislation, the President, though he could not appoint without the consent of the Senate, could remove without such consent in the case of any officer whose tenure was not fixed by the Constitution. The first legislative restriction upon this power was enacted March 3, 1865, by the very provision we are here considering (13 Stat. 489), which subsequently became § 1230, Rev. Stats. Thereafter, on July 13, 1866, Congress took away altogether the power of the President to dismiss an officer of the Army or Navy in time of peace, except in pursuance of a court-martial sentence or in commutation thereof (c. 176, 14 Stat. 92). After that, in the controversy between President Johnson and the Senate, the tenure of office act was passed which cut down the power of the President to remove civil officers. Act of March 2, 1867, c. 154, 14 Stat. 430. The validity of these acts has never been directly passed on by this court in any case. The question has been expressly saved. *Parsons* v. *United States*, 167 U.S. 324, 339.

While, thus, the validity and effect of statutory restrictions upon the power of the President alone to remove officers of the Army and Navy and civil officers have been the subject of doubt and discussion, it is settled, *McElrath* v. *United States*, 102 U.S. 426; *Blake* v. *United States*, 103 U.S. 227; *Keyes* v. *United States*, 109 U.S. 336; *Mullan* v. *United States*, 140 U.S. 240, that the President with the consent of the Senate may effect the removal of an officer of the Army or Navy by the appointment of another to his place, and that none of the limitations in the statutes affects his power of removal when exercised by and with the consent of the Senate. Indeed the same ruling has been made as to civil officers. *Parsons* v. *United States*, 167 U.S. 324.

Between the Brandeis and Taft opinions, the Court held, in an opinion by Justice Day, that where the Congress had vested the power of appointment in the Secretary of the Treasury, it could not be exercised by the President.[26] This, then, was the state of the law when the *Myers* case came before the Court for decision. In cases where the appointment was made by the President with the advice and consent of the Senate, the President clearly could remove the officer with the consent of the Senate, even when that consent came only by way of approval of the nomination of a successor.[27] When the appointment was of an "inferior officer," removal could be made by the authority that had been given the appointing power by the Congress.[28] There was strong support that the President could remove an official appointed with the advice and consent of the Senate even without Senate approval.[29] It was unclear whether, with regard to such appointees, the President had to abide conditions of removal specified by legislation creating the office or amendatory thereto.[30] Such conditions, however, seemed clearly to bind the removal of inferior officers.[31] The President could not appoint "inferior officers" when Congress charged a department head with that power.[32]

Three major themes had run throughout this construction by adjudication. First, that the removal power followed from the appointive power. But this thesis was ambiguous as to the right of the Senate to participate in removal of those whose nominations it had confirmed. The second thesis was unequivocally in favor of presidential power. It argued that the appointment and removal powers were inherently executive powers in their nature and could be limited only by express constitutional provision. This rested on the constitutional language that the President was faithfully to execute the law. The third argument rested on legislative power granted by the Constitution. The power to create the office—inherently a legislative power—included the power to specify the conditions of tenure of the office.

The themes were to be played with some variations in the *Myers* case. Before reaching that case I would first offer discussion on the personal animosity between Brandeis and Taft. "Realists" will find it relevant; "conceptualists" may at least find it interesting. The hostility derived from congressional hearings that involved the removal of a federal government official, alleged cabinet-level corruption, campaign contributions, a presidential cover-up, executive privilege, and many more of the issues that we have come to know through the hearings of the Senate Watergate committee.[33]

The Ballinger-Pinchot affair, like Watergate, had many implicit issues. One was the question whether Theodore Roosevelt's theory of presidential power—that it consisted of everything that Congress did not forbid it—was being abandoned by William Howard Taft in favor of the proposition, for which he became known, that the President had only those powers that were delegated to him. The question arose in the administration of the Republican conservation program. Taft apparently was unwilling to push his authority as far as the conservationists, including Gifford Pinchot, head of the forestry service in the Department of Interior, wished:[34]

> [The Ballinger-Pinchot affair] started with an accusation leveled against Secretary [of the Interior] Ballinger in 1909 by Louis P. Glavis, a young man of twenty-five who was chief of General Land Office field agents within Ballinger's department. Glavis charged that the Secretary of the Interior, his superior, was abandoning the national policy of conservation by letting the Guggenheim interests take over certain coal-bearing public lands in Alaska. Glavis prepared a detailed document explaining his charges. Taft examined them in the

summer of 1909 at his vacation home in Beverly, Massachusetts, then called on Secretary Ballinger to furnish him a detailed reply. The Secretary did so, at great length.

Taft received the Ballinger documents, consulted with George Wickersham, his Attorney General, and within six days made public a letter that Taft said he had sent to Ballinger, exonerating him completely. Ballinger, the President said, should discharge Glavis as a faithless public servant. Secretary Ballinger then told news reporters that the matter was closed. . . . [Glavis was fired, as was his superior Pinchot for supporting him.]

. . . The Taft administration [arranged] to have a joint committee of Congress set up, ostensibly to investigate the charges but really calculated to vindicate Secretary Ballinger. . . . At the urging of editor Hapgood [of *Collier's Weekly*], Brandeis was brought in . . . to take charge of the case for Glavis and for *Collier's* [which had published Glavis's story].

In the course of the long hearings in the spring of 1910, Brandeis completely turned the tables on the committee majority and its chief witnesses, Secretary Ballinger and his close associates. [One of the senators complained that he would not be a party to turning the investigation of Glavis into an investigation of the presidency.] By persistent questioning, and by reconstructing the schedule of activity of the men involved, he brought out the fact that President Taft, busy with golf, social affairs, and ceremonial appearances during his vacation at Beverly, had not really had time to examine the matter. Brandeis proved that in fact Taft's "findings" had been prepared long in advance in Ballinger's own office, with the aid of Attorney General Wickersham. Then the trusting Taft had simply added his signature.

The Ballinger-Pinchot congressional investigation had permitted Glavis and Pinchot to have their own counsel entitled to cross-examine the witnesses. Here, as in the Army-McCarthy hearings, where another Boston lawyer, Joseph Welch, turned the hearings into a full adversary process, the judge and jury became not the congressmen sitting on the committee, but the American public. Thus, although the committee exonerated him by a strict party vote, Ballinger resigned in disgrace. For what Brandeis had proved beyond doubt was that after Taft ordered the discharge of Glavis, and questions began to be asked, Taft and Ballinger had conspired to have a lengthy memorandum prepared to support their action and pre-dated it by two months to make it appear that Taft had acted in reliance on the report which, in fact, he could not have seen until after the firing since it did not exist before then. Partly as a result of the hearings, Theodore Roosevelt entered the 1912 elections, contributing to Taft's defeat. And it was recognized that it was Louis Brandeis who turned the hearings of what was to be a tame committee whitewash into an indictment of the Taft presidency. "Mene, mene, tekel, Upharsin,"[35] the handwriting on the wall.

Gall was added to the wormwood, when Brandeis was appointed to the Supreme Court by Wilson. Taft had always coveted a Supreme Court appointment, which he was ultimately to receive. He thought that he was entitled to the post that Wilson gave to Brandeis. And he was among the leaders of the fight against the Brandeis confirmation.[36] Immediately after the Brandeis nomination, Taft wrote a letter to a Washington confidante, revealing his feelings:[37]

> Our worthy President has developed more qualities of Machiavelli than even I, with a full appreciation of the admirable roundness of his character, had suspected. When I think of the devilish ingenuity manifested in the selection of Brandeis, I can not but admire his finesse. Of course, joking aside, it is one of the deepest wounds I have had as an American and a lover of the Constitution and a believer in progressive conservatism, that such a man as Brandeis could be put in the Court, as I believe he is likely to be.
>
> He is a muckraker, an emotionalist for his own purposes, a socialist, prompted by jealousy, a hypocrite, a man who has certain high ideals in his imagination, but who is utterly unscrupulous in method in reaching them, a man of infinite cunning, of great tenacity of purpose, and, in my judgment, of much power for evil. He is only one of nine on the Court, but one on the Court is often an important consideration; and even if the rest of the Court is against him, he has the opportunity to attack their judgments and weaken their force by insidious demagoguery, and an appeal to the restless element that can do infinite harm. I sincerely hope that he can be defeated in the Senate, but I don't think so.

Walter Lippmann editorialized in *The New Republic* on Taft's opposition to Brandeis: "One would have supposed that ex-President Taft was the last man qualified to express a judgment on Mr. Louis D. Brandeis. . . . It was Mr. Brandeis who demonstrated to the country Mr. Taft's immoral procedure in a disreputable incident."[38]

Taft and Brandeis became the judicial antagonists in the judicial *cause célèbre* of its time. Like many such cases, the facts arose out of a controversy of small proportions, however large the principles at stake. Frank S. Myers was a postmaster in Portland, Oregon. The statute under which he was appointed called for the approval of his nomination by the Senate, which he had received. It also provided a four-year term "unless sooner removed or suspended according to law."[39] With one year of Myers's term left, President Wilson removed him from office without consulting the Senate. Myers brought suit raising the question whether the President was authorized to remove without the advice and consent of the Senate before the expiration of his term, a question which had never been directly faced by the Supreme Court.

The judicial process, seldom swift, moved glacially here. The case was brought to the Court for argument in December 1923; it was reargued in 1925; decision was not rendered until 25 October 1926. After handing down the opinion in *Myers*, Taft wrote: "I never wrote an opinion that I felt to be so important in its effect."[40] That it was written against the background of the Ballinger-Pinchot affair was underlined by the fact that George Wharton Pepper, a senator from Pennsylvania, provided briefs and argument on behalf of the plaintiff's cause. Pepper had been counsel to Pinchot in the congressional hearings.

Taft expressed the underlying motivation for his opinion shortly after the judgment:[41]

> I am very strongly convinced . . . that the danger to this country is in the enlargement of the powers of Congress, rather than in the maintenance in full of the executive power. Congress is getting into the habit of forming boards who really exercise executive power, and attempting to make them independent of the President after they have been appointed and confirmed. This merely makes a hydra-headed Executive, and if the terms are lengthened so as to exceed the duration of a particular Executive, a new Executive will find himself stripped of control of important functions, for which as the head of the Government he becomes responsible, but whose action he cannot influence in any way.

The question for decision stated by Chief Justice Taft was "whether under the Constitution the President has the exclusive power of removing executive officers of the United States whom he has appointed by and with the advice and consent of the Senate."[42] Taft's first argument that the President's power was uninhibited derived from his reading of the 1789 debates. Knowing where he was going, Taft had no difficulty in reaching the conclusion that "there is not the slightest doubt, after an examination of the record, that the vote was, and was intended to be, a legislative declaration that the power to remove officers appointed by the President and the Senate vested in the President alone, and until the Johnson Impeachment trial in 1868, its meaning was not doubted even by those who questioned its soundness."[43]

He then turned to Madison's arguments on the implied assumption that Madison spoke for the Congress when it acted on his motion. First, that the Constitution provided for a strict separation of powers, except where specific variations thereof were made by constitutional language. The power to execute the laws was given to the President and he could conduct his office only through subordinates. The power of appointment and removal were, therefore, essential ingredients in the executive authority. "It is quite true that, in state and colonial governments at the time of the Constitutional Convention, power to make appointments and removals had sometimes been lodged in the legislatures or in the courts, but such a disposition of it was really vesting part of the executive power in another branch of the Government."[44] This was shown by the fact that the power of appointment and removal rested in the Crown at the time of the Revolution, and the power and prerogatives of the Crown were what the Founders necessarily meant by "executive power."

He then endorsed Madison's argument that the power of removal was an implicit part of the power of appointment. And he had no difficulty in concluding that the Senate did not share the power of appointment but only passed on presidential nominations:[45]

> In the discussion in the First Congress fear was expressed that such a constitutional rule of construction as was involved in the passage of the bill would expose the country to tyranny through the abuse of the exercise of the power of removal by the President. Underlying such fears was the fundamental misconception that the President's attitude in his exercise of power is one of opposition to the people, while the Congress is their only defender in the Government, and such a misconception may be noted in the discussions had before this Court. . . . The President is a representative of the people just as the members of the Senate and of the House are, and it may be, at some times, on some subjects, that the President elected by all the people is rather more representative of them all than are the members of either body of the Legislature whose constituencies are local and not countrywide.

As to the notion that the right to prescribe the tenure of office attaches to Congress because the power to create the office is in the legislature, Taft resorts again to Madison, who had not answered it but had only abominated it: "When I consider the consequences of this doctrine, and compare them with the true principles of the Constitution, I own that I can not subscribe to it."[46]

Taft also insisted that giving such power to Congress was inconsistent with his notions about the independence of the executive:[47]

> It could never have been intended to leave to Congress unlimited discretion to vary fundamentally the operation of the great independent executive branch of government and thus most seriously to weaken it. It would be a delegation by the Convention to Congress of the function of defining the primary boundaries of another of the three great divisions of government.

Of course, that is exactly what the constitution makers did. For, as you may recall, the Necessary and Proper Clause gives that residual power to Congress: "The Congress shall have Power . . . To make all Laws which shall be necessary and proper for carrying into Execution the foregoing Powers, and all other Powers vested by this Constitution in the Government of the United States, or in any Department or Officer thereof."[48]

Taft took the Madisonian text as dogma. As for Hamilton's *Federalist* No. 77, that was dismissed on the ground that Hamilton later changed his opinion, which hardly affected the contemporary construction offered to the people of New York in seeking ratification. As for Marshall's opinion in *Marbury* v. *Madison*, his words were only dicta. And, if they were not dicta, the holding was overruled by the dicta in *Parsons* v. *United States*.[49] Moreover, Marshall, too, had changed his mind by the time he wrote his biography of George Washington.[50]

Taft then got carried away with his own function as Constitution writer. Making first the argument that the President had to have control over his cabinet and policy-making officers, he held that a similar control was necessary over every government employee. It was this same kind of reasoning that led Kleindienst to assert that executive privilege existed not only as to presidential advisers but with reference to all two and one-half million government employees.[51] It was this overreaching that rendered the Taft opinion so vulnerable to both contemporary and future attack:[52]

> The duties of the heads of departments and bureaus in which the discretion of the President is exercised and which we have described, are the most important in the whole field of executive action of the Government. There is nothing in the Constitution which permits a distinction between the removal of the head of a department or a bureau, when he discharges a political duty of the President or exercises his discretion, and the removal of executive officers engaged in the discharge of their other normal duties. The imperative reasons requiring an unrestricted power to remove the most important of his subordinates in their most important duties must, therefore, control the interpretation of the Constitution as to all appointed by him.
>
> But this is not to say that there are not strong reasons why the President should have a like power to remove his appointees charged with other duties than those above described. The ordinary duties of officers prescribed by statute come under the general administrative control of the President by virtue of the general grant to him of the executive power, and he may properly supervise and guide their construction of the statutes under which they act in order to secure that unitary and uniform execution of the laws which Article II of the Constitution evidently contemplated in vesting general executive power in the President alone. Laws are often passed with specific provision for the adoption of regulations by a department or bureau head to make the law workable and effective. The ability and judg-

> ment manifested by the official thus empowered, as well as his energy and stimulation of his subordinates, are subjects which the President must consider and supervise in his administrative control. Finding such officers to be negligent and inefficient, the President should have the power to remove them. Of course there may be duties so peculiarly and specifically committed to the discretion of a particular officer as to raise a question whether the President may overrule or revise the officer's interpretation of his statutory duty in a particular instance. Then there may be duties of a quasi-judicial character imposed on executive officers and members of executive tribunals whose decisions after hearing affect interests of individuals, the discharge of which the President can not in a particular case properly influence or control. But even in such a case he may consider the decision after its rendition as a reason for removing the officer, on the ground that the discretion regularly entrusted to that officer by statute has not been on the whole intelligently or wisely exercised. Otherwise he does not discharge his own constitutional duty of seeing that the laws be faithfully executed.

The fact of the matter is that, by Taft's own testimony,[53] his prime objective was to prevent Congress from creating what we have come to call, somewhat euphemistically, independent administrative agencies in theory not responsible to the President and in fact not responsible to Congress. It was necessary, therefore, to bring every officer outside the Article III judiciary and the Congress itself within the presidential power of removal. His judgment was thus to be applicable to all appointments, except judicial appointments as to which the Constitution provided a tenure for "good behavior," *i.e.*, to appointments made with "the Advice and Consent of the Senate," to presidential appointments that did not require such consent, and appointments by heads of departments, both of the latter in the constitutional category of "inferior officers."[54]

It took Taft some seventy pages to dispose of the case for the majority. Justice Holmes took less than a page to reject the Taft position. Short and to the point, he wrote:[55]

> The arguments drawn from the executive power of the President, and from his duty to appoint officers of the United States (when Congress does not vest the appointment elsewhere), to take care that the laws be faithfully executed, and to commission all officers of the United States, seem to me spider's webs inadequate to control the dominant facts.
>
> We have to deal with an office that owes its existence to Congress and that Congress may abolish tomorrow. Its duration and the pay attached to it while it lasts depend on Congress alone. Congress alone confers on the President the power to appoint to it and at any time may transfer that power to other hands. With such power over

its own creation, I have no more trouble in believing that Congress has power to prescribe a term of life for it free from any interference than I have in accepting the undoubted power of Congress to decree its end. I have equally little trouble in accepting its power to prolong the tenure of an incumbent until Congress or the Senate shall have assented to his removal. The duty of the President to see that the laws be executed is a duty that does not go beyond the laws or require him to achieve more than Congress sees fit to leave within his power.

Of this opinion, Harold Laski wrote to Holmes:[56]

And those vast opinions, sent me very kindly by Brandeis, in *Myers* v. *U.S.* in which, frankly, I thought the case for dissent so obvious as hardly to need even your page. For a power to create a post is surely a power to create its conditions; otherwise your President would be an intolerable autocrat.

What Laski might have said was that Holmes's page overrode the need for the lengthy Brandeis opinion, which ran some fifty-six pages.

Just as Holmes's opinion was typical of his style, so was Brandeis's an exemplar of his own. It was a heavily documented point-by-point destruction of the grounds on which the Chief Justice rested. And, also typically, he insisted that the question was narrower than Taft had made it. He spoke of the power of removal of inferior officers, of whom the Portland postmaster was one. His opinion opens with this narrowing of the issue:[57]

Postmasters are inferior officers. Congress might have vested their appointment in the head of the department. The Act of July 12, 1876, c. 176, § 6, 19 Stat. 78, 80, reenacting earlier legislation, provided that "postmasters of the first, second, and third classes shall be appointed and may be removed by the President by and with the advice and consent of the Senate, and shall hold their offices for four years unless sooner removed or suspended according to law." That statute has been in force unmodified for half a century. Throughout the period, it has governed a large majority of all civil offices to which appointments are made by and with the advice and consent of the Senate. May the President, having acted under the statute in so far as it creates the office and authorizes the appointment, ignore, while the Senate is in session, the provision which prescribes the condition under which a removal may take place?

It is this narrow question, and this only, which we are required to decide. We need not consider what power the President, being Commander in Chief, has over officers in the Army and the Navy. We need not determine whether the President, acting alone, may remove high political officers. We need not even determine whether, acting

> alone, he may remove inferior civil officers when the Senate is not in session. . . . All questions of statutory construction have been eliminated by the language of the Act. It is settled that, in the absence of a provision expressly providing for the consent of the Senate to a removal, the clause fixing the tenure will be construed as a limitation, not as a grant; and that, under such legislation, the President, acting alone, has the power of removal. . . . But, in defining the tenure, this statute used words of grant. Congress clearly intended to preclude a removal without the consent of the Senate.

Clearly the data detailed by Brandeis demonstrated that congressional construction was against the Taft position and that, as Holmes had said, there was nothing in the arguments of inherent executive power or in the necessity faithfully to execute the laws that could afford comfort to the majority position. He concluded by resorting not to concepts of separation of powers but rather to the constitutional structure of checks and balances:[58]

> Checks and balances were established in order that this should be "a government of laws and not of men." As White said in the House, in 1789, an uncontrollable power of removal in the Chief Executive "is a doctrine not to be learned in American governments." Such power had been denied in Colonial Charters, and even under Proprietary Grants and Royal Commissions. It had been denied in the thirteen States before the framing of the Federal Constitution. The doctrine of the separation of powers was adopted by the Convention of 1787, not to promote efficiency but to preclude the exercise of arbitrary power. The purpose was, not to avoid friction, but, by means of the inevitable friction incident to the distribution of the governmental powers among three departments, to save the people from autocracy. In order to prevent arbitrary executive action, the Constitution provided in terms that presidential appointments be made with the consent of the Senate, unless Congress should otherwise provide; and this clause was construed by Alexander Hamilton in The Federalist, No. 77, as requiring like consent to removals. Limiting further executive prerogatives customary in monarchies, the Constitution empowered Congress to vest the appointment of inferior officers, "as they think proper, in the President alone, in the Courts of Law, or in the Heads of Departments." Nothing in support of the claim of uncontrollable power can be inferred from the silence of the Convention of 1787 on the subject of removal. For the outstanding fact remains that every specific proposal to confer such uncontrollable power upon the President was rejected. In America, as in England, the conviction prevailed then that the people must look to representative assemblies for the protection of their liberties. And protection of the individual, even if he be an official, from the arbi-

trary or capricious exercise of power was then believed to be an essential of free government.

What the *Myers* opinions—majority and dissenting—reveal is not that the Constitution did or did not provide for presidential removal, for there is no adequate explanation for the silence of the Constitution on this score, not even history, however it is read.[59] What the *Myers* opinions—majority and dissenting—reveal is that political questions will be decided in the courts by political judgments. I do not mean party allegiance when I speak of political judgments. Rather, the questions were answered the way writers of constitutions would answer them. Is it better to afford this power to the executive than to preserve it for congressional control? The issue was not how the Founders answered or would have answered the question; the issue was which alternative the judicial body would say is the better policy. Moreover, it is not what would have been better policy at the time of the founding of the nation, but what was better policy for the issues and conditions at the time of decision.

Taft went into the case with notions of preserving or expanding executive power. Brandeis was more committed to the concepts of representative democracy and executive restraint. The proper answer was as easy for one as it was for the other. And surely their judgments were based more on personal experience and predilections than on the arguments in support of their respective positions. Here, as is the case so often, even on issues that do not clearly involve statecraft, judgment tends to precede argument rather than follow it.

Critics of the *Myers* case are equally likely to approve or disapprove in light of their own conceptions of the proper allocation of power to the executive and legislative branches. Thus, Max Lerner, one of Holmes's most ardent admirers, found it necessary to part company with his hero on the *Myers* decision:[60]

> There was a protest against [the *Myers*] decision both from the right and left on the Court, as also in the country. And the weight of opinion today holds that Justices McReynolds and Brandeis had the better of the historical and constitutional arguments. Nevertheless, Taft would seem to have been writing from a clearer and more functional view of the problem of Presidential leadership in a democracy. While President, he had approached his problems from a judicial standpoint, because of his earlier conditioning as a judge; and while Chief Justice, he approached his problems from an administrative standpoint, because of his earlier conditioning as a President.
>
> Holmes's dissent is difficult to reconcile with such realism about the executive process as he had shown in his *Moyer* decision. He takes here a view of Presidential power that seems far too limited for our day. It could be shown historically that there has been a

> rough sequence in our conceptions of the fundamental locus of our governmental power: first Congressional, then judicial, and latterly—with the growth of a vast administrative structure—Presidential.

Lerner seems to say that since the locus of government power is now in the President, it is incumbent on the Court to enhance rather than limit that power. Lerner was an admirer of Franklin D. Roosevelt as much as of Holmes. In this instance, he could not follow both, as the Court's next decision on the subject revealed.

Franklin Delano Roosevelt, in reliance on the license that he thought was given him by the Taft opinion in *Myers*, removed a member of the Federal Trade Commission. The governing statute provided that removal could be grounded on inefficiency, neglect of duty, or malfeasance in office. Earlier, such legislative conditions had been considered redundant by the Court in *Shurtleff* v. *United States*.[61] Much to Roosevelt's chagrin, however, this time the President was held to have acted unconstitutionally, in spite of *Myers* and *Shurtleff*, both of which were distinguished to death in *Humphrey's Executor* v. *United States*.[62]

Shurtleff was distinguished on the ground that the legislative history in the *Humphrey's* case made it clear that Congress really meant to limit dismissals to those that could be grounded in the causes that it specifically stated. This was not a distinction but an excuse. "We conclude that the intent of the act is to limit the executive power of removal to the causes enumerated, the existence of none of which is claimed here."[63] That ruling put the Court squarely up against the opinion in *Myers*. But this, too, was quickly overcome:[64]

> The office of a postmaster is so essentially unlike the office now involved that the decision in the *Myers* case cannot be accepted as controlling our decision here. . . . Putting aside *dicta*, which may be followed if sufficiently persuasive but which are not controlling, the necessary reach of the decision goes far enough to include all purely executive officers. It goes no farther;—much less does it include an officer who occupies no place in the executive department and who exercises no part of the executive power vested by the Constitution in the President.

Thus, the primary objective of the Taft opinion—the control over administrative agencies—was removed from its scope. What Taft so clearly believed to be an executive agency, since it fell within neither the judicial nor the legislative branches, was held to be outside the ken of executive control. "To the extent that it exercises any executive function—as distinguished from executive power in the constitutional sense—it does so in the discharge of its quasi-legislative or quasi-judicial powers, or as an agency of the legislative or judicial departments of the government."[65] This explanation is less than helpful, since the President in faithfully executing the laws may also be said to be acting as an agent of the legislative and judicial departments.

The Court abandoned all prior rationalizations for the removal power except the incantation of the formula about separation of powers. It espoused, instead, a functional analysis:[66]

> The authority of Congress, in creating quasi-legislative or quasi-judicial agencies, to require them to act in discharge of their duties independently of executive control cannot well be doubted; and that authority includes, as an appropriate incident, power to fix the period during which they shall continue in office, and to forbid their removal except for cause in the meantime. For it is quite evident that one who holds his office only during the pleasure of another, cannot be depended upon to maintain an attitude of independence against the latter's will.
>
> . . . .
>
> The result of what we now have said is this: Whether the power of the President to remove an officer shall prevail over the authority of Congress to condition the power by fixing a definite term and precluding a removal except for cause, will depend upon the character of the office; the *Myers* decision, affirming the power of the President alone to make the removal, is confined to purely executive officers; and as to officers of the kind here under consideration, we hold that no removal can be made during the prescribed term for which the officer is appointed, except for one or more of the causes named in the applicable statute.

Four members of the majority in the *Myers* case, including the author of the unanimous *Humphrey's* opinion, Justice Sutherland, joined in this conclusion. Perhaps decision rests not only on whether a Justice considers expanded executive or legislative power better for the nation but also on who occupies the presidential office.[67] The Court particularly left open for future adjudication the question which jobs were more like those of Federal Trade Commissioners than like those of postmasters.

That question was addressed by the Court in the case of *Wiener* v. *United States*,[68] involving the discharge by President Eisenhower of a War Claims Commissioner who had been appointed by President Truman. The statute, this time, provided neither a term of office nor specific inhibitions on removal from office. The office itself, however, was one whose charter doomed it to extinction three years after the expiration of dates for filing claims.

The opinion for the unanimous Court was written by Justice Frankfurter, who enjoyed the opportunity. First, he took down the *Myers* opinion:[69]

> The assumption was short-lived that the *Myers* case recognized the President's inherent constitutional power to remove officials, no matter what the relation of the executive to the discharge of their duties and no matter what restrictions Congress may have imposed regarding the nature of their tenure. The versatility of circumstances often mocks a natural desire for definitiveness.

The *Humphrey's* opinion substituted the functional analysis for *Myers*'s doctrinal one. But *Wiener* offered no statutory language at all to distinguish it, for example, from *Shurtleff*.

What the Court did in *Wiener* was to reverse the presumption as to congressional intention. Whenever Congress assigns quasi-judicial or quasi-legislative functions—in *Wiener* the functions were essentially judicial—without specifying tenure or conditions of removal, the discretionary power of the President to remove does not exist. "[N]o such power is given to the President directly by the Constitution, and none is impliedly conferred upon him by statute simply because Congress said nothing about it. The philosophy of *Humphrey's Executor*, in its explicit language as well as its implications, precludes such a claim."[70]

What light, if any, does all this throw on the validity of the Cox discharge? The President apparently properly believed that, because the special prosecutor was not appointed by him but by the Attorney General, the power of discharge was vested in the Attorney General. This was a rejection of statements in *Myers* that have not yet been directly overruled by either *Humphrey's Executor* or *Wiener*, statements that claimed plenary authority of removal in the President because he was charged with the execution of the laws, albeit through subordinates.

Was the discharge of Cox by the Acting Attorney General valid? The question is not easy to answer, although it was easily answered in the negative by Judge Gesell in the district court.[71] It must be remembered that, although the special prosecutor was an "inferior officer" in constitutional terms, he was appointed pursuant to a general congressional authorization to the Attorney General to appoint staff in the department. The special prosecutor's post was not specifically created by the Congress. Congress had, therefore, spelled out no legislative conditions for tenure or for removal.

Under the internal regulations, however, as Elliot Richardson has reminded us, "the charter [of the special prosecutor's office] preserved to the Attorney General the power to remove the special prosecutor, but only 'for extraordinary improprieties on his part.' " There was no suggestion that there were any such "extraordinary improprieties" charged against Cox, unless failure to take directives from the President constituted "extraordinary improprieties."

To what extent could internal departmental regulations control the right of a department head to remove? If the lesson later taught by

United States v. *Nixon*[72] is not applicable solely to the facts of that case, a possibility that should not be lightly dismissed, it would appear that the regulatory removal provisions were binding on the acting Attorney General and, if so, the Cox discharge was invalid. For the Court ruled in *United States* v. *Nixon* that the regulatory provisions for the special prosecutor had the force of law and were binding on the Attorney General unless and until they were withdrawn:[73]

> Under the authority of Art. II, § 2, Congress has vested in the Attorney General the power to conduct the criminal litigation of the United States Government. 28 U.S.C. § 516. It has also vested in him the power to appoint subordinate officers to assist him in the discharge of his duties. 28 U.S.C. §§ 509, 510, 515, 533. Acting pursuant to those statutes, the Attorney General has delegated the authority to represent the United States in these particular matters to a Special Prosecutor with unique authority and tenure. The regulation gives the Special Prosecutor explicit power to contest the invocation of executive privilege in the process of seeking evidence deemed relevant to the performance of these specially delegated duties. 38 Fed. Reg. 30739, as amended by 38 Fed. Reg. 32805.
>
> So long as this regulation is extant it has the force of law. . . .
>
> Here, as in [*United States ex rel.*] *Accardi* [v. *Shaughnessy*, 347 U.S. 260 (1954)], it is theoretically possible for the Attorney General to amend or revoke the regulation defining the Special Prosecutor's authority. But he has not done so. So long as this regulation remains in force the Executive Branch is bound by it, and indeed the United States as the sovereign composed of the three branches is bound to respect and to enforce it.

So much then for the proponents of theories that the constitutional power of removal must be in the President or that the legislative power over removal belongs to the Congress. The power to specify terms of removal may now be in the bureaucracy, although the Congress might be able to pretermit this power by legislation and the President by executive order. But, so long as the Department head has not withdrawn his regulation, he may surrender the power of discharge or condition it, and all "three branches [are] bound to respect and to enforce it."

If Cox's removal were in fact illegal, he might have invoked the ancient and honorable writ of *quo warranto*, or its modern equivalent, to prevent his being superseded. But he did not. And the major removal cases brought to the Supreme Court were concerned with the right of the claimant to receive the compensation that he was denied by his premature discharge. We have not had a Supreme Court case in which the incumbent's right to office has been sustained, where the jobholder has sought specific relief against his replacement by a successor. That was the question in *Marbury* v. *Madison*. It is highly unlikely that it would ever be held that the invalidity of Cox's discharge made invalid the subsequent appointment and exercise of duties by Jaworski, although conceptually such a case could be made.

In keeping with Max Lerner's position quoted earlier,[74] the allocation of the power of removal continues to reflect the general movement of governmental power. Where it might once have graced the temporarily dominant Congress, or the temporarily dominant President, it is now appropriately to be found in the bureaucracy and the judiciary in combination. So does the changing Constitution reflect the realities of the changing positions of power within our national government.

Constitutional questions of both the power of appointment and the power of removal came to the fore when the Congress was contemplating the creation by legislation of an office of special prosecutor. The need they sought to meet was the assurance of the independence of such an office. It was feared, on the basis of some experience, that to put the power of appointment or removal in the hands of the very government officials who might themselves be suspected of criminal activity, the President and the Attorney General, could not provide the independence necessary to the office.

We have since had some enlightenment on the constitutional power of the Congress over appointments in a case that could be said to be an outgrowth of Watergate. In 1974, in the aftermath of the revelations of the abuses of political contributions to presidential campaigns, Congress enacted amendments to the Federal Election Campaign Act of 1971.[75] Among its provisions were those creating the Federal Election Commission. The validity of the entire statute was called in question, largely on First Amendment grounds, because the law inhibited some persons and entities from making some expenditures for, and contributions to, candidates for President. The Court, in *Buckley* v. *Valeo*,[76] played loose with the First Amendment rights involved,[77] but became a strict constructionist when the issue of the validity of appointments to the commission was before it.

The statute provided that the Federal Elections Commission should have eight members: the Secretary of the Senate and the Clerk of the House, *ex officio*, and without vote; two members to be appointed by the President *pro tem* of the Senate, on advice of the majority and minority leaders; two members to be appointed by the Speaker of the House, on similar recommendations; and two members to be appointed by the President. The validity of the method of appointment was seen as a problem in separation of powers. For this, the Court resorted to the usual imagery from Madison and his reliance on Montesquieu, but more pointedly on the opinion of Chief Justice Taft in *Hampton & Co.* v. *United States*,[78] where he spoke in the language of the *Myers* case on which he relied.

More directly, the decision of the Court in *United States* v. *Germaine*[79] was invoked for the proposition that "any appointee exercising significant authority pursuant to the laws of the United States is an Officer of the United States, and must, therefore, be appointed in the manner prescribed by § 2, cl. 2, of . . . Article [II]."[80] This meant appointment either by the President with the advice and consent of the Senate, or by the President, the courts of law, or the heads of departments, without the need for approval by the Senate. "While the Clause expressly authorizes Congress to vest the appointment of certain officers in the 'Courts of Law,' the absence of similar language to include Congress must mean that neither Congress nor its officers were included within the language 'Heads of Departments' in this part of cl. 2."[81] The Court found, therefore, that none of the commissioners was appointed in conformity with the requirements of Article II, § 2, cl. 2, including apparently, for some reason not shown, the two presidential appointees.[82] Therefore:[83]

> Insofar as the powers confided in the Commission are essentially of an investigative and informative nature, falling in the same general category as those powers which Congress might delegate to one of its own committees, there can be no question that the Commission as presently constituted may exercise them. . . .
>
> But when we go beyond this type of authority to the more substantial powers exercised by the Commission, we reach a different result. The Commission's enforcement power, exemplified by its discretionary power to seek judicial relief, is authority that cannot possibly be regarded as merely in aid of the legislative function of Congress. A lawsuit is the ultimate remedy for a breach of the law, and it is to the President, and not to the Congress, that the Constitution entrusts the responsibility to "take Care that the Laws be faithfully executed." Art. II, § 3. . . .
>
> . . . They may, therefore, properly perform duties only in aid of those functions that Congress may carry out by itself, or in an area sufficiently removed from the administration and enforcement of the public law as to permit their being performed by persons not "Officers of the United States."
>
> This Court observed more than a century ago with respect to litigation conducted in the courts of the United States:
>
> "Whether tested, therefore, by the requirements of the Judiciary Act, or by the usage of the government, or by the decisions of this court, it is clear that all such suits, so far as the interests of the United States are concerned, are subject to the direction, and within the control of, the Attorney-General." *Confiscation Cases*, 7 Wall. 454, 458–59 (1869).

The *Confiscation Cases*, it should be noted, were decided one year before the creation of the Department of Justice. That its dictum is today an overstatement of the rule limiting representation in the federal courts to the Attorney General is revealed by the Court's decision in *United States* v. *Nixon*, where it was recognized that different parts of the executive branch might engage in litigation in opposition to one another within the jurisdiction of the United States courts.[84]

The Court in *Buckley* v. *Valeo* thereby established two rules relevant to the question whether Congress could establish a special prosecutor's office independent of the President and the Attorney General. First, the Congress cannot vest the power of appointment in itself. Second, the enforcement of the laws through civil litigation—and *a fortiori* through criminal litigation—was an executive function.

The Congress in contemplating the creation of a statutory special prosecutor seems never to have thought of having the appointments made by the Congress.[85] It did, however, consider appointments by a court or judge. Article II, § 2, cl. 2, read literally, would support such authority. The few decisions on the subject would also seem to support the validity of this proposition. The principal case here is *Ex parte Siebold*, which sustained the appointment by the federal courts of supervisors of congressional elections:[86]

> Finally, it is objected that the act of Congress imposes upon the Circuit Court duties not judicial, in requiring them to appoint the supervisors of election, whose duties, it is alleged, are entirely executive in their character. It is contended that no power can be conferred upon the courts of the United States to appoint officers whose duties are not connected with the judicial department of the government.
>
> The Constitution declares that "the Congress may, by law, vest the appointment of such inferior officers as they think proper, in the President alone, in the courts of law, or in the heads of departments." It is no doubt usual and proper to vest the appointment of inferior officers in that department of the government, executive or judicial, or in that particular executive department to which the duties of such officers appertain. But there is no absolute requirement to this effect in the Constitution; . . .
>
> But as the Constitution stands, the selection of the appointing power, as between the functionaries named, is a matter resting in the discretion of Congress. . . . The observation in the case of Hennen, to which reference is made (13 Pet. 258), that the appointing power in the clause referred to "was no doubt intended to be exercised by the department of the government to which the official to be appointed most appropriately belonged," was not intended to define the constitutional power of Congress in this regard, but rather to

> express the law or rule by which it should be governed. . . . But the duty to appoint inferior officers, when required thereto by law, is a constitutional duty of the courts; and in the present case there is no such incongruity in the duty required as to excuse the courts from its performance, or to render their acts void. It cannot be affirmed that the appointment of the officers in question could, with any greater propriety, and certainly not with equal regard to convenience, have been assigned to any other depositary of official power capable of exercising it. Neither the President, nor any head of department, could have been equally competent to the task.

The last quoted sentence would certainly be applicable to the appointment of a special prosecutor charged with investigating questionable behavior of the President and his staff and the Department of Justice itself. Yet examples of the use of courts for appointing nonjudicial aides are few.[87] Happily, the need for such extraordinary appointment processes has been rare.

If one were, then, to advise the Congress on its choice of options for creation of an office of special prosecutor, one might say that there is authority to vest such an appointment in the courts. One could not assure Congress, however, that the present Supreme Court would take kindly to such a notion. But nothing in *Buckley* v. *Valeo* reads directly against it.

The higher hurdle is the question where such an office could be placed. It is possible to argue that it could be taken out of the Department of Justice and established independently thereof. There is nothing in the constitutional provisions for appointment and removal that would preclude this. And there is the Teapot Dome precedent. But the Supreme Court's reiteration in *Buckley* v. *Valeo* of the language in the *Confiscation Cases* would read against the power of prosecution outside the Attorney General's department, even if there is no other gloss on the Constitution to support such a position. The *Confiscation Cases* did not speak of constitutional mandate but only of "the Judiciary Act," "usage of the government," and uncited "decisions of this court."

The Court in *Buckley* v. *Valeo* made clear that the power of prosecution for violation of the civil laws of the United States would be considered an "executive function." "Executive functions" have, however, been assigned to independent agencies before. Indeed, that was exactly what Taft was concerned about in the *Myers* opinion.[88] But then, the Supreme Court in *Buckley* v. *Valeo* sounded more like Taft in *Myers* than like the Court in either *Humphrey's Executor* or *Wiener*. Indeed, there were several places where the *Buckley* v. *Valeo* Court relied on Taft's language in the *Myers* case.

The better part of valor would suggest to Congress that if it did wish to provide for a special prosecutor, it would provide for appointment by the President with the advice and consent of the Senate, carefully specify the functions and powers of the office, place it within the Department of Justice, and make provisions against removal from office that would protect the incumbent against the malversations of the President. This last it would seem able to do under *Humphrey's Executor* and *Wiener*, because the very nature of the office requires even greater independence than any Federal Trade Commissioner or War Claims Commissioner could rightfully claim. As an act of caution, it might also qualify the statutory rule that an indictment must be signed by either a United States Attorney or the Attorney General of the United States in order to be valid.[89]

6

Impeachments

Lest we forget, Richard M. Nixon was not impeached. Had he been, he would have been the second President of the United States to have suffered such obloquy. Instead, he became the first American President to resign his office. And he must have done so with the certain knowledge that he would otherwise have been impeached and, in all probability, convicted and removed from office. His abdication, therefore, was probably his last great contribution to his country. For, while his resignation may not have legally forestalled impeachment and trial, it did make it possible for the nation to shorten the trauma that was Watergate. No one, I expect, would have enjoyed the spectacle of such a trial. And it is not clear that the nation could have survived it. Indeed Nixon's resignation speech might have been improved by quoting Dickens's Sidney Carton, in *Tale of Two Cities*: "It is a far, far better thing that I do, than I have ever done; it is a far, far better rest that I go to, than I have ever known."

The resignation raised no constitutional questions. Presidential resignation is clearly contemplated by Article II and the Twenty-fifth Amendment. There were, of course, no procedural precedents. The President's letter to the Secretary of State was concise: "Dear Mr. Secretary: I hereby resign the office of President of the United States. Sincerely, Richard Nixon."

The alternative course, impeachment and trial, is also specifically contemplated by the words of the Constitution. But, as is so frequently the case, the words do not dispose of all the issues that may be raised under them. For, as Charles Curtis once observed: "Language, at any rate in legal documents, does not fix meaning. It circumscribes meaning. Legal interpretation is concerned, not with the meaning of words, but only with their boundaries."[1] And this is particularly the case where constitutional interpretation is involved. As Felix Frankfurter has pointed out: "The Constitution is, of course, a legal document, but a legal document of a fundamentally different order from an insurance policy or a lease of timberland."[2] And his meaning is enlightened by reference to Justice Holmes's statement of the nature of constitutional language:[3]

> . . . the provisions of the Constitution are not mathematical formulas having their essence in their form; they are organic living institutions transplanted from English soil. Their significance is vital not formal; it is to be gathered not simply by taking the words and a dictionary, but by considering their origin and the line of their growth.

To none of the Constitution's provisions is such an approach more necessary than to those concerned with impeachment. This is all the more true because we have no guidance from judicial opinions. There have been no Supreme Court opinions to tell us what Article II, § 4 of the Constitution means. We can rely only on the words of the Constitution, their purpose and function, and their history, both before and after their inclusion in the basic document.

We are somewhat handicapped in our search for meaning, not only because our judicial masters have not told us what to think, but because most of the available authoritative voices have been those of partisans. Impeachment is hardly a cold, dispassionate event. The literature on the subject is largely polemical rather than objective. Thus, while we should ordinarily welcome and pay heed to the views of Benjamin Curtis and of Luther Martin on the subject—two of the keenest legal minds that this country has produced—when Curtis spoke to the question, he spoke as counsel for Andrew Johnson in his impeachment trial, and Martin did so as the principal lawyer for Supreme Court Justice Samuel Chase when he was brought to the bar of the Senate.[4] And, if the views of our antecedents are tainted by bias, contemporary writers on the subject would seem to suffer no less lack of detachment. They are prisoners of their cause, as we may all be, in the context of the aftermath of Watergate. What we need to guide us, but do not have, is the kind of wisdom Learned Hand once ascribed to Justice Cardozo:[5]

> . . . the wise man is the detached man. By that I mean more than detached from his grosser interests—his advancement and his gain. Many of us can be that. . . . I am thinking of something far more subtly interfused. Our convictions, our outlook, the whole make-up of our thinking, which we cannot help bringing to the decision of every question, is the creature of our past; and into our past have been woven all sorts of frustrated ambitions with their envies, and of hopes of preferment with their corruptions, which, long since forgotten, still determine our conclusions. A wise man is one exempt from the handicap of such a past; . . . he can weigh the conflicting

factors of his problem without always finding himself in one scale or the other.

Article II, § 4 of the Constitution provides: "The President, Vice President and all civil Officers of the United States, shall be removed from Office on Impeachment for, and Conviction of, Treason, Bribery, or other high Crimes and Misdemeanors." The principal point of controversy that arises almost every time a potential impeachment is debated is whether or not "other high Crimes and Misdemeanors" is to be interpreted as acts which the substantive law has made punishable as a crime if committed by anyone.

Dumas Malone, in his brilliant biography of Thomas Jefferson, stated the issue in the context of the impeachment trial of Justice Samuel Chase:[6]

> The crucial question throughout these [proceedings], and the question of most enduring interest, was that of the nature and limitation of impeachment within the constitutional framework. Opinions ranged from the one most strikingly voiced by Senator Giles at the outset, that impeachment was a mere political inquest into which the question of criminality did not enter, to the Federalist contention that no offense was impeachable if not indictable.

The question was put by Malone in terms of the grossest alternatives: one need not choose between political whim and indictable offenses. But the recent debates in the Judiciary Committee often revealed that there were still some who, in 1974, felt that it was necessary to charge indictable offenses in any bill of impeachment. Congressman Edward Hutchinson of Michigan argued:[7]

> The meaning of the words treason and bribery are self-evident. They are crimes, high crimes directed against the State. To me the meaning of the words other high crimes or misdemeanors is equally obvious. It means what it says, that a President can be impeached for the commission of crimes and misdemeanors which like other crimes to which they are linked in the Constitution, treason and bribery, are high in the sense that they are crimes directed against or having great impact upon the system of government itself.
>
> Thus, as I see it, the Constitution imposes two separate conditions for removal of a President. One, criminality, and two, serious impact of that criminality upon the Government.

Those espousing this position were strong supporters of the President and opposed to impeachment, an ever dwindling number. The more common statement of the constitutional requirement, within the committee, was stated well by Congressman Harold Donohue of Massachusetts:[8]

Now the awesome constitutional duty of each member of this committee is to make an impartial determination as to whether or not the evidence before us warrants a reasonable judgment that Richard M. Nixon as President has seriously, gravely, purposefully, and persistently abused and misused the power entrusted to him by the people of these United States.

The textual argument in favor of construing the constitutional phrase "high Crimes and Misdemeanors" as requiring indictable offenses is supported by some of the other phraseology of the Constitution. Article III, § 2 provides: "The trial of all Crimes, except in Cases of Impeachment, shall be by Jury," thus suggesting that an impeachment trial was a criminal trial that would have required a jury were it not for the specific exemption. So, too, with the language of Article II, § 2, which provides for the pardon power with regard to all offenses against the United States, except impeachments, which suggests that—but for the specific exemption—impeachments were concerned with offenses against the United States.

The constitutional provision for trial by the Senate speaks in terms of convictions, a word referable to criminal proceedings although the legal profession also talks of convictions in other contexts, such as civil jury cases. Article I, § 3, cl. 7 reads:

> Judgment in Cases of Impeachment shall not extend further than to removal from Office, and disqualification to hold and enjoy any Office of honor, Trust or Profit under the United States: but the Party convicted shall nevertheless be liable and subject to Indictment, Trial, Judgment and Punishment, according to Law.

This provision can be read both in favor of and against limiting impeachable offenses to indictable offenses. While it speaks of conviction, at the same time it rejects the sanctions applicable to criminal convictions: fine, physical punishment, and imprisonment. Moreover, it prevents a judgment of conviction on impeachment from having the effect a criminal judgment would be required to have as a bar to further criminal trial for the same acts as grounded the impeachment.

Were we confined to a reading of the language of the Constitution, as Justice Roberts once suggested to be the rule,[9] we could conclude that, although there is some ambiguity in the Constitution's language, a case might be made for the proposition that impeachment must rest on charges that would sustain an indictment under the criminal code of the United States. But we would not give even a criminal statute so narrow a reading, no less the Constitution. And so, we must look not merely to the words of the document, but to what those words meant to those who wrote them, to the function that they were intended to serve, to the history of their use before, during, and after their composition.

Impeachment was not a concept created by the Founding Fathers. Like so many of the principles of the Constitution, impeachment was inherited both from the English constitution and from those of the states who survived some thirteen years as loosely allied but independent nations between the Declaration of Independence and the framing of the Constitution. The authors of our basic document were kept peculiarly well informed on the notion of impeachment because of the contemporaneous impeachment of Warren Hastings,[10] taking place at Westminster while the new American government was being created. Edmund Burke, champion of the American cause in Parliament, was, at the same time, the chief mover of Hastings's impeachment. He thought that impeachment was the "great guardian of the purity of the constitution."[11]

For the English, however, impeachment was not a tool available against the constitutional head of state, the king. And it was used not only to sever a man from his office, but also to sever his head from his body. English impeachment was a criminal process as well as a political one. This does not mean that removal and punishment were always the joint objectives of English impeachments. There were instances, as was the case with Warren Hastings and Lord Bolingbroke, for examples, where the accused was no longer in office by the time he was charged and tried. (It should be noted that trial at the House of Lords was appropriate for most, if not all, of those subjected to impeachment processes, because it was there and only there that peers of the realm could then be tried for their crimes. It is, therefore, not surprising that there was much controversy over the question whether a commoner was subject to impeachment.)[12]

One thing that the writers of the American Constitution made clear was that no matter how close to English precedent they wished to come, the American impeachment process was basically a political process for removal and not an alternative to, or substitute for, criminal proceedings. They did this both by restricting the possible sanctions to non-criminal ones, *i.e.*, removal from and disqualification for office, and by specific provision that criminal proceedings could follow upon impeachment proceedings no matter the outcome of the latter.

It is clear that however criminal their nature, British impeachment proceedings need not have been based on charges of indictable offenses. This point was ably made and proved by Raoul Berger's inquiries into the historical record. He summed it up this way:[13]

> The foregoing examples by no means exhaust the list which could be adduced to illustrate that English impeachments did proceed for mis-

conduct that was not "criminal" in the sense of the general criminal law.

These charges fulfill an even more important purpose—they serve, broadly speaking, to delineate the outlines of "high crimes and misdemeanors." For they are reducible to intelligible categories: misapplication of funds . . . , abuse of official power . . . , neglect of duty . . . , encroachment on or contempts of Parliament's prerogatives. . . . Then there are a group of charges which can be gathered under the rubric "corruption."

The problem is obviously complicated by the fact that in English practice, although the word "crimes" was obviously used to include "high crimes and misdemeanors," high crimes and misdemeanors were a separate and special category of misbehavior describing only political wrongs to be dealt with by political trials—political as distinguished from judicial—for impeachment, attainder, and treason. Thus, Blackstone could and did say that "an impeachment before the lords by the commons of Great Britain, in parliament, is a prosecution of the already known and established law."[14] This did not mean only statutory law but also the established common law of "high misdemeanors," which Blackstone defined as "the mal-administration of such high officers, as are in public trust and employment."[15]

The great English legal historian, F. W. Maitland, appeared to read the English constitution to allow Parliament to make impeachable offenses mean whatever the members wanted it to mean.[16] His understanding appears to have been that the High Court of Parliament could, indeed, define the crime, much as did the courts of common law, in the very course of exercising its judgment: *pro re nata* was the phrase used and rejected by Blackstone.[17] It was in the course of applauding the disappearance in England of impeachment as a criminal process that Maitland wrote:[18]

> It seems highly improbable that recourse will again be had to this ancient weapon unless we have a time of revolution before us. If a statesman has really committed a crime then he can be tried like any other criminal: if he has been guilty of some misdoing that is not a crime, it seems far better that it should go unpunished than that new law should be invented for the occasion, and that by a tribunal of politicians and partizans; for such misdoings disgrace and loss of office are now-a-days sufficient punishments.

So far as American impeachment is concerned, of course, "disgrace and loss of office" are the only sanctions. So far as the English are concerned, because of a government responsible to the legislature, the capacity to compel removal from office is in the hands of the Parliament without the need for impeachment processes.

Whether the English inheritance be that described by Blackstone, by which high crimes and misdemeanors consist of "mal-administration of such high officers, as are in public trust and employment," or the Maitland belief that the crime may be newly defined by the Parliament each time, it would seem that the requirement of an indictable offense was not one handed down to us by our English forebears.

It was in 1875 that Justice Swayne reminded us: "The theory of our government is, that all public stations are trusts, and that those clothed with them are to be animated in the discharge of their duties solely by considerations of right, justice, and the public good."[19] This notion seems to underlie the English concept that impeachments require not mere distaste for the officer or his policies but a violation of the fiduciary duties implicit in public office. And this notion clearly comes through the comparatively sparse legislative history of the Impeachment Clause in the 1787 Convention.

All the major constitutional plans brought to the Convention made some provision for the removal of the executive. The New Jersey Plan called for removal of the executive by Congress "on application by a majority of the Executives of the several States."[20] The Virginia Plan called for removal on conviction after impeachment by the House for "malpractice or neglect of duty," with trial by the judiciary.[21] The Hamilton Plan called for removal of "all officers of the United States" on "impeachment for mal- and corrupt conduct; and upon conviction to be removed from office, & disqualified for [*sic*] holding any place of trust or profit—all impeachments to be tried by a Court to consist of the Chief or Judge of the Superior Court of Law of each State, provided such Judge shall hold his place during good behavior, and have a permanent salary."[22]

It is not insignificant that the concern of the Convention from the beginning and throughout was centered on a means for removal from office and not on punishment for misbehavior. On 2 June 1787, it was moved that the executive "be removable on impeachment and conviction of mal-practice or neglect of duty."[23] The motion passed,[24] after the rejection of a provision for removal by a majority of state legislatures.[25] It was Madison and Wilson who opposed the introduction of state authorities.[26]

Madison's leadership here was demonstrated in the only important debate on the question:[27]

> Mr. [Madison] thought it indispensable that some provision should be made for defending the Community [against] the incapacity, negligence or perfidy of the chief Magistrate. The limitation of the period of his service, was not a sufficient security. He might lose his capacity after his appointment. He might pervert his administration into a scheme of peculation or oppression. He might betray his trust to

foreign powers. The case of the Executive Magistracy was very distinguishable, from that of the Legislative or of any other public body, holding offices of limited duration. It could not be presumed that all or even a majority of the members of an Assembly would either lose their capacity for discharging, or be bribed to betray, their trust. Besides the restraints of their personal integrity & honor, the difficulty of acting in concert for purposes of corruption was a security to the public. And if one or a few members only should be seduced, the soundness of the remaining members, would maintain the integrity and fidelity of the body. In the case of the Executive Magistracy which was to be administered by a single man, loss of capacity or corruption was more within the compass of probable events, and either of them might be fatal to the Republic.

There were still some who opposed impeachment, like Pinckney and Rufus King. Elbridge Gerry "urged the necessity of impeachments. A good magistrate will not fear them. A bad one ought to be kept in fear of them. He hoped the maxim would never be adopted here that the chief Magistrate could do [no] wrong."[28] Edmund Randolph thought the impeachment provision necessary as a means for punishment.[29]

The document itself went through several versions before its final draft incorporating the "high crimes and misdemeanors" language. The provision for impeachment for "mal-practice or neglect of duty" was once again approved on July 26.[30] But the Journal for August 20 showed that the reference to the Committee of Five provided: "Each of the Officers above-mentioned shall be liable to impeachment and removal from office for neglect of duty, malversation, or corruption."[31] The September 4 draft, however, provided for impeachment only for "treason or bribery."[32] The words "or other high crimes and misdemeanors" were added on September 8.[33]

Madison's notes for that day show how the adoption of the provision for impeachment for "other high Crimes and Misdemeanors" came about. Mason had objected to impeachment being limited to treason and bribery, and moved to add the term "mal-administration."[34] Madison objected that the term "mal-administration" was "[s]o vague" as to be "equivalent to a tenure during pleasure of the Senate."[35] He should have known better, since "mal-administration" was the term used in the Virginia constitution among others. But Madison did mean to make clear that the Constitution was not authorizing the removal of the President merely at the will of Congress. Mason withdrew the word "mal-administration" and substituted "other high crimes & misdemeanors."[36] Thus, the impeachment clause came for ratification by the states in the words that are now familiar to us.

The Convention history reveals that the Founders were quite familiar with the concept of high crimes and misdemeanors as utilized in English practice. The evidence clearly reflects that the concern was over abuse of official authority rather than concern with personal misbehavior of the officeholder. They were not ready to provide for congressional recall on grounds other than misbehavior in office. Those who would build on Madison's objection to the word "mal-administration" to argue that indictable offenses were to be required as grounds for removal must ignore the total record and Madison's own explanation: the Convention did not intend to make mere congressional distaste a basis for removal of an elected President.

Madison's position was made clear when he, among others, went to the people seeking ratification of the Convention's Constitution. The supporters of the Constitution worked the length and breadth of the land explaining the document and seeking support for it. Certainly the most famous and perhaps the most authoritative of these efforts was *The Federalist Papers*. Although they were directed to residents of New York, they received wider dissemination and have proved an important if not always compelling guide to the Constitution's construction since ratification. As Chief Justice Marshall noted in *Cohens* v. *Virginia*: "Its intrinsic merit entitles it to this high rank [as explicator of the meaning of the Constitution]; and the part two of its authors performed in framing the constitution, put it very much in their power to explain the views with which it was framed."[37] The reference, of course, was to Madison and Hamilton.

It fell to Hamilton to explain the Constitution's impeachment provisions in Nos. 65 and 66 of *The Federalist*. The allocation of authority to the two branches of the national legislature, like so many of the Constitution's provisions, derived from common experience and uncommon reason:

> A well-constituted court for the trial of impeachments is an object not more to be desired than difficult to be obtained in a government wholly elective. The subjects of its jurisdiction are those offenses which proceed from the misconduct of public men, or, in other words, from the abuse or violation of some public trust. They are of a nature which may with peculiar propriety be denominated POLITICAL, as they relate chiefly to injuries done immediately to the society itself. . . .
>
> What it may be asked, is the true spirit of the institution itself? Is it not designed as a method of NATIONAL INQUEST into the conduct of public men? If this be the design of it, who can so properly be the inquisitors for the nation as the representatives of the nation themselves? It is not disputed that the power of originating the inquiry, or, in other words, of preferring the impeachment, ought to be lodged in the hands of one branch of the legislative body. Will not the reasons which indicate the propriety of this arrangement strongly plead

for an admission of the other branch of that body to a share of the inquiry? The model from which the idea of this institution has been borrowed pointed out that course to the convention. In Great Britain it is the province of the House of Commons to prefer the impeachment, and of the House of Lords to decide upon it. Several of the State constitutions have followed the example. As well the latter as the former seem to have regarded the practice of impeachments as a bridle in the hands of the legislative body upon the executive servants of the government. Is not this the true light in which it ought to be regarded?

In setting out the reasons why the trial was not assigned to the Supreme Court, Hamilton noted in No. 65 of *The Federalist* the less than rigidly confined nature of the proceedings, which, he said,

> can never be tied down by such strict rules, either in the delineation of the offense by the prosecutors or in the construction of it by the judges, as in common cases serve to limit the discretion of courts in favor of personal security. . . . The awful discretion which a court of impeachments must necessarily have to doom to honor or to infamy the most confidential and the most distinguished characters of the community forbids the commitment of the trust to a small number of persons.

Here again we find that the essence of the offense for which impeachment will properly lie is "the abuse or violation of some public trust," the exact definition of which must be in the "awful discretion . . . [of] a court of impeachments." There is here a justification for a legislative check on the executive, not in terms of a vote of no confidence, but only in response to a presidential violation of the high duties of his office. There is certainly not to be found here any intimation that the function of the impeachment is to afford a tribunal for a trial of criminal offenses. Hamilton is rather suggesting that the reason for not utilizing a law court for the trial of impeachments is exactly because the issues are so different from those that are meant for the ordinary criminal law processes.

We find this position underlined in *Federalist* No. 70, where Hamilton is justifying the single rather than the plural executive. There he notes: "Responsibility is of two kinds—to censure and to punishment. The first is the more important of the two, especially in elective office. Man, in public trust, will much oftener act in such a manner as to render him unworthy of being any longer trusted than in such a manner as to make him obnoxious to legal punishment."

The reading given by Hamilton was also given by Madison. Although he later voiced objections to the use of the word "mal-administration," Madison urged that incapacity, negligence, or perfidy of the President are proper grounds for impeachment.[38] He also voiced an opinion that would have forestalled the "Saturday night massacre," when he told his fellow congressmen that an unwarranted removal from office by the President of a worthy official would warrant impeachment of the President.[39] As a representative in the First Congress, Madison argued that the President was subject to impeachment even for the wrongdoings of those whom he had appointed to office,[40] certainly a vicarious liability that we have never tolerated for criminal offenses.

The Hamiltonian concept of the basis for impeachment, breach of trust and abuse of office, found support time and time again in the ratifying conventions. Pinckney in South Carolina asserted that impeachment would lie against those who betrayed their "public trust."[41] Randolph at the Virginia convention talked of impeachment for misbehavior.[42] Thomas Iredell argued for impeachment in the event the President gave false information to the Senate.[43] Archibald MacLaine in North Carolina referred to impeachment for "any maladministration in his office."[44] And Samuel Stillman in Massachusetts stated that impeachment would lie for "malconduct."[45]

Thus, both at the Convention that framed the Constitution and at the conventions that ratified it, the essence of an impeachable offense was thought to be breach of trust and not violation of the criminal laws. And this was in keeping with the primary function of impeachment, removal from office.

Neither English history nor the debates that framed the Constitution and its ratification suggested the necessity for an indictable crime as a base for an impeachment, nor did the commentators on the Constitution who expounded that document early in its history. James Wilson, in his lectures on the Constitution, wrote: "In the United States and in Pennsylvania, impeachments are confined to political characters, to political crimes and misdemeanors, and to political punishments."[46] He had already defined "high misdemeanors" as "malversation in office."[47] And the *Oxford English Dictionary* tells us that, even then, "malversation" meant "corrupt behavior in an office of trust."

Joseph Story asserted that ordinary crimes could afford a base for impeachment, but that the constitutional provision authorizing impeachment was far broader than that. In 1833, he wrote:[48]

> Not but that crimes of a strictly legal character fall within the scope of the power . . . ; but that it has a more enlarged operation, and reaches what are aptly termed political offences, growing out of personal misconduct or gross neglect, or usurpation, or habitual disregard of the public interests, in the discharge of the duties of political office. These are so various in their character, and so indefinable in their actual involutions, that it is almost impossible to provide systematically for them by positive law. They must be examined upon

very broad and comprehensive principles of public policy and duty. They must be judged of by the habits and rules and principles of diplomacy, of departmental operations and arrangements, of parliamentary practice, of executive customs and negotiations, of foreign as well as domestic political movements; and, in short, by a great variety of circumstances, as well those which aggravate as those which extenuate or justify the offensive acts which do not properly belong to the judicial character in the ordinary administration of justice, and are far removed from the reach of municipal jurisprudence.

Chancellor Kent, in his *Commentaries*, also clearly delineated the function of the Impeachment Clause as a means "to prevent the abuse of the executive trust." The treatise reads as follows:[49]

> In addition to all the precautions which have been mentioned to prevent abuse of the executive trust in the mode of the President's appointment, his term of office and the precise and definite limitations imposed upon the exercise of his power, the Constitution has also rendered him directly amenable by law for mal-administration.[50] The inviolability of any officer of government is incompatible with the republican theory, as well as with the principles of retributive justice. The President, Vice-President, and all civil officers of the United States may be impeached by the House of Representatives for treason, bribery, and other high crimes and misdemeanors, and upon conviction by the Senate removed from office. If, then, neither the sense of duty, the force of public opinion, nor the transitory nature of the seat, are sufficient to secure a faithful discharge of the executive trust, but the President will use the authority of his station to violate the Constitution or law of the land, the House of Representatives can arrest him in his career, by resorting to the power of impeachment.

Oliver Wendell Holmes, Jr., the editor of the twelfth edition of Kent's *Commentaries*, took cognizance, in a footnote, of Professor Dwight's article contending "that there can be no impeachment except for a violation of a law of Congress, or for the commission of a crime named in the Constitution."[51] He also made note that the contrary argument was made in the same law review by Justice Lawrence. And his chief reference here was to Story's position already noted.

The last of the classic commentators to whom I would make reference, Alexis de Tocqueville, was atypically confused on the issue. At one point, he asserted: "[T]he Senate is generally obliged to take an offense at common law as the basis of its sentence."[52] Later he claimed: "A political sentence in the United States may therefore be looked upon as a preventive measure; and there is no reason for tying down the judges to the exact definitions of criminal law. Nothing can be more alarming than the vagueness with which political offenses, properly so called, are described in the laws of America."[53]

There is still one more major source of evidence for interpreting the language of the Constitution in question here: the experience under the constitutional provision that affords a basis for finding a customary construction. In 1797, William Blount was impeached because of his conduct as a senator of the United States. The Senate had, before Blount's impeachment, expelled him from membership in that body for "having been guilty of a high misdemeanor, entirely inconsistent with his public trust and duty as a Senator."[54] When the impeachment came before the Senate, that body dismissed the impeachment in response to a three-pronged plea in defense: (1) that a senator was not a "civil officer"; (2) that since he had already been removed from office, he was no longer subject to impeachment; and (3) that no crime or misdemeanor had been alleged.[55] We are not told on which ground the dismissal rested. But the case is usually accepted for the proposition that a member of Congress is not a civil officer.[56] And it is clear that the Constitution makes different provision for removing a legislator, charging each House with the discipline of its own membership, and makes no substantive requirement, only the procedural one of a two-thirds vote for expulsion.[57]

I shall omit here reference to the impeachments of judicial officers. The removal of judges it has been suggested—erroneously I think—invokes a different standard from removal of "civil officers." I turn then to the only presidential impeachment in American history—indeed the only serious move towards presidential impeachment before the Nixon presidency. It occurred in the aftermath of the Civil War, in the course of a contest between Congress—or its Radical Republican leadership—on the one hand and the executive on the other, and it was brought against one of the most unpopular Presidents the nation has ever known, Andrew Johnson. Congress sought every means to subordinate the presidency to its will. Finally, Johnson was impeached, primarily as a result of his discharge of Secretary of War Stanton and the appointment of his replacement in violation of the Tenure of Office Act.[58] There were eleven counts in the bill of impeachment, the tenth of which asserted that Johnson[59]

> unmindful of the high duties of his office and the dignity and proprieties thereof . . . designing and intending to set aside the rightful authority and powers of Congress, did attempt to bring into disgrace, ridicule, hatred, contempt, and reproach the Congress of the United States, . . . to impair and destroy the regard and respect of all the good people of the United States for the Congress . . . [made] certain intemperate, inflammatory, and scandalous harangues, . . . [thereby

also subjecting the office of the presidency to] contempt, ridicule, and disgrace, to the great scandal of all good citizens.

There should be little doubt that this portion of the charge did not meet either the indictable offenses standard that Benjamin Curtis, as Johnson's counsel, urged upon the Senate, or the standard of breach of trust of office or fiduciary duty. The essential element of this charge was "seditious libel," a concept that had died with the Alien and Sedition Laws some years earlier. It may be presumed that the President of the United States is entitled to the protections that the First Amendment affords every other person.

The charge that the President had failed faithfully to execute the laws in refusing to enforce the Tenure of Office Act was not a charge of a criminal offense but, at best, one of malversation of office. Here, it turned out, the charge was not insufficient, but the proof that the President had wantonly disobeyed a constitutional statute was inadequate to secure the necessary plurality. He had claimed the right to test the statute's constitutionality.

The acquittal of President Johnson by the Senate has been greatly romanticized by many, including no less a personage than John Fitzgerald Kennedy.[60] For those who abominate the Radical Republicans, Johnson's victory was merely the perseverance of truth and justice over calumny. But with the newly won dominance of revisionist history of the post–Civil War period,[61] it is the Radicals who wear the white hats and Andrew Johnson who is the villain. And there appeared an interesting and cogent volume justifying the impeachment of President Johnson,[62] too late to vindicate the impeachment.

Even revisionist historians, however, recognize that the Johnson impeachment did not fail for want of charges of indictable offenses. They could hardly do otherwise, since some of the articles did in fact charge indictable offenses. The cause of failure of conviction lay elsewhere. Eric McKitrick, one of the revisionist historians, describes the failure this way:[63]

> The impeachment was a great act of ill-directed passion, and was supported by little else. . . . Most people, including the noblest of the recusant Senators, were sick to death of Andrew Johnson and would have given much to see the end of him. But this could be accomplished neither by a popular referendum nor by a legislative vote of "no confidence," though either one would have settled his fate in an instant, and in either event the zeal of Trumbull and Fessenden would have been only too available. But the only form open was that of a judicial trial, and matters had reached such a pass that many men were quite willing to stretch their principles all out of shape, to seize upon any form at all that was plausible, and to face

> their consciences later. "Not a loyal tongue will wag against impeachment," Representative Blair was assured by a constituent from Flint, Michigan; "The people want rest." Yet political principles were one thing, legal principles quite another. The Tenure of Office Act, thanks to the equivocations of a joint conference committee back in February, 1867, was quite unable to bear the intense legal scrutiny to which it was subjected during the trial of Andrew Johnson. The President's counsel, men of the very highest character and ability, showed rather mercilessly how little protection the Act really gave to Lincoln's holdovers, and they argued most effectively that nothing treasonable could be found in the President's effort to test a law which he considered unconstitutional. The Managers of Impeachment, whose composite personality was a curious blend of demagogue and rascal, were not really able to give them much of a battle. More than one observer must have cringed at the spectacle.

McKitrick ignored the closeness of the Senate vote. What Curtis and his co-counsel did was to demonstrate to the satisfaction of nineteen of the fifty-four senators that Johnson had not betrayed the trust that inheres in the highest office of the land, and that he was not required to enforce a law he believed to be unconstitutional in the absence of judicial validation. The close vote did establish that the impeachment process, even under the most trying circumstances, was not convertible into a "no-confidence" vote, that if criminal charges were not required, charges of breach of fiduciary duty were.

For many observers, particularly those "liberals" in and out of academia who had supported and sponsored the growth of the imperial presidency, the Johnson impeachment afforded a different lesson. The aficionados of presidential government tended to mix "memory and desire" in their evaluation of the Johnson impeachment. James MacGregor Burns wrote:[64]

> If Johnson had not barely escaped conviction, a precedent would have been set for the easy dismissal of a President less on legal grounds than on political. Given the constitutional ambiguity over the division of legislative and executive power . . . , given also the many conflicting precedents and doctrines of previous Presidents . . . , it would always have been possible to impeach an aggressive or intractable President on grounds that he was violating the Constitution or the statutes. Even the threat of impeachment would have been a potent weapon for congressmen. As it turned out, the most unpopular President after Johnson could calculate that if impeachment had not worked under the conditions of 1868, it never would. Impeachment became something like the nuclear arm—a weapon too potent to be used in warfare over limited objectives.

The jump from the premise that impeachment was not a political tool to remove an unpopular President to the conclusion that it had no function was too broad by far. The demise of presidential impeachment was prematurely announced. The lessons of constitutional history were not to be disregarded. Presidents, Richard Nixon among them, have surely recognized that impeachment is a last resort and have frequently tested the limits of their power with the certainty of political wisdom that it would take an awful lot of wrongdoing by the executive before the legislative branch could be aroused to the use of the ultimate weapon. But the behavior of the 93d Congress in the Nixon case revealed that duty would be done, even by a reluctant Congress. And if "the most unpopular President after Johnson [did] calculate that if impeachment had not worked under the conditions of 1868, it never would," that calculation was just one more error of judgment that brought him to resignation.

The House Judiciary Committee, which was charged with determining whether charges of impeachment should be brought against President Nixon, proceeded deliberately, judiciously, and conscientiously in its task. No one can read the proceedings of the committee without crediting it with commitment to constitutional standards. The House of Representatives of 1974 was not the House of Representatives of 1868. It was not a foreordained conclusion that impeachment would follow because of its distaste for, or political opposition to, the incumbent President. It proceeded to examine the evidence, not to determine whether the President had been guilty of particular violations of the criminal code, but to seek far more significant violations of the trust of his office. And it brought in a bill of impeachment alleging such wrongdoings as would warrant removal from office because of that breach of faith, not because of acts that violated Title 18 of the United States Code.

The Articles of Impeachment, numbering three, were impressive validations of the concepts that the Founding Fathers inserted in the Constitution in the Impeachment Clause. Some of the charges were criminal acts. Article I asserted that:[65]

> In his conduct of the office of President of the United States, Richard M. Nixon, in violation of his constitutional oath faithfully to execute the office of President of the United States and, to the best of his ability, preserve, protect, and defend the Constitution of the United States, and in violation of his constitutional duty to take care that the laws be faithfully executed, has prevented, obstructed, and impeded the administration of justice, in that:
>
> On June 17, 1972, and prior thereto, agents of the Committee for the Re-election of the President committed unlawful entry of the headquarters of the Democratic National Committee . . . for the pur-

> pose of securing political intelligence. Subsequent thereto, Richard M. Nixon, using the powers of his high office, engaged personally and through his subordinates and agents, in a course of conduct or plan designed to delay, impede, and obstruct the investigation of such unlawful entry; to cover up, conceal and protect those responsible; and to conceal the existence and scope of other unlawful covert activities.

There followed a bill of particulars which made it clear that the violation was not simply that of obstruction of justice, but of "using the powers of his high office" to do so. And this was made clearer by the concluding paragraph:[66]

> In all of this, Richard M. Nixon has acted in a manner contrary to his trust as President and subversive of constitutional government, to the great prejudice of the cause of law and justice and to the manifest injury of the people of the United States.

The second Article invoked the same formula to a different subject:[67]

> Using the powers of the office of President of the United States, Richard M. Nixon . . . has repeatedly engaged in conduct violating the constitutional rights of citizens, impairing the due and proper administration of justice and the conduct of lawful inquiries, or contravening the laws governing agencies of the executive branch and the purposes of these agencies.

Again, there followed a bill of particulars.

The third Article was based on the wilful refusal of the President to respond to the subpoenas of the House committee.

The committee report was never acted upon. The resignation of the President was accepted by the House as adequate reason to go no farther. Whether resignation should be a legal barrier to further impeachment proceedings is an open question. The sanctions available to the Senate on conviction for impeachment are twofold: removal from office and disqualification from holding further office under the United States. Resignation satisfies the removal sanction only. Precedents reveal that, although the constitutional provisions for these sanctions are conjoined, the Senate may choose not to apply both. Thus, in the case of the conviction of Judge Ritter, the Senate voted 76 to 0 not to disqualify him from further office.[68] On the other hand, on the conviction of Judge Archbald, the Senate specifically voted that both sanctions be applied.[69]

One of our most eminent constitutional scholars has asserted, without qualification, that impeachment proceedings may be maintained against a civil officer no longer in office. Bernard Schwartz has written:[70]

> Resignation does not give a federal officer immunity from impeachment for acts committed while in office. In the very first impeachment proceeding . . . counsel for the defendant conceded this. "I shall certainly never contend," he declared, "that an officer may first commit an offense and afterwards avoid punishment by resigning his office." The point was squarely settled in 1876 when the Senate held that the resignation of the officer concerned, in anticipation of the impeachment proceeding, did not deprive it of jurisdiction to try him. Such holding is consistent with the relevant provision of the organic document.

Professor Schwartz may be reading more into the precedent of the proceedings against Secretary of War Belknap than it can support. Clearly on his side is the fact that the Senate voted 37 to 29 that it had the necessary jurisdiction to proceed. But the defendant was not convicted, and twenty-two of the not-guilty votes rested on the ground that the Senate was without jurisdiction. History shows that in each of the other impeachment cases where the defendant had resigned, as in the Nixon case, the proceedings were abated. There was no taste in any of them, any more than with Nixon, for a legislative extortion of revenge. The only justification for further proceedings would have been to air the facts, but there were already facts enough known to all. Never before had the impeachment process been directly witnessed by so many millions. There was little need for a Senate trial to add to their knowledge.

One more constitutional question relevant to the Impeachment Clause: Could there have been an appeal to the courts from a Senate judgment of conviction? Except for the fact that the judicial branch of government has been reaching out for power at a rate that can be equated only with the reach of the executive, the answer would be clearly in the negative. But so long as the Supreme Court's authority is not regularly tethered to some restraining principles, all the plain arguments against such review must be regarded as tentative rather than conclusive.

Charles Black has put forth the strongest argument against such review. "The most powerful maxim of constitutional law," he said, "is that its rules ought to make sense."[71] He goes on to demonstrate that judicial interference in an essentially political process would make no sense at all:[72]

> The president now appeals to the Supreme Court. The jurisdiction of that Court over the appeal is to say the least quite unclear, but it takes jurisdiction anyway. On the merits, the Court disagrees with the House and with the Senate on some point, let us say, as to the

meaning of "high Crimes and Misdemeanors," or on some procedural question of weight (perhaps dividing 5 to 4, perhaps filing nine opinions no five of which espouse the same reasoning.) *So it puts the impeached and convicted president back in for the rest of his term.* And we all live happily ever after.

I don't think I possess the resources of rhetoric adequate to characterizing the absurdity of that position. With what aura of legitimacy would a thus-reinstated chief magistrate be surrounded? Who would salute? When a respectably dressed Londoner approached the Duke of Wellington, saying, "Mr. Smith, I believe," the Duke replied, "If you believe that, you'll believe anything." I would say the same of anyone who can believe that there is hidden away somewhere, in the interstitial silences of a Constitution formed by men of practical wisdom, a command that could bring about such a preposterous result as the judicial reinstatement of a president solemnly convicted, pursuant to the constitutional forms.

It should be noted, of course, that the notion of temporary removal from the presidency is not as impractical as it once may have been. The Twenty-fifth Amendment, if not written as was the original Constitution "by men of practical wisdom," does provide for return to office by a disqualified President, but not after the disqualification from office has been decreed by at least two-thirds of the Senate on accusation by at least a majority of the House.

There are substantial and more objective reasons to conclude that judicial review of a judgment of impeachment would not have been available in the Nixon case. There is, of course, not a word in the language of the Constitution itself to suggest that the judiciary were to have a role in the impeachment process. But then, as is often noticed, there is not a word in the Constitution to suggest the power of judicial review in any situation.[73] The fact that they have taken unto themselves this power in other fields is offered as the principal reason why they should do so here.[74]

Of course, if one thinks of an impeachment trial as merely another form of criminal process, then it may be argued that the person called before the Senate forum is entitled to the forms of due process of law encapsulated in the Bill of Rights, at least insofar as the Constitution itself does not remove their applicability, as was the case with jury trial. Although the constitutional concept of due process has not yet been extended to a guarantee of an appeal, where appeal is afforded to some, it is required to be afforded to all.[75]

There was, in fact, an attempt by Judge Ritter, the last civil officer to be convicted of impeachment, collaterally to attack the Senate judgment of conviction. But it proved a failure. What Ritter did was to sue in the Court of Claims for his salary as a judge on the ground that the removal from office perpetrated by the impeachment processes was invalid. The Court of Claims, however, gave him short shrift:[76]

> We think that when the provision that the Senate should have "the *sole* power to try all impeachments" was inserted in the Constitution, the word "sole" was used with a definite meaning and with the intention that no other tribunal should have any jurisdiction of the cases tried under the provisions with reference to impeachment. . . . The dictionary definition of the word "sole" is "being or acting without another" and we think it was intended that the Senate should act without any other tribunal having anything to do with the case. This would be the ordinary signification of the words and this construction is supported by a consideration of the proceedings of the Constitutional Convention and the uniform opinion of the authorities which have considered this matter.

The Court of Claims then surveyed literature on the subject, state court judicial actions rejecting judicial review under their own impeachment provisions, and a dictum in a Supreme Court case, *Mississippi* v. *Johnson*,[77] where the Court indicated the impropriety of an injunction to prevent the Senate from sitting on a bill of impeachment brought in by the House.

It must be conceded that the modesty displayed by the Supreme Court in 1867 in the *Johnson* case is no longer evident among its more recent exercises of power. Chief Justice Chase's words are instructive if somewhat anomalous today when the courts are more highly regarded as the repository of all wisdom and judgment. "The cult of the robe" did not hold full sway when Chief Justice Salmon P. Chase wrote for the Court:[78]

> The Congress is the legislative department of the government; the President is the executive department. Neither can be restrained in its action by the judicial department; though the acts of both, when performed, are, in proper cases, subject to its cognizance.
>
> The impropriety of such interference will be clearly seen upon consideration of its possible consequences.
>
> Suppose the bill filed and the injunction prayed for allowed. If the President refuse obedience, it is needless to observe that the court is without power to enforce its process. If, on the other hand, the President complies with the order of the court and refuses to execute the acts of Congress, is it not clear that a collision may occur between the executive and legislative departments of the government? May not the House of Representatives impeach the President for such refusal? And in that case could this court interfere, in behalf of the President, thus endangered by compliance with its mandate, and restrain by injunction the Senate of the United States from sitting as a court of

impeachment? Would the strange spectacle be offered to the public world of an attempt by this court to arrest proceedings in that court?

In *Mississippi* v. *Johnson*, the Court ruled that it could neither enjoin the President from enforcing laws of Congress nor issue mandamus to him to enforce those laws. It is interesting to note, too, that the Court then thought that failure to enforce congressional laws—not an indictable crime—could give rise to impeachment. At least as late as 1937, when it denied certiorari in *Ritter*,[79] the Supreme Court gave no hint that it would be prepared to review judgments of a Senate court of impeachment.

The Constitutional Convention considered giving the Supreme Court the jurisdiction over impeachments and decided against it. The Committee on Detail's August 6 draft included this provision:[80]

> The Jurisdiction of the Supreme Court shall extend . . . to the trial of impeachments of Officers of the United States. . . . [I]n cases of impeachment . . . this jurisdiction shall be original. . . . The Legislature may assign any part of the jurisdiction above mentioned (except the trial of the President of the United States) [to] Inferior Courts.

The Convention postponed consideration of these provisions on August 27,[81] on the motion of Gouverneur Morris, who thought the Supreme Court an improper forum.[82]

On 8 September 1787, "Mr. Madison, objected to a trial of the President by the Senate, especially as he was to be impeached by the other branch of the Legislature, and for any act which might be called a [misdemeanor]. The President under these circumstances was made improperly dependent. He would prefer the supreme Court for the trial of impeachments, or rather a tribunal of which that should form a part."[83] Gouverneur "Morris thought no other tribunal than the Senate could be trusted. The Supreme Court were too few in number and might be warped or corrupted."[84] "Mr. Sherman regarded the Supreme Court as improper to try the President, because the Judges would be appointed by him."[85] The Convention voted on Madison's motion to strike the words "by the Senate" after the word "conviction" and rejected it by a vote of nine states to two.[86]

Sherman's position was reflective of an earlier debate in the Convention on the appointment of the judiciary. On July 18, Mason urged:[87]

> The mode of appointing the Judges may depend in some degree on the mode of trying impeachments, of the Executive. If the Judges were to form a tribunal for that purpose, they surely ought not to be appointed by the Executive.

Morris "supposed it would be improper for an impeachmt. of the Executive to be tried before the Judges."[88] The Convention unanimously agreed to remove from the jurisdiction of the courts the category of "Impeachments of national officers."[89]

Hamilton offered an amendment for consideration at the New York State convention providing that a special court for impeachments be created.[90] And, indeed, the New York ratifying convention unsuccessfully recommended an amendment to that effect:[91]

> That the Court for the Trial of Impeachments shall consist of the Senate, the Judges of the Supreme Court of the United States, and the first or Senior Judge for the time being, of the highest Court of general and ordinary Law Jurisdiction in each State.

In *The Federalist*, however, Hamilton made it quite clear that the Supreme Court, under the Constitution as written by the national convention, was properly excluded from participation. In No. 65, he wrote:

> Where else than in the Senate could have been found a tribunal sufficiently dignified, or sufficiently independent? What other body would be likely to feel *confidence enough in its own situation*, to preserve, unawed and uninfluenced, the necessary impartiality between an *individual* accused, and the *representatives of the people, his accusers?*
>
> Could the Supreme Court have been relied upon as answering this description? It is much to be doubted, whether the members of that tribunal would at all times be endowed with so eminent a portion of fortitude, as would be called for in the execution of so difficult a task; and it is still more to be doubted, whether they would possess the degree of credit and authority, which might, on certain occasions, be indispensable towards reconciling the people to a decision that should happen to clash with an accusation brought by their immediate representatives. A deficiency in the first, would be fatal to the accused; in the last, dangerous to the public tranquility.

Impeachment proceedings were not ordinary criminal trials. Moreover, the courts might be called on to try the same defendant for at least some of the same charges:

> These considerations seem alone sufficient to authorize a conclusion, that the Supreme Court would have been an improper substitute for the Senate, as a court of impeachments. There remains a further consideration, which will not a little strengthen this conclusion. It is this: The punishment which may be a consequence of conviction upon impeachment, is not to terminate the chastisement of the offender. After having been sentenced to a perpetual ostracism from

> the esteem and confidence, and honors and emoluments of his country, he will still be liable to prosecution and punishment in the ordinary course of law. Would it be proper that the persons who had disposed of his fame, and his most valuable rights as a citizen, in one trial, should, in another trial, for the same offense, be also the disposers of his life and his fortune? Would there not be the greatest reason to apprehend, that error, in the first sentence, would be the parent of error in the second sentence? That the strong bias of one decision would be apt to overrule the influence of any new lights which might be brought to vary the complexion of another decision? Those who know any thing of human nature, will not hesitate to answer these questions in the affirmative; and will be at no loss to perceive, that by making the same persons judges in both cases, those who might happen to be the objects of prosecution would, in a great measure, be deprived of the double security intended them by a double trial. The loss of life and estate would often be virtually included in a sentence which, in its terms, imported nothing more than a dismission from a present, and disqualification for a future, office. . . .
>
> . . . I forbear to remark upon the additional pretext for clamor against the judiciary, which so considerable an augmentation of its authority would have afforded.

That which Hamilton forbore to remark upon, the exclusion of the judiciary from the political maelstrom of presidential removal procedures, was noted as a happy and necessary choice by later commentators on the question. As Lord Bryce wrote, "Rare as this method of proceeding is, it could not be dispensed with, and it is better that the Senate should try cases in which a political element is usually present, than that the impartiality of the Supreme court should be exposed to the criticism it would have to bear, did political questions come before it."[92]

The argument is made, however, that the Supreme Court has now survived criticism of its political nature and its lack of political impartiality, despite the fact that it has so readily in recent years entered into the political thicket. Since we need no longer fear diminution of Supreme Court authority for this reason, it is suggested that the courts be given authority—or rather assume authority—to review the impeachment processes. Eighteen years ago, Professor Wechsler asked the question: "Who . . . would contend that the civil courts may properly review a judgment of impeachment when article I, section 3 declares that the 'sole Power to try' is in the Senate?"[93] The expected answer was that nobody would make such a contention. Today, the answer would be that many lawyers and all addicts of judicial supremacy would say that such a power exists in the courts. What happened in the interim was that the Court itself jumped into the political sphere with little hesitation and no doubts about its competence.

There is, of course, no statutory provision for direct review of a Senate judgment by the Supreme Court of the United States or, indeed, by any other federal or state court. Perhaps some theory could be concocted to show that the Senate's judgment was reviewable by one of the prerogative writs. Such a judgment would be but another demonstration of judicial prestidigitation. The Supreme Court, at least since Marshall's day, has been adept at lifting itself by its own bootstraps. Indeed, *Marbury* v. *Madison*[94] might be a worthy model on which the Court could fashion an extension of its constitutional authority. As the ultimate authority on the Constitution, it may well be able to see things in that document that cannot be seen by the unanointed, *i.e.*, those who have not taken the judicial oath of office.

More likely the test will be made, if at all, by indirection. In that event, *Powell* v. *McCormack*[95] or *Gravel* v. *United States,*[96] or even *United States* v. *Lovett*[97] may well show the way. One commentator contended that an improper impeachment would be nothing more than a bill of attainder and therefore must be subject to review as was the legislative act that was condemned in the *Lovett* case. He would draw an analogy from the fact that before Congress utilized the courts for enforcement of their contempt orders, contempts of Congress were first held not subject to judicial review on the basis of English precedent[98] but later came within the ken of the judiciary power.[99] It does not matter to him that the Constitution particularly authorizes impeachments—a form of removal that was available to Congress but not chosen in the *Lovett* case—at the same time that it condemns bills of attainder and bills of pains and penalties.

In any event, the mode for review suggested by *Lovett*, where three civil servants were forbidden by legislation to receive further compensation for services in the employ of the United States government, was by suit in the Court of Claims for the money to which they claimed to be entitled. This was the mode of review attempted by Judge Ritter and frustrated by the Court of Claims denial of jurisdiction, a denial with which the Supreme Court declined to interfere.

The means for relief in *Powell* v. *McCormack* were different. There Congressman Powell had been reelected to Congress, but the House refused to seat him because of conduct that the House found obnoxious. Article I, § 5 provides: "Each House shall be the Judge of the Elections, Returns and Qualifications of its own Members." It provides further that "Each House may determine the Rules of its Proceedings, punish its Members for disorderly Behaviour, and, with the Concurrence of two thirds, expel a Member."

Powell brought a declaratory judgment action in the United States District Court for the District of Columbia for a declaration that he was entitled to his seat. The trial court dismissed for want of jurisdiction over the subject matter. The Court of Appeals affirmed the decision, each judge writing an explanation of his own.[100] It was Judge McGowan's position that, since the House vote was in excess of the two-thirds necessary for expulsion, it was not necessary to decide whether Powell was denied his seat for reasons unacceptable to the constitutional provisions of qualifications for election. The Supreme Court of the United States, in an opinion by Chief Justice Warren, held that the courts had jurisdiction to determine the question and that Powell had been improperly excluded because he had established all the requirements for election specified by the Constitution: He was twenty-five years of age, seven years a citizen, and resident of the state from which he was elected. Justice Stewart's dissent, the only dissent, rested on the ground that the term of Congress to which Powell had been elected had expired and the case was, therefore, moot.

Warren found that the case presented a proper "federal question." Interestingly enough, the Court declined to address the case in the terms suggested by Judge McGowan, leaving open the issue whether the case would have been justiciable had it been an expulsion rather than an exclusion case. Clearly, too, it did not address itself to the reviewability of an impeachment judgment which, like an exclusion vote, requires two-thirds of the members to sustain. But the Court did, at one point, suggest acceptance of the analogy between the power to seat, the power to exclude, and the power to convict on impeachment. The analogy cannot be carried far. All the Court did was to repeat respondents' contentions that the three were analogous and then to reject the respondents' conclusion that it followed that there was no jurisdiction in the courts. Thus, Warren said:[101]

> Respondents first contend that this is not a case "arising under" the Constitution within the meaning of Art. III. They emphasize that Art. I, § 5, assigns to each House of Congress the power to judge the elections and qualifications of its own members and to punish its members for disorderly behavior. Respondents also note that under Art. I, § 3, the Senate has the "sole power" to try all impeachments. Respondents argue that these delegations (to "judge," to "punish," and to "try") to the Legislative Branch are explicit grants of "judicial power" to the Congress and constitute specific exceptions to the general mandate of Art. III that the "judicial power" shall be vested in the federal courts. Thus, respondents maintain, the "power conferred on the courts by article III does not authorize this Court to do anything more than declare its lack of jurisdiction to proceed."
>
> We reject this contention . . .

There is no indication that the Court, in its judgment, is accepting the respondents' equation of the power to "judge," to "punish," and to "try": its opinion goes only to the issue of the power of the House to judge the qualifications of its members.

Nevertheless, the opinion, like many of the Warren Court's opinions, reads the judicial authority more broadly than did earlier courts. And it must be conceded that a similar attitude could bring even impeachments within judicial control. Even the opinion in *Powell*, however, acknowledges that the Court may not have the power to order coercive relief rather than simply declaratory relief.[102] And the Court did note, in a footnote, where some of the Court's most important law is frequently made, that "[c]onsistent with [its] interpretation, federal courts might still be barred by the political question doctrine from reviewing the House's factual determination that a member did not meet one of the standing qualifications. This is an issue not presented in this case and we express no view as to its resolution."[103]

As with *United States* v. *Nixon*,[104] the *Powell* case may be summed up by the language at the end of the opinion. "[I]t is the responsibility of this Court to act as the ultimate interpreter of the Constitution."[105] And when one asks where the Court gets this authority to act as the "ultimate interpreter" of the Constitution, one quickly finds that, as in the *Nixon* case, the Court conferred this authority on itself in *Baker* v. *Carr*,[106] allegedly relying on *Marbury* v. *Madison*, which says nothing of the sort.

Justice Douglas in his separate concurring opinion suggests that the decision in *Powell* would not be binding on an "expulsion" case and, *a fortiori*, it cannot be said to control an impeachment question. Douglas said: "By Art. I, § 5, the House may 'expel a Member' by a vote of two-thirds. And if this were an expulsion case I would think that no justiciable controversy would be presented, the vote of the House being two-thirds or more. But it is not an expulsion case."[107]

One might accept the proposition suggested by Martin Shapiro in his analysis of political question jurisdiction in the high court, not as the most propitious solution but as the most likely one. Professor Shapiro wrote in 1964:[108]

> At best then, the whole debate over political questions and reapportionment is inconclusive, leaving the Court perfectly free to choose whatever course it wishes. Actually, however, the proponents of the doctrine seem, to me at least, to lose. Granted that there are certain cases at certain times that a particular court would be well advised, for a variety of reasons, not to decide. Then let them not decide those particular cases at those particular times. The evil of the "political questions" doctrine is that it elevates a single expediential act into a matter of binding Constitutional principle.

What Shapiro and many others like him fail to understand is that there are questions that the Court should not undertake to decide, for once having decided to decide some of them, it will be called upon to decide all of them. Not all political questions are alike, of course. But questions involving the basic conflicts between the legislative and executive branches of the national government will almost always be of sufficient moment to command judicial attention if we concede judicial competence. Or at least the momentum that compels decision of them will constantly increase. And sooner or later, the judicial branch could be ground to dust between the competing forces whose respective powers it is trying to mediate. Just such an ultimate decision could be one that decided that the Senate could not try or convict a President who was impeached by the House of Representatives.

It is clear to me that judicial review of impeachment proceedings was never contemplated by those who wrote the Constitution. It is clear to me that before the decisions of the reapportionment cases, there was no possibility that the judicial branch would undertake such a review. It is, however, equally clear to me that the enhanced self-image of the American judiciary today might very well lead it to decisions, with consequences that could be disastrous, not merely, as Professor Black suggested, for the judiciary itself. The judiciary, as Hamilton noted, has no special information, training, or capacity to render such a decision. It would do well to demonstrate by example rather than edict the proposition that each branch of government ought to stay within the confines set for it by the Constitution and not press at the edges of its authority to see how much power it can accumulate before it engorges itself.

7

Presidential Prosecutions and Presidential Pardons

When President Nixon produced the tapes demanded of him, after the fiasco of the Saturday Night Massacre, the special prosecutor had in his hands devastating evidence of criminal culpability. The question that the prosecutor faced was what to do with that evidence. He requested a report from his staff on the constitutional propriety of indicting a sitting President. That report added to his quandary rather than alleviating it:[1]

> The . . . memorandum, forwarded to the Special Prosecutor . . . concluded that nothing in the text of the Constitution or in legal precedents explicitly barred the grand jury from indicting President Nixon. But the memorandum expressed grave doubts about the institutional "propriety" of indicting a sitting President. [The] conclusion echoed research done by the original Watergate prosecutors. . . . On account of the symbolic damage to the Presidency and the concrete damage to the functioning of the government that might be caused by a criminal proceeding against a sitting President, the Justice Department had concluded in its [earlier] study, the criminal process should not go beyond the point where the President's performance of his official duties would be impaired.

To add to his problems, the Watergate task force in his office informed Jaworski that "the evidence of Nixon's criminal conduct [was] overwhelming—that failure to take action could not be justified for want of a strong enough case."[2] This second report asserted:[3]

> . . . the President might be prosecuted for obstruction of justice, for bribery, for obstruction of a criminal investigation, and for conspiracy to commit all these offenses. In addition, he could conceivably be charged for having "aided, abetted, and counseled" the payment of a bribe, for having failed to report what he knew about the cover-up as an "accessory after the fact," and for misprision of a felony.

In the end, the grand jury, at the behest of the special prosecutor, did not indict the President but authorized him to be named as an "unindicted co-conspirator."

The arguments pro and con on the indictability of an incumbent President are not strong, on either side. Fortunately, the question had never before been proffered.

The primary argument made against indictability derived from language of the Impeachment Clause. Article I, § 3, cl. 7, provides:

> Judgment in Cases of Impeachment shall not extend further than to removal from Office, and disqualification to hold and enjoy any Office of honor, Trust or Profit under the United States: but the Party convicted shall nevertheless be liable and subject to Indictment, Trial, Judgment and Punishment, according to Law.

The obvious purpose of the provision allowing subsequent trial was to avoid the possibility of a plea of double jeopardy by an official impeached by the House and tried by the Senate, if he is brought to trial after his removal from office. Some, including members of the House Judiciary Committee,[4] were of the view that the language of the constitutional provision established a condition precedent to criminal prosecution, *i.e.*, that there could be no criminal prosecution of a President until he had first been impeached and convicted on the impeachment charges.

There was very little to support the thesis thus proffered. Alexander Hamilton, when seeking to have the Constitutional Convention provide a term for life for the chief executive, had at the same time suggested that he be free of criminal sanction until he was impeached and removed.[5] The Convention paid no heed to this suggestion. In *The Federalist* No. 69, Hamilton again stated: "The President would be liable [in impeachment] and would afterwards be liable to prosecution." Gouverneur Morris had observed that the Supreme Court would "try the President after the trial of the impeachment."[6] Few, aside from the partisans, like those on the Judiciary Committee, found any support in these ambiguous statements for the proposition that the Impeachment Clause set up a prescribed sequence for prosecution, with impeachment a necessary precedent to a criminal trial.

The question was twice presented for judicial resolution during the Watergate period. Judge Otto Kerner, a sitting judge of the United States Court of Appeals for the Seventh Circuit, was under criminal indictment. He argued that he could not be subjected to the processes of the criminal law until he had first been impeached and removed from office. The argument was rejected by the Court of Appeals:[7]

> The Constitution does not forbid the trial of a federal judge for criminal offenses committed either before or after the assumption of

judicial office. The provision of Art. I, § 3, cl. 7, that an impeached judge is "subject to Indictment, Trial, Judgment and Punishment, according to Law" does not mean that a judge may not be indicted and tried without impeachment first. The purpose of the phrase may be to assure that after impeachment a trial on criminal charges is not foreclosed by the principle of double jeopardy, or it may be to differentiate the provisions of the Constitution from the English practice of impeachment. R. Berger, [*Impeachment*] at 78–80, citing 1 J. Wilson, Works 324 (McCloskey ed.); 14 Annals of Cong. 423 (1805) (giving an interpretation of the clause by L. Martin, a member of the Constitutional Convention).

The Supreme Court turned down review of the *Kerner* case.[8] The issue was also proffered to the Supreme Court in the Nixon tapes case, but the Court found it unnecessary to decide the question.[9] The impeachment provisions are the same for Presidents as they are for judges.

Less political opponents of presidential prosecution did not attempt to rest their conclusion on the Impeachment Clause. Two Yale Law School professors who took this position were Robert Bork and Alexander Bickel. Professor Bork was Solicitor General at the time. His position was stated in his memorandum for the trial court in the Spiro Agnew case, where he asserted that a President is immune from criminal prosecution but a Vice-President or other government official is not.[10] Bickel's position was stated in the *New Republic*, and he argued that because a President is immune from criminal prosecution, so too must be the Vice-President.[11] Bickel wrote:

> In the presidency is embodied the continuity and indestructibility of the state. It is not possible for the government to function without a President, and the Constitution contemplates and provides for uninterrupted continuity in that office. Obviously the presidency cannot be conducted from jail, nor can it be effectively carried on while an incumbent is defending himself in a criminal trial. And the incumbent cannot be replaced or suspended or deprived of his function as President while he is alive and not declared physically disabled. . . . Hence a sitting President must be impeached [and removed from office] before he can be indicted.

The principal argument against such presidential immunity is that there is no language in the Constitution that affords it. The only provision for immunity from prosecution is that which is granted Congress in Article I, § 6, which provides: "The Senators and Representatives . . . shall in all Cases, except Treason, Felony and Breach of the Peace, be privileged from Arrest during their Attendance at the Session of their respective Houses, and in going to and returning from the same." Solicitor General Bork acknowledged the rule of *inclusio unius, exclusio alterius*:[12] "Since the Framers knew how to, and did, spell out immunity, the natural inference is that no immunity exists where none is mentioned." And there is constitutional legislative history to support this conclusion. Thus, Charles Pinckney, a member of the Convention, spoke out in Congress against the existence of a presidential privilege,[13] and James Wilson told the Pennsylvania ratification convention that "not a *single privilege* is annexed to his [a President's] character."[14]

The fact remains, however, that there is no evidence in the records of the Convention to dispel the notion of a presidential privilege from suit. The congressional privilege was a reaction to English experience of harassment of anti-establishment members of Parliament; there was no similar evidence that executive officials had been similarly imposed upon. And, as usual, the *inclusio unius* argument is something less than persuasive. Many official privileges have been sustained, even without statutory support, and in the absence of constitutional language. As we have already seen, the Supreme Court of the United States acknowledged (or created) the existence of a constitutional executive privilege in *United States* v. *Nixon*.[15] Nor is there doubt that the judicial branch also enjoys a privilege against accountability for acts performed in the course of its judicial duties, although there is no constitutional language or history to support it.[16]

The person directly charged with responding to the question of presidential immunity was the special prosecutor, Leon Jaworski. His staff reports have already been noted. The *New York Times* reported that Jaworski had advised the grand jury not to indict the President. He was reported to have said: "It was researched at the time and the conclusion was that legal doubt on the question was so substantial that a move to indict a sitting President could touch off a legal battle of gigantic proportions."[17] By the time of the publication of his book, Jaworski was still equivocal:[18]

> The evidence, we felt, was sufficient at that early date [7 Jan. 1974] to indicate that the President might be chargeable with conspiring to obstruct justice, to commit bribery, and to obstruct a criminal investigation by endeavoring through bribery to prevent communication of information relevant to criminal violations to the prosecutors. Accordingly, the President might also be chargeable with the substantive offenses of obstruction of justice, bribery, and obstruction of a criminal investigation. Moreover, the President possibly could be charged as an accessory after the fact and misprision of felony.
>
> I had no doubt that the grand jury wanted to indict him. . . .
>
> I had grave doubts that a sitting President was indictable for the offense of obstruction of justice. While legally an indictment could be returned against a sitting President for the offense of murder, say, I did not believe that the U.S. Supreme Court would permit indict-

ment of a sitting President for obstruction of justice—*especially when the House Judiciary Committee was then engaged in an inquiry into whether the President should be impeached on that very ground.* The proper constitutional process, it seemed to me, would be for the Committee to proceed first with its impeachment inquiry.

It is obvious that the special prosecutor had no clear legal reasons in mind for not prosecuting the President. It was enough for him that the Supreme Court might not like it. But the confusion was not of Jaworski's making. There is no clear-cut authority to support either side. The real question is whether the President of the United States must have such a privilege against prosecution as a necessary condition to the performance of his functions. Necessity is the mother of many of our constitutional precepts, including that of judicial review.[19]

My own conclusion is that a President of the United States must be immune from criminal prosecution and that this immunity derives from the structure of our Constitution rather than its language. The President is, by reason of the fact that the executive power of the United States is vested in him, a unique official. He is the only officer of the United States whose duties under the Constitution are entirely his responsibility and his responsibility alone. He is the sole indispensable man in government, and his duties are of such a nature that he should not be called from them at the instance of any other government or branch of government. There is some irony in the fact that the very nature of the "imperial presidency" enhances the necessity that the President be shielded from prosecution.

I am aware that this position was rejected by no less a personage than Chief Justice Marshall, sitting as a *nisi prius* judge in the Aaron Burr case, who was of the opinion that the presidency was not a task that "demanded [the President's] whole time."[20] But there are differences between the subpoena in the *Burr* case, to which Marshall referred, and criminal indictment process directed at the President himself. The first is that Marshall's call was for a small portion, if any, of the President's time, as a witness to produce a document. Indeed, Jefferson was not called upon to appear at all. Marshall's position would seem to be sustained, to this limit—the obligation to respond to a subpoena duces tecum—by the Supreme Court's decision in *United States* v. *Nixon*, the tapes case. The second distinction is the more important one. For Marshall was wrong about the demands of the presidential office, if not in the early nineteenth century, then certainly in the late twentieth. Jefferson disagreed with the Marshall assessment, even then. He refused to acknowledge the power of the Court, because, he said, "The Constitution enjoins his constant agency in the concerns of 6 millions of people."[21] Now there are forty times six millions of people and the President cannot even go to the hospital without taking the presidency with him. We have witnessed the extent of the incapacitation of a President subjected only to congressional inquiries into his misbehavior. How much more debilitating would be a criminal trial, with all the constitutional safeguards, including the right to confront the witnesses against him—and to cross-examine them. An impeachment process does not demand the attendance of the accused; a criminal proceeding does. The impeachment procedure is constitutionally ordained; the criminal prosecution of the President would be derived from the ambiguous silence of the Constitution.

Whatever the correct answer to the question whether an incumbent President may be indicted and tried on criminal charges, there should be no doubt that a removed or retired or resigned President is vulnerable to the criminal processes. Neither the argument based on the Impeachment Clause nor the argument based on his indispensability is any longer available to him. And so when Nixon submitted his resignation, he opened the possibility that a criminal trial was in the offing for him. This time the possibility of criminal proceedings against Nixon was foreclosed by the grant of a presidential pardon.

At his confirmation hearings after his nomination to the Vice-Presidency, Gerald Ford had indicated that a pardon for Nixon was not likely to be tolerated by the American people. After his elevation to the Presidency, in a press conference on 28 August 1974, he said that the question of pardon, while open, was premature:[22]

> . . . I've asked for prayers for guidance on this very important point. In this situation I am the final authority. There have been no charges made. There has been no action by the court. There's been no action by any jury, and until any legal process has been undertaken, I think it's unwise and untimely for me to make any commitment.

Nevertheless, less than two weeks later, on a quiet Sunday morning, 8 September 1974, the new President dropped his bombshell on a sleepy American public. "I, Gerald R. Ford, President of the United States, pursuant to the pardon power conferred upon me by Article II, Section 2, of the Constitution, have granted and by these presents do grant a full, free, and absolute pardon unto Richard Nixon for all offenses against the United States which he, Richard Nixon, has committed or may have committed or taken part in during the period from January 20, 1969 through August 9, 1974."[23]

With this stroke of the pen, he freed Nixon from liability for his federal crimes, and probably doomed his own chances for election to office in his own right. He issued a statement that explained the reasons for his action:[24]

To procrastinate, to agonize, to wait for a more favorable turn of events that may never come, or more compelling external pressures that may as well be wrong as right, is itself a decision of sorts and a weak and potentially dangerous course for a President to follow. . . .

The Constitution is the supreme law of our land and it governs our actions as citizens. Only the laws of God, which govern our consciences, are superior to it. As we are a nation under God, so I am sworn to uphold our laws with the help of God. And I have sought such guidance and searched my own conscience with special diligence to determine the right thing for me to do with respect to my predecessor in this place, Richard Nixon, and his loyal wife and family. . . .

There are no historic or legal precedents to which I can turn in this matter, none that precisely fit the circumstances of a private citizen who has resigned the Presidency of the United States. But it is common knowledge that serious allegations and accusations hang like a sword over our former president's head and threaten his health as he tries to reshape his life, a great part of which was spent in the service of this country and by the mandate of its people. . . .

As a man, my first consideration will always be to be true to my own convictions and my own conscience.

My conscience tells me clearly and certainly that I cannot prolong the bad dreams that continue to reopen a chapter that is closed. My conscience tells me that only I, as President, have the constitutional power to firmly shut and seal this book. My conscience says it is my duty, not merely to proclaim domestic tranquility, but to use every means I have to assure it.

In conclusion, he stated that he regarded it as an act of personal salvation to grant the pardon:

I do believe with all my heart and mind and spirit that I, not as President, but as a humble servant of God, will receive justice without mercy if I fail to show mercy.

Ford's utilization of Lincoln's words from the Second Inaugural Address was obviously meant to set the tone. But the Ford statement lacks Lincoln's elegance and is unduly immersed in piety. It has none of the true ring of the Lincoln language: "With malice toward none, with charity for all, with firmness in the right as God gives us to see the right, let us strive on to finish the work we are in, to bind up the nation's wounds, to care for him who shall have borne the battle and for his widow and his orphan, to do all which may achieve and cherish a just and lasting peace among ourselves and with all nations."[25]

Ford's resort to "higher law" was certainly without justification in the Constitution. Indeed, it was the resort to "higher law" that got his predecessor into his difficulties. Neither presidential conscience nor his witness to God's law is a justifiable alternative to "the law of the land." Unlike the Declaration of Independence, the Constitution derived from the authority of the people. There was no resort in the Constitution to "the Laws of Nature and of Nature's God," or to "unalienable rights" with which the authors were "endowed by their Creator." Instead, it was simply: "We the People of the United States, in Order to form a more perfect Union, establish Justice, insure domestic Tranquility, provide for the common defence, promote the general Welfare, and secure the Blessings of Liberty to ourselves and our Posterity, do ordain and establish this Constitution for the United States of America." Nor did the prescribed constitutional oath, as Ford asserted, invoke the will of the deity: "I do solemnly swear (or affirm) that I will faithfully execute the Office of President of the United States, and will to the best of my Ability, preserve, protect and defend the Constitution of the United States."[26] That the "laws of God," as interpreted by President Ford, are superior to the Constitution and laws of the United States, as he said, is of little constitutional merit, whatever theocratic doctrines may support it. A President who has "implied powers" from Heaven as well as from the Constitution is certainly a fearsome President, without limitation on his authority.

The new anti-Watergate President had salvaged not the country but the Watergate President. The country was disillusioned. The President had engaged in negotiations with Nixon through a secret emissary during the week preceding the pardon. Nixon accepted the pardon, with no signs of contrition or confession. Philip Buchen, Ford's White House counsel, had to tell the press that Ford did not make "a deal" with Nixon and that the grant of a pardon "can imply guilt—there is no other reason for granting a pardon." And the mere fact that it was accepted, he stated, "means that the man believes it is necessary or useful to have it."[27] It became clear that there had been no immediate threat of prosecution, but there was the continued possibility of one.

Jerald ter Horst, the President's press secretary, who had committed himself to a kind of openness with the press that had not marked the Nixon administration, felt it necessary to resign when he had been misinformed about pardon negotiations with Nixon and so had misinformed the media. Most Americans tended to think in the words of one of George Eliot's characters in *Romola*: "There is a mercy which is weakness, and even treason against the common good." The public reaction was such that the President appeared "voluntarily" before the House Judiciary Committee to explain his actions.

Ford explained there that the issue of pardon had first come up when he was still Vice-President in a conversation he had with General Haig, but that he had made no agreement to grant a pardon: "I assure you that there never was at any time any agreement whatsoever concerning a pardon to Mr. Nixon if he were to resign and I were to become President."[28] He stated further: "At no time after I became President on August 9, 1974, was the subject of a pardon for Richard M. Nixon raised by the former President or by anyone representing him."[29]

In response to the committee's resolution of inquiry, he said that he had no "specific knowledge of any formal criminal charges pending against Richard M. Nixon." He explained this:[30]

> I had known, of course . . . that the grand jury investigating the Watergate break-in and coverup had wanted to name President Nixon as an unindicted coconspirator in the coverup. Also, I knew that an extensive report had been prepared by the Watergate Special Prosecution Force for the grand jury and had been sent to the House Committee on the Judiciary, where, I believe, it served the staff and members of the committee in the development of its report on the proposed articles of impeachment. Beyond what was disclosed in the publications of the Judiciary Committee on the subject and additional evidence released by President Nixon on August 5, 1974, I saw on or shortly after September 4, a copy of a memorandum prepared for Special Prosecutor Jaworski by the Deputy Special Prosecutor, Henry Ruth. A copy of this memorandum had been furnished by Mr. Jaworski to my counsel and was later made public during a press briefing at the White House on September 10, 1974.
>
> . . . The memorandum lists matters still under investigation which "may prove to have some direct connection to activities in which Mr. Nixon is personally involved." The Watergate coverup is not included in this list; and the alleged coverup is mentioned only as being the subject of a separate memorandum not furnished to me. Of those matters which are listed in the memorandum, it is stated that none of them "at the moment rises to the level of our ability to prove even a probable criminal violation by Mr. Nixon."

Mr. Buchen explained to the press on 10 September 1974 the reason for the expedited pardon:[31]

> Asked why Mr. Ford had abruptly reversed himself after saying he would wait until the special prosecutor had acted on Mr. Nixon before deciding on a pardon, Mr. Buchen said, "An act of mercy can never be untimely."
>
> But he added that one reason Mr. Ford had changed his mind was that he had not been aware before last week that a President could offer a pardon before there had been an indictment.
>
> Mr. Buchen said that, after the news conference of Aug. 28 at which Mr. Ford had said he would wait for the special prosecutor, "He reflected on the matter and then asked me to find out if he could move more quickly."

A "significant" factor leading to the President's decision to grant the pardon was that he was advised that there would be a year or more delay before a trial of the President could begin, Mr. Buchen said.

The question of the validity of the pardon has been raised only through the media and so-called learned journals. Perhaps the only person who could have made a judicial issue of it, Leon Jaworski, chose not to do so. The means were available to Special Prosecutor Jaworski to seek an indictment against the ex-President and put it to him whether he wished to assert the pardon by way of defense. Had Jaworski so acted, the question of constitutionality would have had to be decided by the courts. Jaworski was either of the view that the arguments against the validity of the pardon were too amorphous or, like President Ford, that Nixon had suffered enough. A recent book on Watergate, by two of the staff of the Watergate task force within the special prosecutor's office, gives evidence that Jaworski's attitude throughout was that the country's needs would be fully met by the removal of the President from office.[32]

In the history of Anglo-American law, pardons have been so much a purely political tool that it is difficult to deal with them in terms of legal doctrine. It is easier to say that the power of pardon was abused than to say that it was illegally exercised. This is not a new phenomenon, as the Reverend Stubbs pointed out in his English constitutional history:[33]

> The more common plan of dispensing by special licence with the operation of a statute in the way of pardons and grants of impunity, was less dangerous to the constitution and less clearly opposed to the theory of monarchy as accepted in the middle ages. Yet against the lavish exercise of this prerogative the commons are found remonstrating from time to time in tones sufficiently peremptory. The power was restricted by the statute of Northampton passed in 1328; but in 1330 and 1347 the king was told that the facilities for obtaining pardons were so great that murders and all sorts of felonies were committed without restraint; the commons in the latter year prayed that no such pardons might be issued without consent of parliament, and the king, in his answer, undertook that no such charters should thenceforth be issued unless for the honour and profit of himself and his people. A similar petition was presented in 1351, and instances might be multiplied which would seem to show that this evil was not merely an abuse of the royal attribute of mercy or a defeat of the ordinary processes of justice, but a regularly systematised perversion of prerogative, by the manipulation of which the great people of the realm, whether as maintainers or otherwise, attempted to secure for their retainers, and those who could purchase their support, an exemption

from the operation of the law. Even thus viewed however it belongs rather to the subject of judicature than to legislation.

It is clear that, at the time of the Federal Constitutional Convention, the pardon power in England was a matter of royal prerogative, to be exercised at the discretion of the Crown. Yet, if the power did not belong to the legislature, English history reveals that it was possible for the Parliament by law to impose restrictions on the utilization of that royal power, witness the Habeas Corpus Act of 1679 and the Act of Settlement of 1701.[34]

After the American rebellion, the states replaced their royal governors by governors with very little authority. What authority they had tended to be restrained by councils of state and these inhibitions extended to the formerly royal prerogative of pardons.[35] It was not unnatural, therefore, that the debates over the pardon power at the Constitutional Convention were primarily concerned with the proper allocation of this, heretofore, royal prerogative. For it was recognized to be a political weapon of no mean proportions.

Neither the Virginia nor the New Jersey Plans, which formed the base for the Convention's actions, made reference to the pardon power at all.[36] Pinckney's Draft of a Federal Government provided that the executive "shall have power to grant pardons & reprieves except in impeachments," obviously modeled on the English scheme.[37] Hamilton would have accorded his governor, as he called the chief executive, "the power of pardoning all offences except Treason; which he shall not pardon without the approbation of the Senate."[38]

Rutledge for the Committee on Detail offered a suggestion which was like that of his compatriot Pinckney: "He shall have power to grant reprieves and pardons; but his pardon shall not be pleadable in bar of an impeachment."[39] Roger Sherman asked that the power be qualified by requiring Senate consent.[40] Luther Martin would have restricted pardons so that they could come only after conviction.[41] James Wilson objected to this on the ground "that pardon before conviction might be necessary in order to obtain the testimony of accomplices."[42] The Martin proposal was withdrawn.[43]

Randolph moved to amend the pardon power to exclude cases of treason,[44] because the President might himself be a party to the treason and use the pardon power to protect his accomplices. Gouverneur Morris said he would rather there be "no pardon for treason, than let the power devolve on the legislature."[45] Wilson thought pardon for treason was necessary and would leave it to the President. If the President were involved in the treason, he could be "impeached and prosecuted."[46] (There was no suggestion that he could pardon himself.) Rufus King thought that the principle of separation of powers required that the power of pardon be vested in the executive, but he was prepared to require the concurrence of the Senate.[47] Madison conceded the deficiencies of leaving pardons to the legislature, but "pardon of treasons was so peculiarly improper for the President" that he would transfer the authority to Congress.[48] The Randolph motion to exclude treason from the presidential pardon power failed.[49]

The administration of the pardon power has never—before the Nixon pardon—excited great public dissatisfaction or question, except after the Civil War.[50] Nor did it arouse much interest at the state ratifying conventions. Critics of presidential authority included the pardon power in their catalog of dissatisfactions.[51] They were particularly perturbed about vesting the power of pardon in treason cases in the President.[52] Like the members of the Constitutional Convention itself, they feared that the President was a likely party to treason and would use his pardon power to exonerate accomplices and thus forestall investigations, especially if he could grant pardon before indictment.[53] The state conventions mirrored the arguments at the national convention and left the results unchanged.

Once more it was left to Hamilton, in *The Federalist* No. 74, to defend what he had not sponsored. It will be noted that in one part of his argument, that relating to treason, Hamilton speaks of a post-conviction action, but, in talking of insurrection, he speaks of negotiations for pardon, obviously before indictment:

> The criminal code of every country partakes so much of necessary severity, that without an easy access to exceptions in favor of unfortunate guilt, justice would wear a countenance too sanguinary and cruel. As the sense of responsibility is always strongest, in proportion as it is undivided, it may be inferred that a single man would be most ready to attend to the force of those motives which might plead for a mitigation of the rigor of the law, and least apt to yield to considerations which were calculated to shelter a fit object of its vengeance. . . .
>
> The expediency of vesting the power of pardoning in the President has, if I mistake not, been only contested in relation to the crime of treason. This, it has been urged, ought to have depended upon the assent of one, or both, of the branches of the legislative body. I shall not deny that there are strong reasons to be assigned for requiring in this particular the concurrence of that body, or a part of it. As treason is a crime levelled at the immediate being of the society, when the laws have once ascertained the guilt of the offender, there seems a fitness in referring the expediency of an act of mercy towards him to the judgment of the legislature. And this ought the rather to be the case, as the supposition of connivance of the Chief Magistrate ought not to be entirely excluded. But there are also strong objections to such a plan. It is not to be doubted, that a single man of prudence and good sense is better fitted, in delicate conjunctures, to balance

> the motives which may plead for and against the remission of punishment, than any numerous body whatever. . . . But the principal argument for reposing the power of pardoning in this case in the Chief Magistrate is this: in seasons of insurrection or rebellion, there are often critical moments, when a well-timed offer of pardon to the insurgents or rebels may restore the tranquility of the commonwealth; and which, if suffered to pass, unimproved, it may never be possible afterwards to recall.

The attacks on the validity of the Nixon pardon were many. No doubt some of them stemmed from pique at the thought that Nixon was to be allowed to escape justice. Although, as the Supreme Court has said, no man is above the law, the pardon, nevertheless, put Nixon beyond its reach, which may amount to the same thing. The objections of some were concerned with the inequality of trying and punishing his aides, while allowing the chief villain to go unscathed. Some saw similar inequality in declining full and free pardons to the Vietnam War resisters while allowing to go free the man who conducted the war for five years. Some were fearful that, if Nixon escaped conviction—they were not so much interested in consequent punishment—he would, Phoenix-like, as he did after his gubernatorial defeat in California, rise again as a political force for evil.[54] But none of these objections could reach the level of substantial legal doubt as to the validity of the pardon. They all spoke rather to the bad judgment of the man who offered it.

There were some who thought that the pardon had been secured by fraud, that the Vice-President had made a deal to secure the presidency by promising pardon to the President in exchange for his resignation. This was the attack that Ford answered in his appearance before the House Judiciary Committee.[55] These skeptics and cynics were not necessarily satisfied with Ford's denial. They were probably right in supposing that fraud in the inducement would have vitiated the validity of the pardon. That, at least, is ancient learning.[56] But if the fraud is not perpetrated on the person exercising the prerogative of pardon, but with his connivance, so that it cannot be said that he was deceived, the rule might be otherwise.

The strongest arguments against the validity of the pardon are two. First, as Ford said in his press conference, it was premature to award a pardon where: "There have been no charges made. There has been no action by the court. There's been no action by any jury, and until any legal process has been undertaken, I think it's unwise and untimely for me to make any commitment."[57] The second is based on the nature of the special prosecutor's authority, as established by the Supreme Court in *United States* v. *Nixon*.[58]

The legal arguments grounded on prematurity have two elements. First, that the pardon was premature because it preceded conviction.

Second, that the pardon was premature because it preceded the filing of any charges of criminality. For again, as President Ford said, he had no "specific knowledge of any formal criminal charges pending against Richard M. Nixon."[59]

The arguments in support of the validity of the pardon despite the fact that it preceded conviction are essentially five.

First. The royal prerogative of pardon was not restricted to post-conviction acts of mercy to relieve against sanctions. The response to this is that there is no evidence that there was any intent or desire to confer any of the royal prerogatives on the President. The primary purpose of the pardon power, here as elsewhere, was to relieve against the rigors of a criminal justice system that could not always assure justice as well as law. It may be recalled that Blackstone[60] and Montesquieu,[61] both patron saints of the law for eighteenth-century America, had argued that the pardon power was appropriate only to a monarchy. And it was no monarchy that was established by the Constitution.

Second. Luther Martin had, at the Convention, urged a qualification on the pardon power so that it could be exercised only "after conviction."[62] The motion was withdrawn on James Wilson's suggestion that a pardon before conviction "might be necessary in order to obtain the testimony of accomplices."[63] The response to this is twofold. To suggest that pre-conviction pardon may be permitted to serve as an immunity device to compel the testimony of witnesses is not to condone a pre-conviction pardon for other purposes. Perhaps the more important response is that, despite this legislative history, the Supreme Court has held that the pardon cannot be used to impose immunity to compel a witness's testimony. In *Burdick* v. *United States*,[64] it held that a pardon, for this purpose, could not be imposed on an unwilling recipient.

Third. It is argued that the power of pre-conviction pardon is established by a Supreme Court dictum in the case of *Ex parte Garland*,[65] where the Court said:

> The power thus conferred is unlimited. . . . it extends to every offence known to the law, and may be exercised at any time after its commission, either before legal proceedings are taken, or during their pendency, or after conviction and judgment.

The response is that this was only dictum and totally irrelevant to the issues before the Court for decision. Moreover, as a commentator noted of these words: "Mr. Justice Field . . . used classic language which neither history nor reason support."[66]

A more telling response, however, is that forty-eight years after *Garland*, in the *Burdick* case, the Supreme Court regarded the question as an open one and not foreclosed by *Garland*. Although the issue was briefed and argued by both sides, the Court resolved the *Burdick* case on other grounds. If the question was still open in 1915, it has not since been either mooted or decided in the Supreme Court.

Fourth. It is urged on behalf of the pre-conviction pardon power that it has certainly been indulged from the time of Washington's presidency forward in granting amnesty. But the analogue between amnesty and pardon is not perfect. True, the Supreme Court said, in *Burdick*, that "it is of little service to assert or deny an analogy between amnesty and pardon," but it went on: "This is so as to their ultimate effect, but there are incidental differences of importance."[67] Clearly, there is a functional difference between individual pardon and group amnesty. It has been described in this manner:[68]

> Before either an amnesty or a full pardon is brought into use, offenses have been committed. An amnesty is usually applied in cases of offenses against the sovereignty of the state, of political offenses, whereas a pardon is employed in cases of infractions of the ordinary laws of the state. The former is often conferred before trial and conviction, but the latter ordinarily is granted only after trial and conviction. An amnesty granted before conviction overlooks the offense in the sense that no legal steps will be taken against the offenders. An amnesty granted after conviction, like a full pardon, absolves one from most of the legal consequences of the offense. Recipients of an amnesty are usually members of a class or of a community, who have committed similar offenses, but the recipients of a pardon are individuals who may or may not be guilty of the same offense or other offenses. In contrast to a pardon, an amnesty displays characteristics of a legislative rather than of an executive act, in the sense that it applies to a defined class, not to a specific individual. Since an amnesty is often granted before trial and conviction, its only purpose in many cases is to arrest the movement of the law. Neither formal acceptance nor pleading of the amnesty is required of the beneficiaries in order to assure to them the resumption of rights lost through the commission of the pardon offense.

This is not to suggest that amnesty does not fall within the presidential pardon power, although amnesty can also be exercised by Congress.[69] It is rather to suggest that there is a functional difference between amnesty and pardon of individuals for individual crimes which may justify pre-conviction relief in one case but not the other. Indeed, as we have seen,[70] Hamilton's argument for the pardon power in the President spoke of post-conviction action with regard to individual crimes and pre-conviction action with reference to group crimes, such as insurrections. Once again, we have had no occasion for the Court to address the question whether amnesties and pardons may be different when the issue is pre-conviction release from criminal liability.

Fifth. The argument for pre-conviction pardon power is also asserted in terms of long-established practice. The difficulty with this argument is that the evidence in support of such a practice has never been adduced. Mr. Buchen, the President's counsel, told us that there were twenty-one precedents for pre-conviction pardon,[71] but, to my knowledge, he never produced them for public scrutiny. The special prosecutor's office, it was said, had also stated that "the pardon power has been used frequently to relieve Federal offenders of criminal liability . . . even where no criminal proceedings against the individual are contemplated."[72] Other statements of sporadic use of the pardon power in this fashion have been reported.[73] The *Congressional Weekly* did report that of the 2,294 pardons granted by Kennedy, Johnson, and Nixon, three preceded conviction, but it is not known at what stage of the proceedings the pardon was offered.[74] As the *Myers* case[75] reveals, the question when repeated actions rise to the dignity of a constitutional construction is one peculiarly within the competence of the Supreme Court to determine.

Finally, on this score, it may be noted that the last major Supreme Court definition before Watergate, that of Justice Holmes in *Biddle* v. *Perovich*,[76] speaks only in terms of post-conviction relief. He said there: "A pardon in our days is not a private act of grace from an individual happening to possess power. It is part of the Constitutional scheme. When granted it is the determination of the ultimate authority that the public welfare will be better served by inflicting less than what the judgment fixed."[77] Alas, this, too, is but dictum, as was Chief Justice Marshall's earlier statement that Holmes contradicted. In *United States* v. *Wilson*,[78] Marshall had written that "a pardon is an act of grace, proceeding from the power entrusted with the execution of the laws, which exempts the individual, on whom it is bestowed, from the punishment the law inflicts for a crime he has committed. It is the private, though official act of the executive magistrate."[79] Certainly the Ford pardon of Nixon sounded more like Marshall than Holmes.

The Holmes dictum points up the primary problem with the arguments on both sides of the question of the validity of pre-conviction pardon. Holmes spoke of "a pardon in our days," suggesting that history alone cannot afford the answer. But the arguments here are essentially historical. With a Constitution that changes with each Supreme Court decision, history of original intent is not enough to command decision. In Justice Brennan's words: "[A]n awareness of history and an appreciation of the aims of the Founding Fathers do not always resolve concrete problems."[80] The point is made by Professor Miller in terms of the *Myers* case this way:[81]

> The postmaster removal case was flawed by history in two ways. First, the history related by the Court was poor history. Second and

more important, history—in the form of a single congressional debate 140 years prior to the decision—was really the Court's only principle of adjudication. The failure to offer additional justifications for the *Myers* holding brought into question its constitutional adequacy from the time it was announced. The historical discussion so weighed down the opinion that it was in constant danger of disappearing from the surface of contemporary constitutional law—which it soon did.

"It ought always to be remembered," Justice Holmes observed, "that historic continuity with the past is not a duty, it is only a necessity."[82] He also told us that "the case before us must be considered in the light of our whole experience and not merely in that of what was said a hundred years ago."[83] The difficulty for us is that there is little "light [from] our whole experience" with the exercise of the pardon power. Clearly the Constitution, though written in 1787, must be applied today. The concerns of the Founders, such as the involvement of a President in treasonous acts, or the necessity for negotiations with insurrectionists, do not concern us today. We are involved with different forms of perfidy by Presidents than treason. What the effect of the development of the imperial presidency should be in this area remains unknown.

For what it is worth, it should be noted that a large plurality of the states, in their modern constitutions, forbid the executive the power of pre-conviction pardons.[84] It should be noted, also, that a functional analysis would suggest that a pre-conviction pardon is *functus officio*. The executive has absolute control over the criminal processes up to the time of conviction, which makes a pardon unnecessary before that time. An indictment may be brought only at the discretion of the Attorney General or his delegate, the United States Attorney.[85] The power of pardon is not necessary to prevent indictment. After indictment, but prior to judgment, the Attorney General also has the authority to dismiss or *nolle pros* a case,[86] effectively eliminating the need for pardon at this stage. Indeed, if the dismissal occurs in this way after the trial has begun by the empanelment of the jury,[87] the Double Jeopardy Clause also will bar a later prosecution.[88] A judgment of not guilty, of course, is as effective as a pardon if not more so. In the event of a judgment of guilt, however, the power of the executive to stay the course of criminal proceedings has ended, except for the utilization of the pardon power.

So, too, is the pardon redundant as a means of conferring immunity to compel the testimony of a witness. The Supreme Court, as I have said, has erased this function by decision.[89] But statutory immunity provisions[90] are effective to this end, if the pardon power is not.

It is true, of course, that the Nixon prosecution was out of the hands of the President and the Attorney General, and thus the power to decline to bring a prosecution or to *nolle pros* the case was not theirs to exercise. Therefore, only the pardon power was left them to exonerate Nixon. But, as we shall see, the fact that these powers had been delegated to the special prosecutor's office reads against rather than for the validity of the pardon.

I do not mean to be saying that the Nixon pardon was invalid because it was rendered prior to conviction. I mean to say only that the question whether the pardoning power is available to that use was an open and not a closed issue. When the question does arise—and it is to be hoped that it will not come again in a pardon from a President to an ex-President—one may expect the presidential power to be sustained, both because of the consistent tendency of the Court to enhance rather than diminish presidential authority and because of a most expansive reading given to the presidential pardon power, since the Nixon pardon, in *Schick* v. *Reed*,[91] argued a few months after the Nixon resignation and decided just before Christmas of 1974.

The petitioner had been sentenced to death by a court-martial, but had had his sentence commuted by the President to a life term, conditioned on the petitioner's never being paroled. He argued that the condition was invalid. The Court delivered a general dissertation on the pardon power and concluded that the President had the authority, under the pardon power, to condition the commutation.

The historical justification for conditioned pardons and reprieves is long and sound. And the Court once again rested its total argument on this history. Much reliance—too much—was placed on the fact that at one point in the debates, Madison referred to the "prerogative of pardon," and that Hamilton in *Federalist* No. 69 spoke of the pardon power "as 'resembl[ing] equally that of the King of Great-Britain and the Governor of New-York.' "[92] From these isolated remarks, the Court concluded: "We see, therefore, that the draftsmen of Art. II, § 2, spoke in terms of a 'prerogative' of the President, which ought not be 'fettered or embarrassed.' "[93]

Madison, at the time, was talking of the power to pardon treason and, it will be remembered, opposed vesting the power in the President. Madison said that "pardon of treasons was so peculiarly improper for the President" that he would be willing to place it in the Congress rather than give it to the President.[94] And when Hamilton spoke of the king of England and the governor of New York, he was not saying their powers were the same, but different. As he said, the governor of New York could grant pardon in cases of impeachment but not in cases of treason or murder.[95] The whole function of the 69th *Federalist* from which Chief Justice Burger took his Hamilton quotation was to show how much less power and authority the President would have under the Constitution than the king had in England. To make it into an argument for the existence of royal prerogative in the President is a gross distortion.

The strength of the Burger opinion lay in the fact that he was able to explicate a long and continuous history from England through the American experience of the executive granting conditional pardons. Most of the other portions of the opinion are less than logical in their arguments. Burger derives from the fact that the Senate was not joined with the executive in the pardon power the conclusion that Congress could not legislate on the subject.[96] At the same time, he suggests that the power of pardon follows the English practice and acknowledges that legislative restraints had been imposed on the use of the prerogative power of pardon.[97] Indeed, the fact of the matter is that Parliament itself exercised the pardon power at this point in English history.[98] Burger says that the draftsmen of the American Constitution originally tracked the English in excluding impeachments from the pardon power,[99] but fails to note that the Constitution itself imposed a far greater limitation on the President with regard to impeachments than the English imposed on their sovereign. In fact, Justice Marshall, in dissent, takes apart most of the majority's historical analysis, except for that which rests on long-standing custom and use.

The point here is not concerned with whether "conditional pardons" are constitutionally valid. It is, rather, that the Supreme Court, once again, was prepared to support any inflated concept of presidential power proffered to it for its stamp of *nihil obstat*. And, when it comes time to pass on the question of pardons before conviction, it will, in all probability, react in the same jejune manner.

As Professor Corwin wrote some forty-three years ago:[100]

> . . . the Supreme Court . . . has steadily favored the aggrandizement of the "executive power" of the President. The net result is that our constitutional law and theory today ascribes to the President an indefinite range of "inherent" powers . . . enables the President to receive and exercise delegated legislative powers of indefinite range, and attributes to him alone all nonjudicial discretion which either the Constitution or the laws of Congress permit.

What then of the argument that the invalidity of the Nixon pardon rests on the failure of any indictment or other criminal charges sufficiently definite to identify any crime for which the pardon was issued? The President, when he issued the pardon, knew of no criminal charges pending against Nixon. The list he secured from the special prosecutor's office of pending investigations contained none in which there had been developed any substantial evidence against the former President. It was known of course that a prosecution was pending against Nixon's "co-

conspirators." For what crimes was Nixon pardoned: "for all offenses against the United States which he, Richard Nixon, has committed or may have committed or taken part in during the period from January 20, 1969 through August 9, 1974."

The answer to the question of the need for certainty in the designation of the crimes for which pardon is offered is of even less clarity than those with which we have heretofore been concerned. Ancient English history suggests that a pardon must be directed to specified crimes, but it is so immersed in the technicalities of the English common law and the even more amorphous English constitution that none can speak with certainty of its meaning.[101] There is nothing in American constitutional history or law that suggests an answer. This question, too, was raised but not decided in the *Burdick* case.[102]

So long as the document of pardon clearly indicates what further criminal prosecutions it is intended to foreclose, it is unlikely to be held void for vagueness. It is true that the language in the Ford pardon sounds more like a forbidden "dispensation" from the operations of the law than like any ordinary pardon. But unlike the ban on "dispensations" that derives from the English Bill of Rights, the presidential act here related only to past events and did not excuse future noncompliance with the law.

I come then to the most substantial attack on the validity of the pardon, the failure of the pardon to conform to the regulations of the Department of Justice. I do not speak of those regulations concerned with the applications for pardons and their administrative disposal within the Department and the White House.[103] I speak rather to those regulations held by the Supreme Court to be binding on the President in *United States* v. *Nixon*, the regulations establishing the office and duties of the special prosecutor.[104]

The regulations provided that "the President will not exercise his Constitutional powers to effect the discharge of the Special Prosecutor or to limit the independence that he is hereby given." That independence included the authority to decide who should be prosecuted and for what. And the special prosecutor was not subject to removal or interference except with the prior approval of the majority and minority leaders and the chairman and ranking minority members of the judiciary committees in both houses of Congress. Whether this limitation on the executive authority was constitutional is dubious in light of the decision of the Supreme Court in *Buckley* v. *Valeo*.[105] Yet the Supreme Court had little difficulty in sustaining the regulations in *United States* v. *Nixon*:[106]

> So long as this regulation remains in force the Executive Branch is bound by it, and indeed the United States as the sovereign composed of the three branches is bound to respect and enforce it. Moreover,

the delegation of authority to the Special Prosecutor in this case is not an ordinary delegation by the Attorney General to a subordinate officer: with the authorization of the President, the Acting Attorney General provided in the regulation that the Special Prosecutor was not to be removed without the "consensus" of eight designated leaders of Congress.

Did these regulations which were held to be binding on all three branches of the government constituting the sovereignty of the United States—notice that the people are no longer sovereign in the minds of the Supreme Court Justices—make invalid the grant of pardon? Certainly the pardon foreclosed the exercise of jurisdiction that had been given to the special prosecutor, the right and power to prosecute President Nixon for any Watergate-related crimes. That this invasion was foreclosed by the binding regulations might rest on the interpretation of those regulations by their promulgator, Solicitor General Bork. In response to a question from Senator Kennedy, Bork stated that:[107]

> In establishing a charter for Mr. Jaworski, the "consensus" provision was inserted for the purpose of providing additional safeguards for the Special Prosecutor. Although public discussion has focused on removal, it was intended that the "consensus" provision apply to any attempt to limit the Special Prosecutor's independence, including his jurisdiction.

Mr. Jaworski, however, apparently did not understand the "consensus" provision to apply to a pardon. He was certain that the regulations imposed no inhibitions on the pardon power. But if the regulations did require his consent to presidential interference with the special prosecutor's functions, there is nothing on the public record to suggest that such consent was afforded. At the time of the Nixon pardon, the special prosecutor's office had made no decision on whether to prosecute the ex-President. The public record does not show that Jaworski was consulted on the issuance of the pardon, but only that he was informed of it shortly before it was announced to the public.

Strangely enough, some solid historical precedent exists for the position that where power of prosecution was not in the hands of the Crown, the king was powerless to render a pardon. Maitland, after stating that the power of royal pardon may be effected either before or after conviction, goes on to state "that during the Middle Ages there were two methods of proceeding against a felon—the appeal brought by the person injured by the crime, for instance, the person whose goods were stolen, or the next kinsman of the murdered man—and the indictment, a royal procedure at the king's suit. The king by pardon might free a man from indictment, but not from appeal."[108]

That there are substantial questions about the validity of the Nixon pardon is, I think, evident. That none but the special prosecutor, with regard to Watergate-related crimes, or the Attorney General, with regard to any other crimes during the period of activity pardoned, may test the validity of the pardon is even more evident. Even if actions were brought in which a challenge to the validity of the Nixon pardon was properly raised, the odds are strong that it would be upheld—if for no other reason than because the burden of persuading the Supreme Court that the President had acted beyond his constitutional authority, given its historical predilection, cannot be carried by the arguments available to the attackers of the pardon.

We are left then with an analogue to Maitland's analysis:[109]

> The legal power of pardon then is very extensive indeed. The check upon it is not legal but consists in this, that the king's secretary may have to answer in the House of Commons for the exercise that he makes of this power.

In this country it could be said, rather, that the President "may have to answer [to the people] for the exercise that he makes of this power." In November of 1976, Mr. Ford may well have answered to the people for the "mercy" he dispensed in 1974.[110]

8

Separation of Powers and Checks and Balances

The primary evil revealed by the events of Watergate was the presidency: not the man but the office. It was and is bloated with unrestrained power, available for use for good or evil, with little or no accountability for the use to which it is put.

In a letter to the *International Herald Tribune* published on 24 September 1974, Barbara Tuchman, a distinguished nonacademic historian, vented her spleen following the Nixon pardon. She addressed fundamental questions still unanswered:

> The American presidency has become a greater risk than it is worth. The time has come to seriously consider the substitution of cabinet government or some form of shared executive power.
>
> The Framers may have been the most intelligent and farsighted political men ever to operate at one time in our history but they could not foretell the decline of Congress. . . .
>
> The Presidency has gained too great a lead; it has bewitched the occupant, the press and the public. While this process has been apparent from John F. Kennedy on, it took the strange transformation of good old open-presidency Gerald Ford to make it clear that the villain is not the man but the office.
>
> Hardly had he settled in the ambience of the White House than he began to talk like Louis XIV and behave like Richard Nixon. If there was one lesson to be learned from Watergate it was the danger in overuse of the executive power and in interference with the judicial system. Within a month of taking office Mr. Ford has violated both at once. The swelling sense of personal absolutism shows in these disquieting remarks: "The ethical tone will be what I make it. . . ." "In this situation I am the final authority . . ." and, in deciding to block the unfolding legal procedure, "My conscience says it is my duty. . . ." Our judicial system can operate well enough

> without the dictate of Mr. Ford's conscience. To be president is not to be czar. . . .
>
> . . . The only way to defuse the presidency and minimize the risk of a knave, a simpleton or a despot exercising supreme authority without check or consultation is to divide the power and the responsibility. Constitutional change is not beyond our capacity.

There is, I think, little doubt that Tuchman's attack on the imperial presidency was accurate. Whether her solution is possible, or even desirable, is more dubious. For, if the political processes fail to provide us with presidential candidates who are "first-rate" men, as Tuchman argues, how and where will we find the quality of men necessary to frame a new Constitution? Even when we discount our romantic notions, the roster of members of the Constitutional Convention of 1787 is an impressive one. No body of solons that can be considered its equal has ever since been conjoined: not in the Senate or House of Representatives, not in the Cabinet, not on the Supreme Court—not even on university faculties. One has only to look at the constitutional conventions that have occurred in the several states in recent years to arouse severe doubts about charging any group of persons with the task of redrawing the American Constitution.

While Tuchman's description may be accurate, still it must be asked whether the Constitution we were given in 1787 is at fault or whether the perversions of that Constitution are to blame; even whether the conditions that command an ever-shrinking world in international relations and a "service state" in the domestic sphere would permit a less expansive presidency to function adequately for the needs of our time. While it may be true that no other nation utilizes our system of government, it cannot be said that any of these other governments functions better than ours does. I do not mean here to suggest pride or pleasure in the functioning of our existing political structure. It is rather a note of despair that I strike. Parochially, I am reminded of Robert Hutchins's dictum that the University of Chicago is not a good university, it is only the best.

We have recently been treated to some inside views of the functioning of the English cabinet system in Richard Crossman's *Diaries of a Cabinet Minister* and Harold Wilson's *The Governance of Britain*. Neither can make a reader believe that the answer to the problem of proper governance is surely to be found in the cabinet system. And the argument for such a change has been spelled out for us by Professor Hardin, with much promise but little hope.[1]

There can be little doubt that the overpraised and overmaligned Founding Fathers were cognizant and wary of the problems of concentration of power in government. They wrote, however, against a stereoptic background. First was the earlier hateful experience under the English monarchy. The lesson from that was spelled out in the Declaration of Independence, which placed the blame for the tyranny largely on the king and his royal judges, *i.e.*, on the executive and the judiciary. Second was the unfortunate experience under the Articles of Confederation. The Constitutional Convention was called specifically to cure the deficiencies of the Confederation Congress, but here, unlike the case of the king of England, it was the weakness and not the strength of government that created the problems, the weakness of a powerless Congress and a nonexistent executive and judiciary.

From the outset, the Convention was tendered plans all of which utilized a tripartite system of national government to be framed under some concept of separation of powers. The state governments had long since subscribed to that concept. Thus, the first order of substantive business was the receipt of the Virginia Plan with provisions for three branches, including a bicameral legislature, an executive, and a judiciary.[2]

The work of the Convention from that time on was to put flesh on the bare bones of the commonly accepted concept of three branches with different functions for—and restraints on—each. The other major problem for resolution was also one concerned with distribution and separation of powers. The question was what authority was to be given to the government to be created and what left to the states whose sovereignty had been almost undiminished under the Confederation.[3] This division of functions, too, was a means for inhibiting concentration of governmental power.

No less an authority on government than William Ewart Gladstone hailed the American Constitution as "the most wonderful work ever struck off at a given time by the brain and purpose of man."[4] He spoke at a time when our Constitution was functioning more effectively than it has in recent times.

If there was genius in the formation of the new government, it came by way of adapting old notions to new conditions. The two novelties in the Constitution were the form of federalism for which it provided and the equally new conception of checks and balances, the latter a combination of the ideas of "separation of powers" and a "balanced government," neither of those new except in the way of their joinder. Both new concepts were directed to limiting the power of government to avoid such concentration as might lead to tyranny.

Of the new federalism, the English expert on the subject, K. C. Wheare, has written: "[T]here is found in the Constitution of the United States a principle of organization which distinguished it as an association from those other associations . . . which are sometimes grouped with it as examples of federal government."[5] He described the novel structure in this fashion:[6]

> . . . the Constitution of the United States establishes an association of states so organized that powers are divided between a general government which in certain matters . . . is independent of the governments of the associated states, and, on the other hand, state governments which in certain matters are, in their turn, independent of the general government. This involves, as a necessary consequence, that general and regional governments both operate *directly* upon the people; each citizen is subject to two governments. It is not always easy to say what matters are within the spheres of the general and the regional governments respectively. The words of the Constitution are sometimes ambiguous, contradictory or vague. But however vague the Constitution may be about where the line is to be drawn, it is quite clear on the point that, once granted that a government is acting within its allotted sphere, that government is not subordinate to any other government in the United States. If we examine the American Constitution we must conclude that, as a matter of law there laid down, the field of government is divided between a general authority and regional authorities which are not subordinate one to another, but co-ordinate with each other. . . . The principle of organization upon which the American association is based is that of the division of powers between distinct and co-ordinate governments.

However old-fashioned and unreal this may sound to contemporary Americans, the concept of the Constitution was accurately described in these remarks. Federalism of the form described was seriously limited as a consequence of the Civil War and the postwar constitutional amendments, particularly the Fourteenth. It lingered until the Great Depression and World War II, when it was seriously shrunken by the Roosevelt administration, and it has continued to decline until it has all but disappeared. I do not propose here to dwell on the demise of federalism. There are some, such as Nelson Rockefeller, who would tell us that federalism is alive and well and living in the United States.[7] This argument, however, rests on the proposition that state governments are, each year, asserting more authority over the people within their jurisdiction; they employ more people; they spend more money. But this overlooks the nature of the federalism described by Wheare. For it is no longer true that there are any substantial areas of government that cannot be exercised by the national government or any that can be exercised only by the states. Much of the business of state government is the execution of policies and laws made by the national government; indeed, much of the money that is spent by the states is disbursed to the state governments as allowances from the central authority.

The only point I should add here is that, throughout our history, the Supreme Court has persistently and consistently acted as a centripetal force favoring, at almost every chance, the national authority over that of the states. It made substantial contributions to the ultimate demise of federalism.

The fate of separation of powers and checks and balances is not different from that of federalism. For it, too, came to life at the Convention with some vigor but is now so debilitated as hardly to be recognizable. And as Louis Heren noted a decade ago: "Indeed, it can be said that the main difference between the modern American President and a medieval monarch is that there has been a steady increase rather than a diminution of his power. In comparative historical terms the United States has been moving steadily backward."[8] And, "The modern American President can be compared with the British monarchy as it existed for a century or more after the signing of Magna Carta in 1215."[9] This was not said in derogation but in admiration of the working of the American system of government.

Nevertheless, it would appear that this was not exactly what the framers had in mind when they delivered the Constitution to the people for ratification. The respective positions of the democratically inclined, pro-legislature members, such as Sherman of Connecticut, and those who favored the executive power, like James Wilson of Pennsylvania, were stated early in the debates.

Madison records that on 1 June 1787, when the subject for consideration was the motion of Wilson for a one-man executive as opposed to the suggested multiple executive, Rutledge of South Carolina opened by saying that "he was for vesting the Executive power in a single person, tho' he was not for giving him the power of war and peace. A single man would feel the greatest responsibility and administer the public affairs best."[10] He was followed in debate by Sherman of Connecticut:[11]

> Mr. Sherman said he considered the Executive magistracy as nothing more than an institution for carrying the will of the Legislature into effect, that the person or persons ought to be appointed by and accountable to the Legislature only, which was the depositary of the supreme will of the Society. As they were the best judges of the business which ought to be done by the Executive department, and consequently of the number necessary from time to time for doing it, he wished the number might [not] be fixed, but that the legislature should be at liberty to appoint one or more as experience might dictate.

Obviously, Tuchman's ideas were in fact the subject for consideration at the Convention. Whether their rejection under the conditions existing then should be equally cogent for today's circumstances, of course, the framers were in no position to tell us.

Wilson of Pennsylvania was certainly pro-nationalist, anti-legislature, and pro-executive, but even he recognized that the new executive could not take on the role of a king. He said that he[12] did not consider the Prerogatives of the British Monarch as a proper guide in defining the Executive powers. Some of these prerogatives were of a Legislative nature. Among others that of war & peace &c. The only powers he conceived strictly Executive were those of executing the laws, and appointing officers, not appointed by the Legislature.[13]

Mr. Randolph [of Virginia] strenuously opposed a unity in the Executive magistracy. He regarded it as the foetus of monarchy. We had he said no motive to be governed by the British Governmt. as our prototype. . . . the fixt genius of the people of America required a different form of Government. He could not see why the great requisites for the Executive department, vigor, despatch & responsibility could not be found in three men, as well as in one man. The Executive ought to be independent. It ought therefore [in order to support its independence] to consist of more than one.[14]

Wilson replied to Randolph:[15]

. . . that Unity in the Executive instead of being the fetus of Monarchy would be the best safeguard against tyranny. He repeated that he was not governed by the British Model which was inapplicable to the situation of this Country; the extent of which was so great, and the manners so republican, that nothing but a great confederated Republic would do for it.

The issue of a single or plural executive was postponed. Madison thought it more appropriate to deal with the question of what powers the executive should have before dealing with the question of how many executives there should be:[16]

. . . as certain powers were in their nature Executive, and must be given to that departmt. whether administered by one or more persons, a definition of their extent would assist the judgment in determining how far they might be safely entrusted to a single officer. He accordingly moved that [the provision for the national executive should afford it] "power to carry into effect. the national laws. to appoint to offices in cases not otherwise provided for, and to execute such other powers ("not Legislative, nor Judiciary in their nature.")[17] as may from time to time be delegated by the national Legislature."

This debate revealed some of the multitude of currents and contending forces at work at the Convention. There were nationalists and states' rights advocates; there were big states and little states partisans; there were pro-legislative and pro-executive factions; there were democrats and royalists; there was a very large variety of interests to be accommodated. None of the individuals at the Convention, here or later, represented the attitudes of the Convention as a whole, which was more than the sum of its parts. The achievement of the Convention was its capacity for compromise on the major issues. And the evolving principle of separation of powers as modified by a system of checks and balances was one of those compromises. If there was a dominant theme at the Convention, it related to no particular issue but rather to a consensus that whatever government was created, it must be one of limited powers. Concentration of power led to tyranny, whether the power was in the national government as a whole or in the legislative or executive branches of it. There was even concern that the federal judiciary might unduly aggrandize itself.[18]

It has become common learning—in Dean Swift's words, usually attributed to Macaulay, "what every schoolboy knows"—that the principle of checks and balances devolved from the Convention primarily as a means for restraining the legislative power. This conclusion rests largely on the unjustified notion that Madison's voice at the Convention was to be considered the voice of the Convention. And that *The Federalist* on that subject represents the ideology of the Convention rather than the polemics of its authors. The fact is that the expressions of the fear of legislative democracy that underlay the arguments of Madison and his cohorts at the Convention were frequently to be found in support of motions to limit the congressional power, most of which failed of acceptance by the Convention itself. Thus, the repeated attempts of Madison and Wilson to establish a council of revision made up of the executive and judicial branches to control the powers of the legislature gave voice to their fears of a strong legislative branch. Each time, however, the Convention rejected this proposal. Rather than supporting the Madisonian position, the Convention abjured it.[19] Similarly, when it was moved that the legislature could reject appointments only by a two-thirds vote, and an anti-legislative speech was made, the Convention voted against it.[20]

There is little doubt that Messrs. Madison and Wilson and Gouverneur Morris wanted to curb the powers of the legislative branch. They regarded the Glorious Revolution, as Burke would come to regard the French Revolution, as an evil example of totalitarian power rather than a movement toward liberal democracy. Thus, Wilson, perhaps even more the "Executive Party" theoretician than Madison or Hamilton,[21]

> remarked that the prejudices agst the Executive resulted from a misapplication of the adage that the parliament was the palladium of liberty. Where the Executive was really formidable, *King* and *Tyrant*, were naturally associated in the minds of the people; not *legislature* and *tyranny*. But where the Executive was not formidable, the two last were most properly associated. After the destruction of the King in Great Britain, a more pure and unmixed tyranny sprang up in the parliament than had been exercised by the monarch. He insisted that

> we had not guarded agst. the danger on this side by a sufficient self-defensive power either to the Executive or Judiciary department.

Gouverneur Morris, of the same group, extolled the presidency in seeking to remove a proposed ban on reelection, for "in the strength of the Executive would be found the strength of America."[22] Madison objected to the trial on an impeachment in the Senate,[23]

> especially as [the President] was to be impeached by the other branch of the Legislature, and for any act which might be called a misdemeanor. The President under these circumstances was made improperly dependent. He [Madison] would prefer the supreme Court for the trial of impeachments, or rather a tribunal of which that should form a part.

Here, as elsewhere, Madison revealed not only his anti-legislative bias but his reiterated support for the combined authority and power of the executive and judiciary, both of which he saw as performing similar if not the same governmental functions. Thus, when opposing the appointment of the executive by the legislature, *i.e.*, a parliamentary system of responsibility, he argued both the necessity for separation of powers in terms very different from what he contended for in *The Federalist*, and the analogy to the independence from legislative appointment and removal that the Convention had already conferred on the judiciary:[24]

> If it be essential to the preservation of liberty that the Legisl: Execut: & Judiciary powers be separate, it is essential to a maintenance of the separation, that they should be independent of each other. . . . There was an analogy between the Executive & Judiciary departments in several respects. The latter executed the laws in certain cases as the former did in others. The former expounded & applied them for certain purposes, as the latter did for others.

There can be no question that Madison and cohorts were anxious to cabin the authority of Congress and expand the powers of the presidency and judiciary. But the evidence is substantial that in many instances their fears of legislative supremacy outran those of their colleagues at the Convention. This is not to say that there were no fears of parliamentary hegemony. It is rather to say that the fear of legislative dominance was not unmatched by concerns for limited authority in the other two branches of government as well. And when we see how Madison spoke of the dangers of the presidency in the impeachment debates,[25] it is clear that his fears of tyranny did not derive from a single source.

The primary limits on the powers of Congress were to be found in the express authorization of a presidential veto and an implied authorization of judicial review of the constitutionality of national laws. But the power of removal of both the executive and the judiciary was entrusted to Congress. And it must not be forgotten that we might look to the actual words of the Constitution not less than to those of its framers and commentators in order to discover its meaning. And if we do look less at what was said at the Convention and more at what was done there, we quickly discover that most, if not all, the substantive powers of the national government were conferred upon the legislature and little or none on either of the other two branches.

It was essentially the separation of powers that was to restrain the overreaching by the second and third branches, since the only substantive authority they were to have was to be derived not from the Constitution but from the legislature. They were both, as Madison had said, executors of the laws of the Congress. They might, each of them, negative the legislative authority. There was no suggestion that they could substitute for it.

When it came time to defend the proposed Constitution against attack on the ground that it had rejected the concept of separation of powers, Madison's essays in *The Federalist* were sophistical rather than forthright. The views he put forth were those that he had espoused at the Convention, clothed in the argument that the checks and balances that had been asserted were really not modifications of separationist theory.

In No. 47, he acknowledged the complaint: "The several departments of power are distributed and blended in such a manner as at once to destroy all symmetry and beauty of form, and to expose some of the essential parts of the edifice to the danger of being crushed by the disproportionate weight of other parts." Not so, he said. The separation of powers was truly a necessary ingredient in any government dedicated to liberty of its people. But the concept of separation of powers requires definition:

> The accumulation of all powers, legislative, executive, and judiciary, in the same hands, whether of one, a few, or many, and whether hereditary, self-appointed, or elective, may justly be pronounced the very definition of tyranny. Were the federal Constitution, therefore, really chargeable with this accumulation of power, or with a mixture of powers, having a dangerous tendency to such accumulation, no further arguments would be necessary to inspire a universal reprobation of the system. . . . In order to form correct ideas on this important subject it will be proper to investigate the sense in which the preservation of liberty requires that the three great departments of power should be separate and distinct.

Where does one look to discover the "correct ideas on this important subject"? Strange as it may seem, the answer was to be found, according to Madison, in the British constitution, for, "The British Constitution was to Montesquieu what Homer has been to the didactic writers on epic poetry." And clearly, Madison was right in concluding: "On the slightest view of the British Constitution, we must perceive that the legislative, executive, and judiciary departments are by no means totally separate and distinct from each other." But then, none, other than the romantic Montesquieu, had ever believed that the British constitution of that time, or any time before or since, could be said to be one based on separation of powers among three branches exercising different governmental functions.

The English did have an amorphous notion of limited government by the time of the American Revolution, and if the theory of separation of powers cast a shadow on it, it was certainly neither a dark nor a deepening one. It is described most favorably to the Madisonian thesis by Professor Vile:[26]

> The theory of the balanced constitution had been evolved from the ancient theory of mixed government, which held, as the basis of its opposition to the exercise of arbitrary power, the belief that power could only be checked by the creation of a system of government in which the three classes of society were nicely balanced against each other. The transformation of the theory of mixed government into the theory of the balanced constitution, in which the King, Lords, and Commons operated a complex system of checks and balances upon each other, demanded, however, a second theorem. This demand was met by the theory of the separation of powers, with the assertion that the functions of government could be divided up among the parts of the system in such a way that each branch could be limited to the exercise of its "proper function," and the balance was completed by allowing each branch a limited right of interference in the functions of the others in order to prevent the encroachment of any one of them upon the function of any other.

However functional the theory of balanced government, *i.e.*, the division of power among three classes of English society, the division into three functionally distinct branches had no reality in the English system. As that uncouth young man, Tom Paine, had written in 1776: "To say that the Constitution of England is a *union* of three powers, reciprocally *checking* each other, is farcical; either the words have no meaning, or they are flat contradictions."[27] Nor was even the system of balanced government, let alone separation of powers, working well at the time of the creation of the new American system. George III had control of his ministers who had control of Parliament, both Lords and Commons. The judiciary was also manipulated by the Crown, and, in any event, had no power of judicial review.

It indeed took no small amount of gall on Madison's part to defend the proposed American Constitution on the ground that it resembled the English model. None had expressed such sentiments at the Convention. The exclusion of members of Congress from participation in office by the Constitution was, by itself, a distinct reprobation of the very essence of the reality of the contemporary British constitution.

In *Federalist* No. 48, Madison, having established his premise that the separation of powers "does not require that the legislative, executive, and judiciary departments should be wholly unconnected," proceeds to the argument "that unless these departments be so far connected and blended as to give to each a constitutional control over the others, the degree of separation which the maxim requires, as essential to a free government, can never in practice be duly maintained."

Simply to provide in the Constitution for each branch to wield its own powers would be "to trust to . . . parchment barriers against the encroaching spirit of power. . . . But the experience assures us, that the efficacy of the provision has been greatly overrated; and that some more adequate defence is indispensably necessary for the more feeble, against the more powerful, members of government. The legislative department is everywhere extending the sphere of its activity, and drawing all power into its impetuous vortex." This last sentence derives from Jefferson's *Notes on Virginia*.[28] It is also a reprise of Madison's words at the Convention.[29]

His argument in No. 48 followed that of Wilson at the Convention, again an argument that failed to carry the point at the Convention, that the dangers of tyranny inhered in the legislative branch. But he was not prepared to allow the power to check government to be vested in the people.[30] And, unlike Jefferson, he lacked any fears that the judiciary might overstep its bounds.

History has proved Madison a false prophet, both because the federal judiciary has shown itself to be an ever-increasing seeker of power and because the Congress, far from intruding on the authority of the other two branches, has come persistently to surrender to them the powers given to it by the Constitution.

What then were the checks and balances to which the antifederalists could object as marring the symmetry of separation of powers but which the Madisonians thought necessary to preclude concentration of governmental power,[31] particularly in the Congress? The first was the division of the legislature into two branches. But bicameralism served other necessities. It primarily afforded a compromise for the small and large states, the latter seeking representation by population and the former by state in the national legislature. Moreover, this was not a check of one branch on another, but an internal check. For the Madisonians it was essentially a check by the Senate, which was to be made up of proper persons chosen by the state legislatures, on the House, which they considered dangerously democratic. This was the same dilution of democracy that was to be found in the provision for choosing the President, not by the people, or the Congress, but by the electoral college.

The power to cast a deciding vote given to the Vice-President where the Senate was equally divided could be considered a check in favor of the executive on the upper house, although the Vice-President was, then, more likely to be the chief executive's primary opponent. Of similar importance was the power of the President to convene either or both houses and to provide for adjournment where both houses could not agree.

The primary check on the Congress by the President was the veto power, but it was subject to being overridden where a two-thirds majority could be secured in each house to do so. And a ban was provided on members of Congress serving either as executive officials or as members of the electoral college. Finally, Congress was forbidden to reduce the emoluments of his office during the term of a President.

The primary power of the legislature to check the President was to be found in the impeachment provisions. And the power that the judiciary was to have in checking the legislature was not a specified power, but rather the power of judicial review of national legislation, inferred from, but not stated in, the functions assigned to the judiciary. But the legislature had a check on the judiciary and the executive by the required concurrence of the Senate in executive and judicial appointments, except where the Congress otherwise provided. The power over the jurisdiction of the courts, except for that vested directly in the Supreme Court's original jurisdiction, was also to be determined by Congress.

These then were to be the real barriers to consolidation of power in the hands of any one branch. There were other restraints on congressional power, but they didn't fall into the category of checks and balances, and are to be found in §§ 9 and 10 of Article I. So far as the separation of powers itself was concerned, this was attained by specific provisions giving all legislative powers to the Congress, by vesting the executive power in the President, and by vesting the judicial power in one Supreme Court and such inferior courts as the Congress might choose to establish.

Although, given Madison's interpretation, the Convention read the simplistic notion of separation of powers out of the Constitution in favor of a "mixed Constitution," in which each branch shared some of the duties of the other, the pure separation-of-powers doctrine has continued to have a hold on the minds if not the deeds of the American people. Even Madison, it will be recalled, relied on the pure notion of implicit executive power in the hiring and firing of government officials. And the Supreme Court of the United States in *United States* v. *Nixon*[32] rested its conclusion about the existence of an executive privilege on undefined constitutional provisions for "separation of powers." The fear that a conjunction of powers in one branch threatens the liberties of the people is of such long-standing acceptance that not even *The Federalist* could destroy it. It took a century and a half of time to make it obsolete.

George Washington's decision not to be available for a third term as President of the United States was undoubtedly based on mixed, if not ambivalent, motives. Certainly he was tired of the ordeal, but equally was he concerned that the presidency not be considered a lifetime office. He announced his decision in what has come to be known as his "Farewell Address." Everyone knows about Washington's Farewell Address, but, except for the injunction to abstain from all entangling alliances,[33] its contents have been obscured by time and circumstance.

Richard B. Morris has told us: "Written after the style of eighteenth-century European statesmen, Washington's political testament had far more durability than that of Frederick the Great or other monarchs who fancied this form of address to their respective nations."[34] And yet, it must be conceded that none of the advice so painstakingly given has been abided by.

Washington warned against political parties and they have come to dominate American political affairs. He advised against "overgrown military establishments which, under any form of government, are inauspicious to liberty, and which are to be regarded as particularly hostile to republican liberty." He admonished us that: "It will be worthy of a free, enlightened, and at no distant period a great nation to give to mankind the magnanimous and too novel example of a people always guided by an exalted justice and benevolence."

He spoke, too, in 1796, of the necessities for observing the principles of separation of powers:[35]

> It is important . . . that the habits of thinking in a free country should inspire caution in those intrusted with its administration to confine themselves within their respective constitutional spheres, avoiding in the exercise of the powers of one department to encroach upon another. The spirit of encroachment tends to consolidate the powers of all the departments in one, and thus to create, whatever the form of government, a real despotism. . . . If in the opinion of the people the distribution or modification of the constitutional powers be in any particular wrong, let it be corrected by an amendment in the way which the Constitution designates. But let there be no change by usurpation; for though this in one instance may be the instrument of good, it is the customary weapon by which free gov-

ernments are destroyed. The precedent must always greatly overbalance in permanent evil any partial or transient benefit which the use can at any time yield.

We are governed today by a constitution far different from that which Washington bequeathed to us. And the most basic changes have been brought about by means other than constitutional amendment, as Washington would have had it. We have seen a concentration of power in the presidency achieved to some degree by usurpation but more largely by the abdication of responsibility by the Congress. We are, indeed, threatened by the despotism that Washington decried, whether it be called "benevolent" or not.

The affair called Watergate brought to the attention of the American public the specter of totalitarianism. The removal and pardon of the President was meant to, and effectively did, except perhaps for sporadic television exhibitions by the former President, put the quietus on that fear. But removal of Nixon did not eliminate the root causes that contribute to the "imperial presidency."

The failure of separation of powers and checks and balances to perform their anticipated function is a long and complex subject which can only be adumbrated here. Despite the rhetoric of their sponsors, they, too, were no more than the "parchment barriers" that Madison had denigrated. Madison himself placed his faith in the nature of the men to be chosen for office; not in their goodness, but in their ambition. In the 51st *Federalist*, he wrote, as I have already noted:

> But the great security against a gradual concentration of the several powers in the same department, consists in giving to those who administer each department the necessary constitutional means and personal motives to resist encroachments of the others. The provision for defence must in this, as in all other cases, be made commensurate to the danger of attack. Ambition must be made to counteract ambition. The interest of the man must be connected with the constitutional rights of the place.

As Hannah Arendt said, Madison thought that " 'ambition would be checked by ambition'—the ambition, of course, to excel and be of 'significance,' not the ambition to make a career."[36] It turned out that most congressmen have had no ambition to excel, only ambition "to make a career." The party system made them subordinates of the party leadership. Where the congressional leadership was fiercely independent, as it has been on occasions in the distant past, Congress was strong. Where the party leadership was subordinate to the will of the President, Congress has been weak. Thus, party allegiance has tended to blur if not obliterate the concept of separation of powers. More, the ambition of so many congressmen has been to achieve high executive or judicial office that the independence of their own offices has been compromised. Senator Ervin is known to have said, during his last term in office, that he was the only member of the Senate who was not a candidate for presidential nomination. Obviously there is hyperbole in that statement, but it states a truth about senatorial behavior.

If the Madisonian concept of ambition as a guide to independence was not to come true, neither was the Jeffersonian concept that the restraints on excessive concentration of governmental power would derive from what Madison acknowledged, also in *The Federalist* No. 51, to be the ultimate authority: "A dependence on the people is, no doubt, the primary control on government." Not that Madison trusted the people, as is evident from the papers following No. 51. He was wrong in his reasons for that distrust; he was right in recognizing that their control would not be sufficient.

Thus, almost a half-century ago, Felix Frankfurter was able to observe what is still the case:[37]

> Perhaps the dominant feeling about government today is distrust. The tone of most comment, whether casual or deliberate, implies that ineptitude and inadequacy are the chief characteristics of government. I do not refer merely to the current skepticism about democracy, but to the widely entertained feeling of the incapacity of government, generally, to satisfy the needs of modern society. . . . At one and the same time, we expect little from government and progressively rely on it more. We feel that the essential forces of life are no longer in the channels of politics, and yet we constantly turn to those channels for the direction of forces outside them. . . . the large abstention from voting in our elections must certainly bespeak an indifference not without meaning.

Frankfurter's thesis was that government and the Constitution had to adapt to the times and not the times to government and the Constitution, and so he saw no virtue in a rigid doctrine of separation of powers:[38]

> On the whole, "separation of powers" has been treated by the Supreme Court not as a technical legal doctrine. . . . the Court has refused to draw abstract analytical lines of separation and has recognized necessary areas of interaction among the departments of government. Functions have been allowed to courts as to which Congress itself might have legislated; matters have been withdrawn from courts and vested in the executive; laws have been sustained which are contingent upon executive judgment on highly complicated facts. By these means Congress has been able to move with freedom in modern fields of legislation, with their great complexity and shifting facts, calling for technical knowledge and skill in administration. Enforce-

ment of a rigid conception of separation of powers would make modern government impossible.

So much for the intent of the framers. But, if this is an explanation for the need to blur the lines between and among the three branches, it is not explanation of the concentration of power in the executive that has come to this nation.

The imperial presidency was not a concept invented by Nixon, although he brought it to its highest, or lowest, form. The imperial presidency had its birth in the crises of the Great Depression and the Second World War. The national governmental structure of the original Constitution as defined by the Founders was transmuted into an executive government upon which an accommodating judicial power was grafted in the fifties, sixties, and seventies. We still have the forms of a tripartite government. But the division of powers contemplated by the Founders has long since disappeared.

I shan't spend much time here on the growth of judicial power. That must await another book. But a portion of the problem was recently stated by Justice Rehnquist in a dissenting opinion in *Trimble* v. *Gordon*.[39] Although it addresses the question of the utilization of the Fourteenth Amendment to strike down state laws, the incorporation of the standards of the Equal Protection Clause of the Fourteenth Amendment in the Fifth Amendment,[40] which applies to acts of Congress, makes it equally appropriate commentary on the national sphere:[41]

> It is too well known to warrant more than brief mention that the Framers of the Constitution adopted a system of checks and balances conveniently lumped under the descriptive head of "'federalism," whereby all power was originally presumed to reside in the people of the States who adopted the Constitution. The Constitution delegated some authority to the federal executive, some to the federal legislature, some to the federal judiciary, and reserved the remaining authority normally associated with sovereignty to the States and to the people in the States. In reaching the results that it did, the Constitutional Convention in 1787 rejected the idea that members of the federal judiciary should sit on a council of revision and veto [national] laws which it considered unwise; the Convention also rejected a proposal which would have empowered Congress to nullify laws enacted by any of the several States.
>
> Following the Civil War, Congress propounded and the States ratified the so-called "Civil War Amendments"—the Thirteenth, Fourteenth, and Fifteenth Amendments, which, together with post–Civil War legislation, sharply altered the balance of power between the Federal and State Governments. See *Mitchum* v. *Foster*, 407 U.S. 225, 238–242 (1972). But they were not designed to accomplish this purpose in some vague, ill-defined way which was ultimately to

> be discovered by this Court more than a century after their enactment. Their language contained the mechanisms by which their purpose was to be accomplished. Congress might affirmatively legislate under § 5 of the Fourteenth Amendment to carry out the purposes of that Amendment; and the courts could strike down state laws found directly to violate the dictates of any of the Amendments.
>
> This was strong medicine, and intended to be such. But it cannot be read apart from the original understanding at Philadelphia: The Civil War Amendments did not make this Court into a council of revision, and they did not confer upon this Court any authority to nullify state laws which were merely felt to be inimical to the Court's notion of the public interest.
>
> That much is common ground at least at the conscious level. But in providing the Court with the duty of enforcing such generalities as the Equal Protection Clause, the Framers of the Civil War Amendments placed it in the position of Adam in the Garden of Eden. As members of a tripartite institution of government which is responsible to no constituency, and which is held back only by its own sense of self-restraint, see *United States* v. *Butler*, 297 U.S. 1, 79 (1936) (Stone, J., dissenting), we are constantly subjected to the human temptation to hold that any law containing a number of imperfections denies equal protection simply because those who drafted it could have made it a fairer or a better law. The Court's opinion in the instant case is no better and no worse than the long series of cases in this line, a line which unfortunately proclaims that the Court has indeed succumbed to the temptation implicit in the Amendment.

What Justice Rehnquist was saying—and he is no less guilty than any of his brethren—is that the Court acts as a superlegislature to decide whether the legislation that comes under its scrutiny would have been worthy of its support at the enactment stage. That there is no license for this authority, either under the original Constitution or its Amendments, including the Bill of Rights and the Fourteenth Amendment, should be clear. The power of judicial review as described by Marshall in *Marbury* v. *Madison*[42] is very different from the power of judicial review as exercised today. The modern power is more akin, as Rehnquist suggested, to a concept of a council of revision—the more so since the Court now rewrites statutes as well as construing them. The Founders clearly did not contemplate this to be within the authority conferred on the judiciary when they provided that the judicial power be vested in one Supreme Court and such other courts as Congress might determine to be required.

Watergate, however, was not directly concerned with the overreaching of the judicial branch. Watergate was an executive branch disaster, an outcome of the imperial presidency.

Arthur Schlesinger was more wont to place the blame on the occupant of the office than on the inherent defects of an office that had become overgrown with powers not subject to limitation. His explanation of the problem, nevertheless, affords us insight into the difficulties:[43]

> The imperial Presidency, born in the 1940s and 1950s to save the outer world from perdition, thus began in the 1960s and 1970s to find nurture at home. Foreign policy had given the President the command of peace and war. Now the decay of the parties left him in command of the political scene, and the Keynesian revelation placed him in command of the economy. At this extraordinary historical moment, when foreign and domestic lines of force converged, much depended on whether the occupant of the White House was moved to ride the new tendencies of power or to resist them.
>
> . . . .
>
> With Nixon there came, whether by weird historical accident or by unconscious national response to historical pressure and possibility, a singular confluence of the job with the man. The Presidency, as enlarged by international delusions and domestic propulsions, found a President whose inner mix of vulnerability and ambition impelled him to push the historical logic to its extremity.

Some years earlier, Schlesinger had written of Nixon: "He is the only major American politician in our history who came to prominence by techniques which, if generally adopted, would destroy the whole fabric of mutual confidence on which democracy rests."[44] That statement was written in 1960, before the campaigns of 1968 and 1972, which are adequately, if more in admiration than distaste, described by T. H. White in his *Making of The President* books.[45] White had to write still another book explaining what he considered Nixon's treachery to those who had thought so highly of him.[46]

It was, however, not only the President but the presidency that was at fault in the Watergate affair. The witnesses at the Senate hearings who were most revealing of the functioning of the office rather than the man were, not the President, who declined the invitation to appear, but Haldeman and Ehrlichman, Dean and Magruder, Butterfield and Moore.[47]

The Watergate problem has its parallel in English history during the period of the American Revolution. The historical analogy is described by Bernard Bailyn, speaking of the discontent with British government of that time:[48]

> The most common explanation, however—an explanation that rose from the deepest sources of British political culture, that was a part of the very structure of British political thought—located "the spring

> and cause of all the distresses and complaints of the people in England or in America" in "a kind of fourth power that the constitution knows nothing of, or has not provided against." This "overruling arbitrary power, which absolutely controls the King, Lords, and Commons," was composed, it was said, of the "ministers and favorites" of the King, who, in defiance of God and man alike, "extend their usurped authority infinitely too far," and throwing off the balance of the constitution, make their "despotic will" the authority of the nation. . . . This "junto of courtiers and state-jobbers," these "court locusts," whispering in the royal ear, "instill in the King's mind a divine right of authority to command his subjects" at the same time as they advance their "detestable scheme" by misinforming and misleading the people.

This is a most fitting description of the Executive Office of the President under Nixon, and particularly of the branch of that office called the White House. This perversion of the English balanced government was called the "corruption of the constitution." And, as Bailyn wrote, "the primary goal of the American Revolution . . . was . . . the preservation of political liberty threatened by the apparent corruption of the constitution."[49]

The control of all government by the king's henchmen was "a kind of fourth power that the constitution knows nothing of, or has not provided against."[50] The American Constitution, however, was thought by its authors to have made provision against this "corruption of the constitution," by adhering to the notion of separation of powers subject to certain checks and balances. But history has come to repeat itself, and it seems true once again that we learn nothing from history except that we learn nothing from history. "The great mass of human calamities, in all ages," Justice Story once told us, "has been the result of bad government, or ill adjusted government; of a capricious exercise of power, a fluctuating public policy, a degrading tyranny, or a desolating ambition."[51]

Part of the problem has been that which the French historian Guizot noted more than one hundred and thirty years ago:[52]

> The disposition of the most eminent men, and of the best among the most eminent, to keep aloof from public affairs, in a free democratic society, is a serious fact. . . . It would seem as if, in this form of society, the tasks of government were too severe for men who are capable of comprehending its extent, and desirous of discharging the trust in a proper manner.

This tendency toward abstention has been exacerbated by the post-Watergate mentality. Because the structural problems of Watergate have never been addressed, but only the shades of these problems, the conditions now imposed on men who would undertake public office are so burdensome that talented and sensitive persons, who do not seek power for the sake of exerting power, are not readily recruited for any administration. The recent notion that the exaltation of the forms of ethical conduct over its substance will avoid "mal-administration" is ingenuous or disingenuous. But then we live in a society in which the symbolic is all and substance nothing. This, too, is a lesson of the Nixon years, but it has not prevented his successors from emulating him, on this score at least.

The structure that gave rise in the United States to the corruption of the Constitution reached in Watergate, strangely enough, derived from the need for an additional, an extraconstitutional, form of checks and balances. With the growth of government and governmental functions came three judicial constructions of the Constitution that effectively licensed the executive branch to secure the dominant voice in our society with the acquiescence of the legislature, which has been forthcoming.

The first of these three judicially created constitutional doctrines was that the national power over foreign affairs was derived not from the Constitution but from the nature of the national government. This, then, was not a delegated power but an inheritance of the royal prerogative directly from our English antecedents. It was put this way by Justice Sutherland, speaking for the Court, in *United States* v. *Curtiss-Wright Export Corp.*:[53]

> The two classes of powers [domestic affairs and foreign affairs] are different, both in respect of their origin and their nature. The broad statement that the federal government can exercise no powers except those specifically enumerated in the Constitution, and such implied powers as are necessary and proper to carry into effect the enumerated powers, is categorically true only in respect of our internal affairs. In that field, the primary purpose of the Constitution was to carve from the general mass of legislative powers *then possessed by the states* such portions as it was thought desirable to vest in the federal government, leaving those not included in the enumeration still in the states. . . . That this doctrine applied only to powers which the states had, is self evident. And since the states severally never possessed international powers, such powers could not have been carved from the mass of state powers but obviously were transmitted to the United States from some other source. . . .
>
> As a result of the separation from Great Britain by the colonies acting as a unit, the powers of external sovereignty passed from the Crown not to the colonies severally, but to the colonies in their collective and corporate capacity as the United States of America. . . . Rulers come and go; governments end and forms of government

> change; but sovereignty survives. A political society cannot endure without a supreme will somewhere. Sovereignty is never held in suspense. When, therefore, the external sovereignty of Great Britain in respect to the colonies ceased, it immediately passed to the Union.

Moreover, not only was this authority in foreign affairs a national power, it was essentially an executive power, termed by Sutherland as "the very delicate, plenary and exclusive power of the President as the sole organ of the federal government in the field of international relations—a power which does not require as a basis for its exercise an act of Congress."[54]

The Supreme Court construction of the presidential authority in foreign affairs was made up of whole cloth, but has been a major contributor to the notion of the imperial presidency. Never mind that the Constitution specifically provided only for the reception of foreign ambassadors—and no more—by the President. Never mind that the power to declare war was given to Congress. Never mind that it was thought necessary specifically to command the states to abstain from foreign relations—a ban that would not be necessary if it was a power they never possessed. Section 10 was a redundancy, at least insofar as it provided that: "No State shall enter into any Treaty, Alliance, or Confederation; . . . No State shall . . . enter into any Agreement or Compact with . . . a foreign Power, or engage in War, unless actually invaded, or in such imminent Danger as will not admit of delay."

That the power of foreign relations passed directly from the hands of the Crown to the hands of the President is certainly of dubious validity. That, if the power was national, it was for the President's execution alone seems equally unjustified. But, since the declaration by the Supreme Court, the Constitution means not what it says but what the Justices say it says. And the President has taken full advantage thereof, which explains both Korea and Vietnam. It explains, too, what Clinton Rossiter has pridefully called "constitutional dictatorship." The concluding paragraphs of his book by that name read:[55]

> One final word. In describing the emergency governments of the western democracies, this book may have given the impression that such techniques of government as executive dictatorship, the delegation of legislative power, and lawmaking by administrative decree were purely transitory and temporary in nature. Such an impression would be distinctly misleading. There can no longer be any question that the constitutional democracies, faced with repeated emergencies and influenced by the examples of permanent authoritarian government all about them, are caught up in a pronounced, if lamentable trend toward more arbitrary, more powerful, and more "efficient" government. The instruments of government depicted here as tem-

> porary "crisis" arrangements have in some countries, and may eventually in all countries, become lasting peacetime institutions.
>
> . . . No sacrifice is too great for our democracy, least of all the temporary sacrifice of democracy itself.

For those to whom democracy and freedom are equations, the sacrifice of democracy cannot be considered the "least sacrifice" to be made. But once again, we are told that the Constitution must adapt to the times, even if the times require its destruction.

The second line of cases contributing to the imperial presidency is that which licensed the national government to occupy the entire field of government and regulation despite the existence of the states. It starts with *United States* v. *Butler*,[56] which holds that the General Welfare Clause—Article I, § 8, cl. 1, says that "Congress shall have Power To lay and collect Taxes . . . to pay the Debts and provide for the common Defence and general Welfare of the United States"—was a grant to Congress of substantive power. Madison, in *The Federalist* No. 41, had argued that this spending power was limited to the expenditures for the specific functions elsewhere authorized in the Constitution. Hamilton had argued that this clause conferred a separate authority to spend moneys, limited only by the necessity that they be spent for the general welfare of the United States. In *Butler*, the Court chose the Hamiltonian construction, although rejecting the expenditure in that case—funds to be paid to farmers under the Agricultural Administration Act—because expenditures were constitutionally authorized only for "matters of national, as distinguished from local welfare."[57] And these payments were for local welfare.

The broader reading has since been sustained. The Court next found a "general welfare" in unemployment compensation payments, by way of grants-in-aid to state programs.[58] And an expansion of the Commerce Clause power soon made the controversy between Madison and Hamilton irrelevant, as it did the *Butler* case distinction between national and local welfare. Thus, the Commerce Clause came to be held to cover the most local of business activities, such as a farmer's crop grown for home consumption[59] and a local restaurant's sale of food to its customers.[60]

The spending power and the commerce power as construed by the Supreme Court have afforded national government hegemony over all affairs of the citizens and residents of this nation. The national government is free to regulate everything, except that it must conform to the Supreme Court's interpretation of the limitations imposed by the Bill of Rights and other specific limitations spelled out in the Constitution itself. From a government of delegated powers it has become a sovereignty with jurisdiction no different from that of the nation from which it seceded in 1776.

The third set of Supreme Court decisions making for the growth of national and executive power is to be found in the area concerned with the validity of the delegation of powers. It will be recalled that, at the Convention, Madison offered a definition of executive power as: "power to carry into effect. the national laws. to appoint to offices in cases not otherwise provided for, and to execute such other powers as may from time to time be delegated by the national Legislature."[61] Pinckney made a motion to qualify the last clause providing for delegation by inserting the words "not Legislative nor Judiciary in their nature." This was rejected as redundant, because the legislature could not delegate legislative or judicial powers to the executive. But the fact is that such delegations have taken place, particularly since the Roosevelt administration, and at a more and more rapid pace, until we have now arrived at the stage where the Congress authorizes the President to write and enact the legislation subject only to congressional veto.[62]

The Supreme Court has generally endorsed this transfer of legislative power to the executive branch. Starting with *Wayman* v. *Southard*[63] in 1825, the Court held that while "important subjects . . . must be entirely regulated by the legislature itself," that was not true of subjects of "less interest, in which a general provision may be made, and power given to those who are to act under such general provisions, to fill up the details."[64] This case always brought forth from my mentor Thomas Reed Powell his old saw that when he got married it was agreed that he would decide all the important questions and his wife all the unimportant ones. "And you know," he would say, "that after forty years of marriage we haven't had an important question yet."

Thus, with the Court's approval, Congress delegated the authority to the Secretary of Agriculture to write rules, the violation of which would subject the violator to penal sanctions.[65] Delegations to the so-called independent agencies were almost without congressional definition, but nevertheless sustained by the Court. The Interstate Commerce Commission was authorized to fix rates so long as they were "just and reasonable."[66] The Federal Radio Commission, now the Federal Communications Commission, was to license radio stations whenever the commission decided that it was in the "public convenience, interest or necessity" so to do.[67] By sustaining these delegations, the Court was also expanding its own authority, for it was left to the courts to determine whether in fact "the public convenience, interest or necessity" was served, or whether the rates were "just and reasonable."

In *J. W. Hampton, Jr. & Co.* v. *United States*,[68] Chief Justice Taft announced that the propriety of delegation "must be fixed according to common sense and the inherent necessities of the governmental coordination."[69] And guess who was to be the arbiter of common sense and inherent necessities.

During the New Deal period, the Court called a temporary halt to this willy-nilly abdication of responsibility by the Congress. In a series of cases concerned with the framing of the National Industrial Recovery Act codes, the Court, unanimously or with strong majorities, held that the power delegated to frame governing codes had been invalidly surrendered by Congress.[70] After Roosevelt's Court-packing plan failed, but his court-packing itself succeeded, the doctrine of invalid delegation fell out of sight and has since showed only feeble signs of life.[71] There have been recent stirrings in the academic world for the restoration of some semblance of integrity to the legislative function.[72] But there yet is no indication that these have had or will have any serious effect on limiting congressional abdication.

The separation of powers as a doctrine restraining the exercise of power by the executive branch has all but disappeared. There are still some old checks and one or two new ones, the latter of dubious constitutional validity. Thus, theoretically Congress still has the power over the purse as a limit on executive power, but the budget—in spite of modern innovations in the Congress[73]—remains largely an executive budget and in its appropriations bills only minor variations are made by the Congress from the demands of the executive departments. The power of congressional inquisition remains, but subject to the still undefined scope of the newly recognized, constitutionally founded, "executive privilege." The comptroller general, an official responsible to Congress, still has auditing authority. And there is a provision for the required reporting of expenditures that may burgeon though it is still largely unused.[74]

The result of this Supreme Court license and congressional irresponsibility is that the nation is now governed essentially, not by laws enacted by Congress, but by rules and regulations promulgated by the executive branch and by independent agency actions, purporting to be in compliance with the congressional will, *i.e.*, where congressional will can be derived from something besides silence, but frequently in opposition to it. With this greatly expanded governmental function, the executive branch has become a series of bureaucracies uncontrolled even by the upper echelons of executive officials and only occasionally subjected to judicial scrutiny.

The countervailing authority that was sought to be developed by the President, who had lost control of the executive government machinery simply because it was too overgrown to be subject to his personal control, was the Executive Office of the President. The Executive Office of the President is a constantly expanding body with frequently changing labels for its internal offices. The 1976 *Congressional Directory*, the latest at my disposal, includes the Office of Management and Budget, the largest of the offices and the most important outside the White

House itself. Its director is certainly the second most powerful man in Washington and is often one unknown to the public at large. But he wields the power of life and death over every program and office in the executive branch. It is here rather than in the departments themselves that the ultimate decisions are made. OMB is essentially the President's primary check on all bureaucratic programs, if not on all bureaucratic decisions. Aside from the concentration of power in a comparatively small force of officials—and power necessarily gives rise to abuse from time to time—the OMB has maintained a reputation for talent and integrity that is at least as high as that enjoyed by any other governmental body, the personal lives of some of its directors notwithstanding.

There are also in this Executive Office of the President: the Council of Economic Advisers, whose substantive powers are nil; the National Security Council and Central Intelligence Agency, whose substantive powers are unlimited because undefined; the Domestic Council; the Office of the Special Representative for Trade Negotiations; the Council on Environmental Quality; the Federal Property Council; the Council on Wage and Price Stability; the Energy Resources Council; the Economic Policy Board; the President's Labor-Management Committee. Some of these are made up almost entirely of cabinet or cabinet-rank officials, grouped for special purposes; some are less lofty. In totality, they represent three functions, that of giving advice to the President, that of administering certain programs that are too sensitive for public administration by old-line departments, and that of providing a check and balance against a runaway bureaucracy.

The CIA apart, none of these agencies was involved in the criminalities and incriminations of Watergate. There is, however, another office, the White House Office, which did in fact house most of the culprits of Watergate. This office, too, originated as a means for the President to check the activities of the bureaucracy. These persons were, it was said, to have provided the eyes and ears for a President whose immobility made it difficult to oversee the growing domain of which he was supposed to be the master. During World War II, this office also housed some of the more vital machinery for the conduct of the war. And since President Kennedy moved McGeorge Bundy into the White House basement, the foreign relations of the nation have been largely conducted from this office.

The difficulty with accommodating this office and its many barons to a concept of responsible government has been great. Starting, perhaps, with Harry Hopkins, the members of this staff were frequently regarded by others—and worse, by themselves—as the President's alter egos. And so, while the Constitution says, "The executive Power shall be vested in a President of the United States of America," it has become accepted that "the President," as the term is used in the Constitution, encompasses the members of the White House Office. Whether or not a President would be constitutionally authorized to engage in wiretaps or break-ins, or appoint secret political police, or abuse the CIA's authority, or attempt to subvert the FBI, or abuse Internal Revenue Service records, or distribute large sums of money for unauthorized purposes, Watergate revealed that the White House staff thought itself imbued with presidential power to do so. We shall never know to what degree these people were acting under presidential order, to what degree they assumed presidential acquiescence and approval, to what degree they regarded themselves as adequately charged with the power to carry out these missions simply by reason of their office. These misdeeds were extraordinary. But the nonconstitutional authority exerted by "The White House" has always been great and frequently invalid.

Patrick Anderson has provided us with an interesting book, written some years before Watergate, about the men in the White House Office.[75] It is not an unsympathetic view. But he concedes: "The role of the presidential assistant comes into serious question when he moves beyond coordination to become the de facto administrator and policymaker for one or more of the departments or programs of the government."[76] Nevertheless, Anderson is unwilling to submit these actual governors of our society to even the limited, normal restraints, ineffectual as they are: Senate approval and a definition of function, whether by Executive Order or by legislation. His reasons are these:[77]

> For the most part, the Presidents have brought men of outstanding ability onto their staffs. Sometimes, men of less obvious gifts have grown to meet the challenges of the job, just as Presidents have grown in office. It would be pointless to try outside regulation of the White House staff, as by Senate confirmation; the only way to get good men around a President is to elect good Presidents. And even then, even at best, the President's men will let him down from time to time. . . .
>
> Yet, the same men will often perform admirably, even heroically, rendering genuine, little-known services to the country, with . . . a good conscience their only sure reward—and even that not always sure. These seekers of power are also men of paradox. Well-intentioned men generally, with a fair share of vanities and frailties, they operate within a political framework that offers many pitfalls and few protections, a system that does not always reward idealism and candor or punish deception and compromise.

One wonders whether after learning of the contents of the Pentagon Papers, after the revelations of CIA behavior, after the Watergate affair, even so sympathetic a voice as Anderson's could be raised to the same defense.

The ancient concept of separation of powers and checks and balances has been reduced to a slogan, to be trotted out by the Supreme Court from time to time as a substitute for a reasoned judgment. The concentration of power has certainly reached the point that made the Founding Fathers fear the necessary consequent tyranny. If it is not to be expected that the constitutional balances can be restored, if it is clear that the Congress has neither the will nor the capacity to act as a strong counterbalance to the executive authority, it is equally clear that some alternatives must be sought. I doubt, as I have said, whether the Tuchman suggestion of movement to a cabinet government is either possible or desirable. But we need reform—before "1984."

9

Reforms

A generation ago there was active in Chicago affairs an extraordinarily adept, old-time politician named Paddy Bauler. Straight out of Finley Peter Dunne and Thomas Nast, Bauler held court as 42d Ward alderman in his saloon. He will go down in history, if at all, for a shrewd and ingenuous remark. Shrewd because of an instinctual understanding of the political world; ingenuous as the child who commented on the absence of the emperor's clothing. Bauler said, when some self-styled reformers were trying to displace what they called "the machine": "Chicago ain't ready for reform yet."

It is a "great leap" from the observations of Paddy Bauler to those of William James. And William James's lesson is different. At the time of the Dreyfus case—the European event in modern history most closely parallel to Watergate—James wrote in a letter home:[1]

> Talk of corruption! We don't know what the word corruption means at home, with our improvised and shifting agencies of crude pecuniary bribery, compared with the solidly entrenched and permanently organized corruptive geniuses of monarchy, nobility, church, Army, that penetrate the very bosom of the higher kind as well as the lower kind of people in all European states . . . and sophisticate their motives away from the impulse of straightforward handling of any simple case.

Three-quarters of a century have not changed the American conception of corruption. We still tend to think of it in terms of "crude pecuniary bribery." We apparently are still committed to the notion that "the love of money is the root of all evil."[2] We have not yet learned from experience that love of power is the grosser evil. And so we think of reform in terms of preventing officials from making pecuniary gain from public office. Certainly that is a goal devoutly to be wished.

But its attainment will not likely afford us relief from the Watergate syndrome. The money there strewn around was not primarily secured for personal gain but for political use. Francis Bacon, who understood those things, wrote: "Money is like muck, not good except it be spread."[3]

The primary malignancy uncovered by the Watergate era was the growing cancer of the dictatorial presidency. Thus, as Arthur Schlesinger wrote in his book, *The Imperial Presidency*:[4]

> Watergate's importance was not simply in itself. Its importance was in the way it brought to the surface, symbolized and made politically accessible the great question posed by the Nixon administration in every sector—the question of presidential power. The unwarranted and unprecedented expansion of presidential power, because it ran through the whole Nixon system, was bound, if repressed at one point, to break out at another. This, not Watergate, was the central issue.

If Schlesinger was right about the question being the scope of the imperial presidency, he was wrong in the implication that this was a blight that originated with the Nixon administration. Schlesinger's book itself demonstrates that the imperial presidency was not an innovation by Nixon but rather the culmination of a historical trend that has deep roots developed over at least four decades. But Schlesinger was a White House staffer under Kennedy, when the concept of presidential hegemony was regarded as desirable rather than undesirable, constitutional rather than unconstitutional. If Schlesinger was correct that the imperial presidency is only a result of "the whole Nixon system," then the removal of Nixon and his minions has provided all the reform that would be needed. But as Tom Wicker of the *New York Times* put it in a 1973 column that he may now consider "inoperative":[5]

> . . . it was "strong" Democratic Presidents who did the most to expand the Presidency to its present imperial status. . . . [T]he doctrine of implied powers . . . is primarily the product of liberal Democratic thought and policy and ultimately was bound to lead to abuse.
>
> This is not a justification for Watergate or any other excessive use of state power; it ought to be a warning, however, that liberal Democrats will not automatically end the threat to liberty inherent in the imperial Presidency merely by coming back to power in 1976.

The American constitutional system, we have been told both by participants[6] and commentators,[7] has prevailed. If so, there may be a question whether any reforms are required. The problem of reform, however, depends on how one sees the issues of Watergate. If, as was so frequently urged upon us by the special prosecutors and the courts, among others, the prime problem of Watergate was to bring the guilty to judgment for their crimes, then the books should, indeed, be closed on the Watergate affair. The list of those convicted for the Watergate burglary, the coverup, and the Fielding affair, reads like a Who's Who of the Nixon White House. Nixon's guilt, we are told, is established by the Ford pardon.[8] Those actually convicted and sentenced included Chapin, Colson, Dean, Ehrlichman, Haldeman, Kalmbach, Kleindienst, LaRue, Magruder, Mitchell, Porter, and Stans. Corporations convicted of illegal campaign contributions do not constitute a list of *Fortune* magazine's top 100 corporations in the United States—perhaps because the list of wrongdoers is not complete—but there certainly are a substantial number of our most eminent corporations on the list, which includes American Airlines, American Shipbuilding Co., Ashland Oil Inc., Braniff Airways, Carnation Co., Diamond International Corp., Goodyear Tire & Rubber Co., Greyhound Corp., Gulf Oil Corp., Lehigh Valley Co-operative Farmers, Minnesota Mining & Mfg. Co., Northrop Corp., and Phillips Petroleum Co. Not strangely the convicted corporations tended to be either a part of a regulated industry or a prime contractor with the government.

This is obviously not the place to argue the question whether the objective of the criminal law is reform of the criminal. Certainly it is unlikely that any one of the defendants found guilty is going to commit the same crimes again.

Not even Archibald Cox, however, now contends that the prime issue in Watergate was the conviction of the guilty. As he recently explained it to a Canadian audience in an article with the brilliantly conceived title: *Watergate and the Constitution of the United States*:[9]

> To the question, "why did Watergate occur," I would have to answer that Watergate occurred because serious personal shortcomings converged with sundry moral and institutional trends: with the relativism and disinclination to make moral judgments which for several decades characterized the ethical climate, especially the academic environment; with the tendency to justify the use of devious, obstructive, or forcible means of imposing one's own will upon others by referring to some passionate belief in the righteousness of one's objectives; with the obsession of portions of the government with gathering intelligence by electronic bugging and other snooping in the name of internal security; and with the aggrandizement of the presidency and the resulting conflict between the President and Congress.

For Cox, too, the essential constitutional questions derived from the expanded power of the presidency, the cause of which he explained:[10]

> For forty years prior to Watergate the size and power of the executive branch of the federal government had been growing at an extraordinary rate, chiefly for three reasons:

1 The revolutionary decision made during the 1930s to use government to meet the social and economic problems of industrial and urban society necessitated an enormous expansion of the executive branch. Putting broad aspirations into concrete government programs requires masses of information and skills from numerous disciplines, which Congress lacks and only an executive bureaucracy can provide. Congress is not only ill-equipped but probably unwilling to equip itself to deal with such complexities. The initiation and formulation of major legislative measures and also their implementation after the enactment of sketchy outlines have passed to the executive branch.

2 The United States' assumption of a leading role in world affairs built up the presidency by focussing world attention upon the president. The constitution, combined with necessity, gives the president greater personal authority in foreign affairs than domestic matters. A succession of presidents pushed these powers to, and sometimes beyond, their limits. The personal manner in which they conducted international relations doubtless influenced their style in dealing with domestic affairs.

3 Radio and television give a president unique ability to focus attention upon his acts and words, and thus to choose the subjects and frame the terms of political debate. Neither senator nor congressman, nor all senators and congressmen together, can approach this source of presidential power.[11]

Here then was the accurate diagnosis of the affliction. When it came time for reform, however, the usual tendency prevailed, to provide treatment for the symptoms rather than the disease. The results were proposals for various palliatives rather than cures. And even most of these have never been effected.

The essential charge to the Senate Select Committee was the investigation of improper campaign practices in the 1972 presidential campaign, with emphasis on financing. And it was with reference to financing of such campaigns that there evolved the primary, if not the sole, legislative "reform" of any consequence.

The Final Report of the Select Committee[12] called for an independent, nonpartisan elections commission with powers to enforce the election laws.[13] It would ban all cash contributions in excess of $100 in any campaign for federal office.[14] Presidential candidates would be allowed a single campaign committee which was to use designated banks for its deposits.[15] A limit of $3,000 in contributions was to be allowed individuals in pre-convention activity and another $3,000 in post-convention campaigning.[16] The committee also proposed an overall limit on presidential campaign expenditures.[17] The committee majority recommended against public financing of political campaigns, but would provide for some tax credits toward private contributions.[18] It would ban solicitation or receipt of campaign contributions from foreign nationals.[19] It would bar officials appointed by the President with the advice and consent of the Senate from soliciting or receiving campaign contributions.[20] And it would place "stringent limitations" on the rights of organizations, including corporations, to make contributions to presidential campaigns.[21]

The arguments against public financing were concisely stated by Senator Howard Baker in his individual report:[22]

> Although public financing probably would solve a limited number of problems afflicting the present process, it would almost certainly create an equal number of potentially greater dangers. Some of those would stem, no doubt, from the incestuous nature of the Government's financing the process by which it is selected. The Responsiveness portion of the Select Committee's report[23] details the repeated efforts of members of the administration to influence or abuse the various departments and agencies for purely political purposes. Would it not be possible under a system of public financing, in which an arm of the Government was responsible for allocating funds, to abuse that authority on behalf of one candidate or party under the guise of bureaucratic red tape? . . .
>
> Another serious problem with comprehensive public financing, in my judgment, is the effect it will have upon the individual's first amendment right of freedom of political expression. I believe that right gives each citizen the right of expressing himself politically, whether by contribution, or otherwise, or conversely, refraining from such expression. . . . I, therefore, urge that it is essential to maintain participation in our political process on a voluntary basis, while attempting to increase the opportunities and incentives to participate.
>
> Public financing, however, provides no such choice. Rather, it states that the need to eliminate the influence of large sum contributors and special interests is so compelling that we must abandon the use of all voluntary private financing in favor of mandatory, public financing; and in the case of the latter, we have no control over which candidate receives our tax dollars, nor whether they are actually used for that purpose. In fact, taxpayers would be directly supporting candidates whom they consider repugnant.

The Congress rejected these arguments. It enacted legislation for reform of the election laws, the prime element of which was public financing.[24] Its effort to inhibit the abuse of the administering agency by the executive, by providing for appointment to the agency by Congress as well as the executive, was struck down as unconstitutional.[25] The free speech arguments, too, were substantially rejected by the Supreme Court when the statute came before it for legitimation.[26]

First, the Court epitomized the limitations on expenditures and contributions:[27]

> The major contribution and expenditure limitations in the Act prohibit individuals from contributing more than $25,000 in a single year or more than $1,000 to any single candidate for an election campaign and from spending more than $1,000 a year "relative to a clearly identified candidate." Other provisions restrict a candidate's use of personal and family resources in his campaign and limit the overall amount that can be spent by a candidate in campaigning for federal office.

The Court held that the limitations on campaign expenditures were unconstitutional:[28]

> A restriction on the amount of money a person or group can spend on political communication during a campaign necessarily reduces the quantity of expression by restricting the number of issues discussed, the depth of their exploration, and the size of the audience reached. This is because virtually every means of communicating ideas in today's mass society requires the expenditure of money. The distribution of the humblest handbill or leaflet entails printing, paper, and circulation costs. Speeches and rallies generally necessitate hiring a hall and publicizing the event. The electorate's increasing dependence on television, radio, and other mass media for news and information has made these expensive modes of communication indispensable instruments of effective political speech.
>
> The expenditure limitations contained in the Act represent substantial rather than merely theoretical restraints on the quantity and diversity of political speech.

The right of politicians to spend could not be inhibited, but the right of contributions by individuals and groups could be constitutionally limited:[29]

> A limitation on the amount of money a person may give to a candidate or campaign organization thus involves little direct restraint on his political communication, for it permits the symbolic expression of support evidenced by a contribution but does not in any way infringe the contributor's freedom to discuss candidates and issues. While contributions may result in political expression if spent by a candidate or an association to present views to the voters, the transformation of contributions into political debate involves speech by someone other than the contributor.
>
> Given the important role of contributions in financing political campaigns, contribution restrictions could have a severe impact on political dialogue if the limitations prevented candidates and political committees from amassing the resources necessary for effective ad-

vocacy. There is no indication, however, that the contribution limitations imposed by the Act would have any dramatic adverse effect on the funding of campaigns and political associations.

Against these broad principles, the Court determined that the limitation of $1,000 on contributions by individuals and groups was valid.[30] On the question whether Congress could limit contributions by political committees to $5,000, the Court sang the same tune.[31] So, too, with expenses incurred by volunteers incidental to carrying out their activities[32] and the $25,000 annual contribution limit.[33]

Direct expenditures, however, even when made by the same persons forbidden to make contributions, are protected by the First Amendment.[34] The limitation on a candidate's expenditure of his own moneys or that of his family is equally void.[35]

The disclosure requirements of the law were upheld with certain qualifications:[36]

> It is undoubtedly true that public disclosure of contributions to candidates and political parties will deter some individuals who otherwise might contribute. In some instances, disclosure may even expose contributors to harassment or retaliation. These are not insignificant burdens on individual rights, and they must be weighed carefully against the interests which Congress has sought to promote by this legislation. In this process, we note and agree with appellants' concession that disclosure requirements—certainly in most applications—appear to be the least restrictive means of curbing the evils of campaign ignorance and corruption that Congress found to exist.

If the disclosure requirements were valid on their face, as they were held to be, it was nevertheless admitted that with regard to some minor parties, they could be invalid in their application:[37]

> Minor parties must be allowed sufficient flexibility in the proof of injury to assure a fair consideration of their claim. The evidence offered need show only a reasonable probability that the compelled disclosure of a party's contributors' names will subject them to threats, harassment, or reprisals from either Government officials or private parties. . . . We cannot assume that courts will be insensitive to [such showings].

The requirement that anyone expending more than $100 other than by contribution to a candidate or committee must also report such expenditures is valid.[38]

The campaign contribution limitations and the disclosure requirements were, in fact, but variations on old themes. These were devices long used for the policing of elections. Only in detail was the new law distinct from the old ones in these regards. Its novelty consisted of provision for public financing of presidential campaigns. These provisions were complex, and may only be synopsized here.[39] The major parties were each entitled to $2,000,000 for the costs of their nominating conventions, provided that they did not spend more than this amount and none of it was allocated for the benefit of individual candidacies. Minor parties would receive a share measured by the proportion of their votes at the last election to the average of the votes for the two major parties. Independent candidates and new parties would get nothing. The same distribution was provided for the national election campaigns, except that the amount each major party was to receive was $20,000,000. Federal moneys were also available to candidates, in the form of matching funds, for primary contests, on condition that they raised the necessary funds in twenty or more states where they were primary candidates. No moneys were available for those who sought nomination by petition.

Only Chief Justice Burger took exception to the proposition that Congress was authorized to spend the taxpayers' money in this way by reason of the General Welfare Clause.[40] The major attack was not on Congress's power to act but on its alleged discrimination against minor party and independent candidates. But these were brushed off as involving distinctions validly based on factual differences.

The proposition that the expenditure limitation in the public financing provision was an invalid invasion of First Amendment rights was easily disposed of by the Court. For, it would seem that the First Amendment right, proclaimed earlier by the Court to be uninhibited in campaign expenditures, was subject to being bought up by the government. If the candidates and parties wanted the moneys that the government dangled before them, they could only acquire them by surrendering their First Amendment right to expend moneys that they might otherwise collect on their own. Thus, First Amendment rights—like Fifth Amendment rights—are defeasible, where the government offers a *quid pro quo*.

There was nothing in the Watergate record to require or even to justify public funding of national elections. The committee recommended against it. And yet this is the one "reform" that can be said to have resulted from the Watergate affair. Justice Rehnquist's proposition that the public funding of elections enshrines in the Constitution not only the two-party system but the two parties, Democratic and Republican, is well taken.

Whether public financing is a good idea, even if it is a constitutional one—the two standards are not the same—must be left to experience. We have had but one: the 1976 elections. The American public's political memory is short, for which our elected officials must be grateful. But a glance back at the news reports of the day may remind us that the bulk of the American public was not happy about the presidential alternatives that were afforded it in 1976. This is not to say that what was regarded, at least then, as the lack of appeal of both candidates should be attributed to public financing. We have had equally glum choices in earlier presidential elections. It can be said, however, that public financing did not appear measurably to raise the quality of candidates. But then, we must not expect too much of reforms such as this one. Even if it only saved money for erstwhile large contributors, it has some virtues. And, as the Court said, "Of almost equal concern as the danger of actual *quid pro quo* arrangements is the impact of the appearance of corruption stemming from public awareness of the opportunities for abuse inherent in a regime of large individual financial contributions."[41] We live in a world where appearances are equivalent to realities. "Congress could legitimately conclude that the avoidance of the appearance of improper influence 'is also critical . . . if confidence in the system of representative Government is not to be eroded to a disastrous extent.' "[42] If the expected appearance of a new political morality in the election process did not bring an outpouring of voters to the polls the first time it was tried, it may yet have that effect in some future elections.

For some, there were more frightening aspects of Watergate than the huge amounts of money that were available for squandering by the Nixon election team, than the milk money allegedly used to buy price supports,[43] or than the ITT contribution to secure favored treatment under the antitrust laws.[44] The major sins were the creation and use by the Nixon White House of its own political police, "The Plumbers," and its abuse of the CIA, the FBI, and the IRS for partisan political goals.

Nothing denotes totalitarian government so clearly as a political police. The shortest historical memories must recall that the way of the European dictators to power and the way for the retention of that power was through the political police. The acronyms "Gestapo" and "OGPU" can still cause tremors of fear in those who have only a reading acquaintance with them, no less those with any personal experience. For those who prefer fictional versions, the story is told in an American setting by Sinclair Lewis in his 1935 novel *It Can't Happen Here*. Even more frightening, perhaps, is Orwell's *1984*, because that date represents a prophecy as well as a description. And we are but a handful of years away from 1984. Even Ehrlichman's somewhat smaller literary achievement, his novel *The Company*, points up the problem of politicized police. They are dangerous to the liberties of the citizens if they are subordinate to presidential control, and even more so when they are not.

Indeed, the problem with political police is that they effectively function outside the law. They become a government unto themselves, demanding and receiving a loyalty from their operatives stronger than that given to country or constitution. When James McCord turned state's evidence for the Watergate burglary, he obviously did it to buy a lesser sentence from Judge Sirica. But he also did so in order to see that the blame for Watergate was not visited upon his beloved CIA:[45]

> I could not use as my defense the story that the operation was a CIA operation because it was not true. . . . Even if it meant my freedom, I would not turn on the organization that had employed me for 19 years. . . . I was completely convinced that the White House was behind the idea and ploy which had been presented, and that the White House was turning ruthless, in my opinion, and would do whatever was politically expedient at any one particular point in time to accomplish its own ends.
>
> I was also convinced that the White House had fired Helms in order to put its own man in control at CIA. . . . It appeared to me that the White House had for some time been trying to get control over the CIA estimates and assessments, in order to make them conform to "White House policy."

Some of the prime criminal characters in the Watergate affair were either CIA affiliates or alumni, from the Cuban burglar Martinez to Hunt and Liddy. Apparently few CIA agents ever totally "come in from the cold." Alumni seem to have a claim on CIA cooperation, as Howard Hunt's behavior in the Fielding and Watergate break-ins clearly indicates. And when the intelligence agencies are put to use by the civilian White House, whether by Nixon or Haldeman or Ehrlichman or Colson, their visage is a fearsome one. The power of the CIA, the FBI, and even the IRS, lies in the potential use of the data they have collected about individuals, which may be perverted, as the White House sought to pervert them, to partisan political ends. There need be no "midnight knock on the door" to intimidate other government officials and public figures.

Its involvement in Watergate was the smallest tip of the CIA iceberg and even much of that received little attention. But in addition to the effort to turn off the FBI, there were other incidents. Thus, as Senator Baker's staff reported to him:[46]

> The results of our investigation clearly show that the CIA had in its possession, as early as June of 1972, information that one of their paid operatives, Lee R. Pennington, Jr., had entered the James McCord residence shortly after the Watergate break-in and destroyed documents which might show a link between McCord and the CIA. This information was not made available to this Committee or anyone else outside the CIA until February 22, 1974, when a memorandum by the then Director of Security was furnished to this Committee.

The response of the CIA seems to be twofold. First, that the Director of Security did not become "aware of the reports concerning the burning of documents at Mr. McCord's home [until] 20 February 1974."[47] Moreover, "The CIA never directed Pennington to engage in activities in violation of the CIA's charter."[48]

Another example of questionable CIA Watergate behavior, strangely enough, relates to tapes of conversations and phone calls. The Baker staff report said:[49]

> In a meeting in Senator Baker's office with Director Colby and George Murphy, following a discussion of the Cushman tape, Murphy asked Colby if there were other tapes, and he replied in the affirmative. . . . Colby further acknowledged the prior existence of a central taping capability at the CIA. Senator Baker then requested that relevant tapes be reviewed and delivered to the Committee, to which Colby agreed. Shortly thereafter, Colby confirmed to Senator Baker recent press accounts that the tapes had been destroyed. . . .
>
> Shortly before Director Helms left office, and approximately one week after Senator Mansfield's letter requesting that evidentiary materials be retained, Helms ordered that the tapes be destroyed. . . . While the CIA claims that the destruction was not unusual and was one of several periodic destructions, two facts seem clear. First, the only other destruction for which the CIA has any record was on January 21, 1972, when tapes for 1964 and 1965 were destroyed (there are no records of periodic destructions); and secondly, never before had there been a destruction of all existing tapes. . . .
>
> The January, 1973, destruction pertained only to recordings of room conversations. However, on Helms' instruction, his secretary destroyed his transcriptions of both telephone and room conversations. The evidence indicates that among those telephone transcriptions were conversations with the President, Haldeman, Ehrlichman, and other White House officials.

It would appear from the record evidence either that the CIA, too, was engaged in a coverup of its own, or that the word "intelligence" was being sadly perverted when used as a description of CIA activities.[50] The Rockefeller Commission would seem to have come down on the side of CIA stupidity. Thus, in reporting on the cooperation afforded Hunt and Liddy in their Watergate escapades, the commission said:[51]

> The providing of assistance to Hunt and Liddy was not within the Agency's authorized foreign intelligence functions. The Commission has found no evidence, however, indicating that the Agency was aware that Hunt's request would involve it in unauthorized activities. . . .
>
> Nor has the investigation disclosed facts indicating that the CIA knew or had reason to believe that the assistance it provided to Hunt

> and Liddy would be used in connection with the planning of an illegal entry. . . .
>
> The responsibility for involvement of the Agency in providing support ultimately used for illegal activities must rest primarily on the White House staff. It is to some extent understandable that the Agency would want to accommodate high-level White House requests which on their face do not appear to be improper. Nevertheless, the Agency is subject to criticism for having used insufficient care in controlling the use of the materials it supplied. Inasmuch as the assistance provided in this case differed from the foreign intelligence services normally provided by the CIA to the White House, the responsible Agency officials would have been well advised to insist on compliance with the normal procedures for control of materials of this kind, notwithstanding (or perhaps particularly because of) the air of mystery that surrounded Hunt's request. . . . The Agency should also use particular care in accommodating requests by or on behalf of former employees or contractors.

The one question on this subject that the Rockefeller Commission report neither asked nor answered was what possible legal activities could the CIA have attributed to Hunt that would have justified the cooperation they afforded him. Or was it just a mistake of the heart rather than the head?

Again, on the question of the tape-burning episode described by the Baker staff, the commission's conclusion cast less credit on the wisdom and intelligence of the CIA, again necessarily assuming good faith on the part of that agency:[52]

> It must be recalled that in January 1973 the Watergate affair had not yet assumed the dimensions which subsequent revelations gave it. Neither the activities of the Plumbers nor the extent of the White House involvement in the cover-up had come to light. Accordingly, destruction of Helms' personal office records cannot be judged with the benefit of hindsight, derived from subsequent revelations.
>
> For the same reasons, however, Helms' stated interpretation of what was Watergate-related presumably was narrower than it would have been after all the facts disclosed to the Watergate Grand Jury in April, 1973, and other information had come to light. Hence, no comfort can be derived from Helms' assurances that no Watergate-related material was destroyed, since what was destroyed had not been reviewed for relevance in light of the later disclosures.
>
> The destruction of the tapes and transcripts, coming immediately after Senator Mansfield's request not to destroy materials bearing on the Watergate investigation, reflected poor judgment. It cannot be justified on the ground that the Agency produced its Watergate-related papers from other files; there is no way in which it can ever be estab-

> lished whether relevant evidence has been destroyed. When taken together with the Agency's general non-responsiveness to the ongoing investigation, it reflects a serious lack of comprehension of the obligation of any citizen to produce for investigating authorities evidence in his possession of possible relevance to criminal conduct.

And again the commission neither asked nor answered the vital question, why were the tapes destroyed at all?

One can only speculate about what the recent history of this nation might have been had President Nixon demonstrated the same "poor judgment" as did the CIA and destroyed the White House tapes after he was told that they were wanted by the grand jury and the Watergate committee. Yet, I must say that I find some comfort in a corrupt, hapless, inefficient intelligence service, more than I would in an effective, efficient one, at least so far as the liberties if not the safety of Americans are concerned. Such a picture does not, however, conform to the results of later investigations. The Watergate Committee recommended more rigid congressional oversight[53] and Senator Baker called for "extensive further examination."[54]

The most extensive and important of these post-Watergate studies was conducted by the Senate Select Committee to Study Governmental Operations with Respect to Intelligence Activities which was established under the chairmanship of Senator Frank Church on 27 January 1975 and reported on 26 April 1976.[55] The Church committee examined not only the CIA and the FBI, but also the National Security Agency, the Department of Defense, and the Department of State intelligence operations. The committee conducted the study and made recommendations for reform, to be effected by later action, if any were to occur. The problems encountered by the Church committee were epitomized in the Report in this manner:[56]

> It is clear that a primary task for any successor oversight committee, and the Congress as a whole, will be to frame basic statutes necessary under the Constitution within which the intelligence agencies of the United States can function efficiently under clear guidelines. Charters delineating the missions, authorities, and limitations for some of the United States' most important intelligence agencies do not exist. For example, there is no statutory authority for the NSA's intelligence activities. Where statutes do exist, as with the CIA, they are vague and have failed to provide the necessary guidelines defining missions and limitations.
>
> The Committee's investigation has demonstrated, moreover, that the lack of legislation has had the effect of limiting public debate upon some important national issues.
>
> The CIA's broad statutory charter, the 1947 National Security Act, makes no specific mention of covert action. The CIA's former

General Counsel, Lawrence Houston, who was deeply involved in drafting the 1947 Act, wrote in September 1947, "we do not believe that there was any thought in the minds of Congress that the CIA under [the authority of the National Security Act] would take positive action for subversion and sabotage." Yet, a few months after enactment of the 1947 legislation, the National Security Council authorized the CIA to engage in covert action programs. The provision of the Act often cited as authorizing CIA covert activities provides for the Agency:

> . . . to perform such other functions and duties related to intelligence affecting the national security as the National Security Council may from time to time direct.

Secret Executive Orders issued by the NSC to carry out covert action programs were not subject to congressional review. Indeed, until recent years, except for a few members, Congress was not fully aware of the existence of the so-called "secret charter for intelligence activities." Those members who did know had no institutional means for discussing their knowledge of secret intelligence activities with their colleagues. The problem of how the Congress can effectively use secret knowledge in its legislative processes remains to be resolved. It is the Committee's view that a strong and effective oversight committee is an essential first step that must be taken to resolve this fundamental issue.

Legislative actions have been less than forthcoming as a result of the many studies. But the Congress would seem to be easily satisfied that reform has occurred. On 18 May 1977, the Senate's Select Committee on Intelligence announced its belief that "the nation's intelligence agencies were now fully accountable to the President and Congress, but it said that strict legislative charters would be needed to insure against a repetition of 'widespread abuses of the past.' "[57] And the committee was hard at work creating those parchment guidelines.

At the same time it was busy creating a monster of which Dr. Frankenstein might be proud. For it proposed to create a single, combined intelligence unit, whose oversight would be charged to a single congressional committee. The ease with which the regulated has coopted the regulator in our history, especially when the regulated is a bureaucracy and the regulator is a congressional committee, is a lesson apparently to be ignored. And what is forgotten about Watergate is that it was the FBI that blew the whistle where the CIA would have been compliant. What if there had been only the CIA? Equally forgotten is the lesson that the dangers of power derive from its concentration, not its dispersal. These proposed changes suggest a giant step backward. The specters of the CIA's CHAOS program and the FBI's COINTELPRO become more ominous rather than less, with the prospect that they could be combined under a single director, with a monopoly on intelligence information. (The step has since been taken by executive order of President Carter.)

For eighteenth-century America, the great fear was of a standing army that could be put to use by the executive to pervert the government from a democracy to a dictatorship. Thus, as Benjamin Fletcher Wright has written:[58]

> One of the striking characteristics of *The Federalist* is the large amount of space devoted to the question of a standing army. The constitutional provision enabling the central government to maintain a standing army in time of peace was among those most frequently singled out for viewing with alarm. Living in the shadow of the Revolution, remembering the declamations against the army of England, and fearful that a standing army might be employed by an American Caesar as an instrument for overthrowing the republic and establishing a dictatorship, the men of that age were, as a result of recent experience and the reading of Roman history, susceptible to this argument to a degree we find it difficult to understand. . . . Hamilton and Madison could not state with certainty that a standing army would never be used for such a purpose. . . . They could argue from the experience of the Greek and English peoples that strength was essential to independence and stability. . . .
>
> They could, and did, also argue that in England control over the army had been transferred since 1688 from the King to the Parliament. Similarly the control by Congress, and the limitation to two years of appropriations for the armies, insured against the use by the executive of an army to overthrow the republic and establish monarchy or a military dictatorship.

Our founding fathers' fears of a standing army are equally applicable today to the so-called intelligence establishment. The safeguards of congressional control are not a present reality. The intelligence community may be a necessity for the "independence and stability" of the nation. But remembering the twentieth-century events in Europe, including Greece and Rome, Berlin and Moscow, Lisbon and Madrid, there remains a fear of subversion implicit in their power. And this is particularly true when, as the Watergate record reveals, the intelligence services are put at the disposal of the White House staff.

This fear is reflected in the recommendation of the Watergate committee that "Congress enact legislation making it unlawful for any employee in the Executive Office of the President, or assigned to the White House, directly or indirectly to authorize or engage in any investigative or intelligence gathering activity concerning national or domestic security not authorized by Congress."[59] This was joined with the recommendation "that the appropriate congressional oversight committees should more closely supervise the operations of the intelligence and law enforcement 'community.' "[60] To date these reforms are not visible.[61]

The major thrust of the reform movement consequent upon the Watergate revelations was to create a new policeman or new policemen to guard the guardians of our criminal justice establishment. Senator Ervin's 1974 efforts, which came before the impeachment move and the consequent resignation of the President, called for the re-creation of the Department of Justice outside the executive branch.[62] Aside from some questions of the constitutionality of such an effort, the bulk of the committee's witnesses testified heavily against the wisdom of such proposals, and they came to naught.

Following the discharge of the Select Committee on Watergate, Senator Ervin drafted the Watergate Reorganization and Reform Act. In its 1975 version, much of it was derived from the Select Committee report. In one part it followed the recommendation "that Congress give careful consideration to the bill now before the Senate (S.2569) that would establish a Congressional Legal Service and thus give Congress a litigation arm that would allow it to protect its interest in court by its own counsel."[63] A second part would have provided for a special prosecutor for crimes committed by high government officials. A third was concerned with making congressional subpoenas enforceable through the courts. Still another provided for limited access by "White House personnel to CIA materials, IRS records, and other sensitive material."[64] The functions of a special prosecutor, in this line, were to be combined with the office of congressional legal counsel. The concept of a special prosecutor continued to thrive without ever garnering enough support for enactment in Congress.[65] On the other hand, the notion of congressional counsel seems to have disappeared. And yet the latter is far more important than the former. The need for an efficient enforcement procedure for congressional subpoenas remains unabated. The idea of extensive financial disclosure by public officials before assuming office and while occupying it still bemuses the Congress. But almost everyone knows that it is window dressing, shadow rather than substance.

I once had the temerity to deliver an opinion to the Government Operations Committee on the Watergate Reform Act, which I repeat here:[66]

> The proposed Public Attorney is obviously patterned on the role of the Watergate Special Prosecutor. While I admire the work that Cox and Jaworski performed, I am by no means convinced that for the kinds of malfeasance they addressed, criminal trials were the best answer. They were, of course, properly ancillary to the work of the Senate Select Committee on Presidential Campaign Finances and the House Judiciary Committee's impeachment processes, but not alternatives to these efforts.

My suggestion is that the investigatory and prosecutorial function of the new Congressional Legal Counsel be confined to the legislative and impeachment processes set forth in the Constitution. As you know, impeachment is not limited to the office of the President or Vice-President, but extends to all executive branch officials, as well as the judiciary. Moreover, its function may be extended to persons who have already separated themselves or been separated from the service of the nation. If, as I believe, the primary obligation in the case of defalcation or dereliction of duty of an important government official is not so much his imprisonment as publicizing the wrongdoing in order to seek legislative means of preventing its recurrence, then the legislative processes are better geared to the proper end than the judicial. And, as the impeachment provisions provide, in the event that the legislative or impeachment processes reveal criminal activity, criminal prosecutions may be brought after the legislative processes have ended, whatever conclusion the Congress may reach.

I would, therefore, suggest the creation of an office of Congressional Legal Counsel, which would be charged with the duty to investigate and prosecute misbehavior of executive and judicial officials—and legislative officials as well—either before the House Judiciary Committee, in the event of a formal impeachment process, or before an appropriate committee of either the House or Senate, where the objective is not removal but curative legislation, and before the proper legislative committee, where the question is the misbehavior of a member of the House or Senate.

For these purposes, the office would have to have all the investigative capacities which the bill proposes to make available to the Office of Public Attorney, except the power of judicial prosecution. But granting these powers as consequent upon the legislature's power of investigation and oversight would raise none of the questions of constitutionality that derive from the creation of a separate office of Public Attorney for criminal prosecutions. I should think it clear that such an official could be appointed by the legislative leadership, perhaps with the approval of the Judiciary Committees, or even the approval of both Houses. . . .

I should add that I think that the Office of Congressional Counsel should have, as well as the functions I have suggested above, the duties and powers that are now provided in S.495 for that office [i.e., representing congressional interests in court]. And I would add still one more important function, that of the oversight of the execution of the laws legislated by Congress. For one of the problems that is not adequately addressed by Congress now is that once legislation has been enacted, it tends to become a license for executive and judicial action which frequently does not conform either to the language or the spirit of the laws as enacted. Some mechanism should be created to keep Congress informed, through its appropriate committees,

> perhaps, of what both the executive and the judicial branches of the government are doing when they allegedly enforce its laws. This function could be performed by the Office of Congressional Legal Counsel. Congress would then be in a position to redesign or restructure the governing legislation if its enforcement does not truly conform to the legislative purpose and intent at the time of enactment.

Nothing has come of this suggestion.

Although Congress remained active but ineffective, steps have been taken within the Department of Justice to provide mechanisms that were lacking at the time of Watergate. Much of their success will depend on who happens to be Attorney General when the crunch comes. In large measure, the independence of the Department of Justice turns upon the independence of the Attorney General. If he's a political relative of the White House, as he usually is, or a moral weakling, as he sometimes may be, the inspector general's task will not be performed, whatever the mechanism. But there is now in the department, as a result of Edward H. Levi's incumbency, an Office of Professional Responsibility, which is concerned with misbehavior of departmental personnel, and the Public Integrity Section in the Criminal Division, with responsibility for the prosecution of cases of public corruption. The latter office is not directly responsible to the Attorney General, so there is a buffer between its operations and the cabinet officer on whom White House staff might be inclined to put pressure. Since an external special prosecutor presents many serious constitutional hurdles to overcome, this internal check may be the only, if not the best, available tool. We won't know until it comes time again to prosecute a White House staff member. It is to be hoped that such an occasion will not arise soon.

There were other sporadic attempts at reform that failed, or at least that have not yet come to fruition. Bills to provide for appropriate procedures and definitions of executive privilege have had no more success since Watergate than they did before or during that period. One such effort[67] in 1974 was scuttled by a combination of those who opposed restraints on the President and those who would tolerate no qualifications on the power of the Congress to secure data from the executive branch. Thus, Congressman Jack Brooks complained that "this bill would confer upon . . . the judiciary the power to determine what information the Congress has a right to obtain. To give any judge . . . such authority is an abdication of congressional responsibility. . . . Congress has adequate authority now to get the information it needs. We should concentrate upon exercising that authority."[68]

Indeed, after the Watergate fiasco, Congress did show some backbone, by threatening to hold both Secretary of Commerce Morton and Secretary of State Kissinger in contempt for failing to produce materials demanded of them by the House of Representatives.[69] In both instances the confrontation was avoided by production of the documents demanded.

In another area, however, Congress has again and again proved its lack of backbone. Just before the Watergate events started to turn on him, President Nixon, having failed to get authority for executive reorganization from Congress, executed a reorganization without congressional acquiescence. On 5 January 1973, he dubbed three cabinet members, the secretaries of Agriculture, HEW, and HUD, to be White House counselors; in addition to their cabinet duties, they were to serve under five presidential assistants: Haldeman for administration; Ehrlichman for domestic affairs; Kissinger for foreign affairs; Roy Ash (OMB) for executive management; and George P. Shultz for economic affairs.[70] The three secretaries were to be responsible for three broad areas, nothing less than natural resources, human resources, and community development. This plan had the worthy objective of attempting to pry control from the bureaucracies, where it had been placed by legislation. However desirable the goal, it had the unfortunate effect of further centralizing the power of the executive branch, not in the President, but in his alter egos, the senior White House staff. Nixon had proposed such a reorganization to Congress in 1971 and again in 1972.[71] Congress had wisely denied it. It was Watergate that killed the unauthorized reorganization, with the discharge of Haldeman, Ehrlichman, and others.

If there were two distortions of constitutional government revealed by Watergate, they were the failure of Congress to perform adequately its function as a check on the executive, and the inordinate concentration of power in the hands of the White House staff. Remedies for neither of these distortions has been afforded.

In 1974, a bill was introduced in the House to cut down the size of the White House staff.[72] It failed because of a conflict engendered by Senator Weicker, who wanted to tack on restraints against use of Internal Revenue Service information. The reason behind the bill was stated by then Senator, now Vice-President, Walter Mondale, who may or may not be of the same opinion today:[73]

> "Along with the growth in the White House staff's size and arrogance has come the corresponding ability to hide behind bloated notions of executive privilege in seeking to avoid responsibility to the Congress," Mondale said. Often, he charged, members and committees working on legislation bargained with Nixon administration cabinet officers and "reached agreement—or what we thought was agreement—only to be told at the last minute that the cabinet officer with whom we were dealing was really only a front man, a PR official sent out by the White House to fend off inquisitive congressmen. The real decisions, we were then told, were being made in the White

> House, by staff members not subject to congressional scrutiny, who could claim executive privilege at will, and who did an excellent job of thwarting the will of the cabinet officers, whose job it should be to make government policy."
>
> Mondale said Franklin D. Roosevelt's Committee on Administrative Management, which first proposed the creation of an Executive Office of the President during the late 1930s, recommended that presidential assistants "not be assistant presidents in any sense," and that they would "remain in the background, issue no orders, make no decisions, emit no public statements."
>
> "This is surely a far cry from the White House staff of today," Mondale added.

It should be noted that things are not yet different under the Carter administration. The numbers of the White House staff were first drastically enlarged,[74] and later cut back by transfer to other offices in the Executive Office of the President. And to underline their importance, many of the White House Office, if not all, are salaried at the highest government levels, in excess of salaries paid to the Haldemans, Ehrlichmans, Deans, and Magruders of an earlier White House,[75] and far in excess of their earnings before they joined the Carter bandwagon in its early stages. And the Congress granted to Carter what it had denied Nixon, a *carte blanche* to reorganize the executive branch to his own satisfaction.[76] Whether this, too, will enhance the power of the White House staff remains to be seen, even though the staff is now referred to as "the President's boys" rather than the President's men.[77] Once again the White House Office is staffed with campaign staff whose expertise is in getting a President elected, not in helping him to govern.

It would appear that, in the prescient words of Paddy Bauler, the United States, like Chicago, "ain't ready for reform yet."

10

The Plebiscitary Presidency

Sir Robert Peel once wrote: "Infamous as Robespierre and Marat unquestionably are, it would be no easy matter to assign each their due share of infamy without a very dispassionate enquiry into many minute events which contributed to shape their course, and into the degrees of conflicting dangers between which they had to choose."[1] The same thought may be ventured about Richard Nixon. No such "dispassionate enquiry" has yet been afforded to us by either the popular or the academic press. If and when it is forthcoming, it is no more likely to change the judgment about Nixon's infamy than it did history's judgment on Marat or Robespierre.[2] For historical judgments, like judicial judgments, are seldom based on data. But we pretend.

Nixon's defenders of the moment, like William Safire and Patrick Buchanan, were once paid by him for their services as apologists and continue so to act through the good graces of the very news media that they once damned. But Nixon cannot be defended by a refusal to accept established facts without an explanation of them or an addition to them. Nor will the judgment on Nixon be affected by the argument that Nixon was only the latest of a long line of perfidious presidents. Victor Lasky is surely right in the title of his latest book, *It Didn't Start with Watergate*.[3] Unfortunately, his next book may well be titled *It Didn't End with Watergate*, which would be a better defense. But it should be remembered that it didn't start with Charles I, either, nor did it end with him.

Nixon may one day be succored the way Caesar was by Marc Antony. But none of Nixon's defenders has yet displayed the gifts of Antony's ghost writer. And it will probably take a poet, even if one of smaller magnitude, to make out the case for Nixon. Yet, even Antony speaking through Shakespeare conceded:[4]

The noble Brutus
Hath told you Caesar was ambitious;
If it were so, it was a grievous fault;
And grievously hath Caesar answered it.

It seems to be harder for academics than for poets to avoid self-righteousness, not to be disdainful of those who are professionally engaged in politics or business, which most of us eschew,[5] except as kibitzers. Politicians' motives, especially, cannot be nearly so pure as our own, and hindsight constantly demonstrates to us the fallibility, if not venality, of those persons in the "real world." In criticizing their efforts, we tend to assume an omniscience that only newspaper writers or television commentators are, by their nature, entitled to assert. But it nevertheless remains the function of academics to aspire to the "dispassionate enquiry" of which Sir Robert Peel spoke.

Attempting—without entire success—to put to one side my long and deep-seated distaste for the person of Richard Nixon, I conclude that the best reasons for Nixon's removal from office are not to be found in the three articles of impeachment voted by the House Judiciary Committee or even in all five of those that the committee considered. This is not to say that these charges were inadequate for impeachment and conviction. It is rather that, just as Watergate was but the symbol of the problems of the imperial presidency, so too were the impeachment articles but the symbols of Watergate. If there were no more to Watergate than concealment of a crime, lying about it, and refusing to respond to congressional demands for information, it could not have been the traumatic event that it was. The impeachment charges will always remain as proof of malversations unique to President Nixon, but to concentrate only on these issues is to exalt shadows and demean substance.

The President's trespasses were recorded not in the bills of indictment but in the evidence from which they were adduced. The published Watergate tapes and the published volumes of evidence before the House Judiciary Committee revealed not only the criminality of a President of the United States but also his immorality or, more properly perhaps, his amorality.

When Nixon took to the air to excuse his behavior in his initial interview with David Frost in May of 1977, the *New York Times* wrote an uncharacteristically acute editorial, displaying more doubts than editorial writers are usually willing to acknowledge:[6]

> Watergate exposed an enduring dilemma that explains a strength of the Presidency but also says much about excess. . . . To become President requires calculation, single-mindedness and ferocity, quali-

> ties which can, abruptly, become far less admirable after an election, depending on the character of the man. Even if the electorate judges character wisely, not even the most upright President can wholly immunize himself against the compulsions of office.
>
> The nation has, so far, responded to this dilemma with a tide of reform. . . .
>
> Are such reforms adequate? Cynics already wonder whether they will not quickly degenerate into perfunctory piety. Some legislators seem resigned to enacting lifeless monuments to a fleeting national attention span. It will take years to find out; the ultimate Watergate trial lies ahead. It will test not our capacity to blame Richard Nixon but our ability to monitor and adjust the checks and balances we profess to be precious—to understand the infectious imperatives of power.

Therein lies the basic constitutional problems that beg for attention if our Watergate experience is to be a lesson learned. As a second-class poet put it in a second-class poem:[7]

> And when midst fallen London, they survey
> The stone where Alexander's ashes lay,
> Shall own with humbled pride the lesson just
> By Time's slow finger written in the dust.

Or, to stick to Shakespeare:[8]

> I shall the effect of this good lesson keep,
> As watchman to my heart.

The question remains, however, What is the lesson to be learned from Watergate? We can readily say that the evils revealed were the failure of our system of checks and balances to inhibit the imperial presidency and the abuse of governmental institutions for the personal gratification of the President. But how was Nixon's presidency different from those of his predecessors and how must it differ from those of his successors?

Arthur Schlesinger put forth a cogent thesis about the special nature of the Nixon presidency:[9]

> As one examined the impressive range of Nixon's initiatives—from his appropriation of the war-making power to his interpretation of the appointing power, from his unilateral determination of social priorities to his unilateral abolition of statutory programs, from his attack on legislative privilege to his enlargement of executive privilege, from his theory of impoundment to his theory of the pocket veto, from his calculated disparagement of the cabinet and his calculated discrediting of the press to his carefully organized concentration of federal management in the White House—from all this a larger

> design ineluctably emerged. It was hard to know whether Nixon, whose style was banality, understood consciously where he was heading. He was not a man given to political philosophizing. But he was heading toward a new balance of constitutional powers, an audacious and imaginative reconstruction of the American Constitution. . . .
>
> . . . It may be that he was the first President in American history to conclude that the separation of powers had so frustrated government on behalf of the majority that the constitutional system had become finally intolerable—and to move boldly to change the system. For Congress, it could be argued, had failed majority government in the high-technology society. It had proved itself incapable of the swift decisions demanded by the twentieth century. It could not make intelligent use of its war-making authority. It had no ordered means of setting national priorities or of controlling aggregate spending. It was not to be trusted with secrets. It was fragmented, parochial, selfish, cowardly, without dignity, discipline or purpose. The Presidency had not stolen its power; rather Congress had surrendered it out of fear of responsibility and recognition of incapacity. Congress was even without pride and, if ignored or disdained, waited humbly by the White House and licked the hand of its oppressor.

Then, providing the philosophical framework of which Nixon was not conscious, Schlesinger undertook to set forth the theory of government that Nixon's actions revealed:[10]

> What Nixon was moving toward was something different: it was not a parliamentary regime but a plebiscitary Presidency. His model lay not in Britain but in France—in the France of Louis Napoleon and Charles de Gaulle. A plebiscitary Presidency, unlike a parliamentary regime, would not require a new Constitution; presidential acts, confirmed by a Supreme Court of his own appointment, could put a new gloss on the old one. And a plebiscitary Presidency could be seen as the fulfillment of constitutional democracy. Michels explained in *Political Parties* the rationale of the "personal dictatorship conferred by the people in accordance with constitutional rules." By the plebiscitary logic, "once elected, the chosen of the people can no longer be opposed in any way. He personifies the majority and all resistance to his will is anti-democratic. . . . He is, moreover, infallible, for 'he who is elected by six million votes, carries out the will of the people; he does not betray them.' " How much more infallible if elected by 46 million votes! If opposition became irksome, it was the voters themselves, "we are assured, who demand from the chosen of the people that he should use severe repressive measures, should employ force, should concentrate all authority in his own hands." The chief executive would be, as Laboulaye said of Napoleon III, "democracy personified, the nation made man."

Any doubts about the validity of Schlesinger's thesis may seem to have been put to rest by Nixon himself in a third television interview with David Frost that was broadcast on 19 May 1977.[11] In that broadcast he unashamedly announced that the President, like the ancient kings of England, could do no wrong. What was a crime when committed by others was legal if done by the President, or by the members of his staff to whom he had issued orders or given permission to ignore the laws and Constitution of the United States.

If there is no doubt about the accuracy of Schlesinger's conclusion, there is still some problem with his analysis. For, the fact is that the "plebiscitary Presidency" has long been justified and advocated by many, if not all, of our academic students of the presidency. It is well described by Clinton Rossiter in his appropriately entitled book, *Constitutional Dictatorship*, and reiterated later in *The American Presidency*. It is the direction of Harold Laski as early as 1940, in *The American President*. One can read similar directions in Richard Neustadt's *Presidential Power* and Louis Koenig's *The Chief Executive*. And I have already quoted Louis Heren's flattery of the presidency that resembles the rule of the kings of England for a century after Magna Carta.

The position of the academic pro-presidential power forces was well described by Robert Hirschfield in an encomium to the presidency and its new occupant, John F. Kennedy, which was published in an English journal:[12]

> Although theoretically the twin fountainheads of executive power are the "Constitution and the laws," in fact the sources of this prodigious authority are democracy and necessity.
>
> The Presidency, like all offices of government, is only a paper institution until the political process supplies the personality which brings it to life. . . . The real foundations of presidential power, therefore, are those forces which elevate the executive to a focal position in government, allowing him to interpret his authority broadly and to exercise it boldly.
>
> The most important of these forces lies in the democratic nature of the modern Presidency. Not only constitutionally, but also politically and psychologically, the President is *the* leader of the nation. . . . [T]he fact remains that its power flows from and is primarily dependent on its tribunate character.
>
> . . . .
>
> The other, and no less important, source of presidential power is necessity. Not only the psychological need for clearly identifiable and deeply trusted authority, but also the governmental necessity for centralized leadership and decisive action in times of crisis.
>
> . . . The separation of powers, federalism, even the Bill of Rights and the rule of law, must sometimes be transcended under conditions

of grave national emergency. Even under less pressing circumstances, the need for purposeful and efficient government is increasingly evident. But the legislative process—complex, deliberative, cumbersome, and designed to assure the compromise of manifold local interests—is ill-suited to meet these challenges. Only the President, possessing (as Alexander Hamilton noted) both unity and energy, can meet the demand for leadership under critical conditions. . . .

. . . under critical conditions there are no effective constitutional or governmental limits on executive power, for democracy and necessity allow the President to transcend the limitational principle and assert his full authority as trustee of the nation's destiny.

Clearly, Schlesinger is right in his assertion that Nixon lacked the contemplative state of mind to define the "plebiscitary Presidency" which was the unstated premise of his actions. But there really was no need for him to provide such a rationalization. "Liberal" scholars had long since justified his notions of the scope of the presidential power, although when they did so, they did not have Nixon in mind, but rather Roosevelt and Kennedy.

When one examines the rhetoric of presidential campaigns, both before and after Watergate, it may be readily noted that all the candidates assume the validity of the "plebiscitary Presidency." Each candidate speaks of what he will do when elected to office, on the assumption that all power over foreign and domestic affairs falls into the hands of the victor. The speech is not in terms of leadership but in terms of command. And the public is called upon to choose between the candidates in the expectation that its choice will not be the representative of the people but the surrogate for the people. Even if the Supreme Court no longer speaks of the people as sovereign, the Court is still bemused by the notion of separation of powers, however often it has sustained presidential overreaching. It has not yet succumbed to the language of a constitutional "plebiscitary Presidency." Surely, it had not yet done so in the 1950s, when it uttered its major ruling on separation of powers.

In 1952, in reviewing and rejecting the constitutionality of a presidential seizure of the American steel mills, which purported to be an exercise of presidential power that rested, in part at least, on the constitutionally specified authority of commander-in-chief and the constitutionally implied powers over foreign relations, the Court's opinion, written by Justice Black, stated:[13]

The President's power, if any, to issue the order must stem either from an act of Congress or from the Constitution itself. There is no statute that expressly authorizes the President to take possession of property as he did here. . . .

. . . it is not claimed that express constitutional language grants this power to the President. The contention is that presidential power should be implied from the aggregate of his powers under the Constitution. . . .

The order cannot properly be sustained as an exercise of the President's military power as Commander in Chief. . . . The Government attempts to do so by citing a number of cases upholding broad powers in military commanders engaged in day-to-day fighting in a theater of war. Such cases need not concern us here. . . .

Nor can the seizure order be sustained because of the several constitutional provisions that grant executive power to the President. In the framework of our Constitution, the President's power to see that the laws are faithfully executed refutes the idea that he is to be a lawmaker. The Constitution limits his functions in the lawmaking process to the recommending of laws he thinks wise and the vetoing of laws he thinks bad. And the Constitution is neither silent nor equivocal about who shall make laws which the President is to execute.

. . . .

It is said that other Presidents without congressional authority have taken possession of private business enterprises in order to settle labor disputes. But even if this be true, Congress has not thereby lost its exclusive constitutional authority to make laws necessary and proper to carry out the powers vested by the Constitution "in the Government of the United States, or any Department or Officer thereof."

The Founders of this Nation entrusted the lawmaking power to the Congress alone in both good and bad times. It would do no good to recall the historical events, the fears of power and the hopes for freedom that lay behind their choice. Such a review would but confirm our holding that this seizure order cannot stand.

In the *Steel Seizure Case*, Justice Frankfurter displayed a healthier respect for separation of powers than he had shown as Professor Frankfurter. With the responsibility for judgment on his shoulders, he wrote:[14]

A constitutional democracy like ours is perhaps the most difficult of man's social arrangements to manage successfully. Our scheme of society is more dependent than any other form of government on knowledge and wisdom and self-discipline for the achievement of its aims. For our democracy implies the reign of reason on the most extensive scale. The Founders of this Nation were not imbued with the modern cynicism that the only thing that history teaches is that it teaches nothing. They acted on the conviction that the experience of man sheds a good deal of light on his nature. It sheds a good deal of light not merely on the need for effective power, if a society is to be at once cohesive and civilized, but also on the need for limitations on the power of governors over the governed.

> To that end they rested the structure of our central government on the system of checks and balances. For them the doctrine of separation of powers was not mere theory; it was a felt necessity. Not so long ago it was fashionable to find our system of checks and balances obstructive to effective government. It was easy to ridicule that system as outmoded—too easy. The experience through which the world has passed in our own day has made vivid the realization that the Framers of our Constitution were not inexperienced doctrinaires. These long-headed statesmen had no illusion that our people enjoyed biological or psychological or sociological immunities from the hazards of concentrated power. It is absurd to see a dictator in a representative product of the sturdy democratic traditions of the Mississippi Valley. The accretion of dangerous power does not come in a day. It does come, however slowly, from the generative force of unchecked disregard of the restrictions that fence in even the most disinterested assertion of authority.

And, indeed, it was "the generative force of unchecked disregard of the restrictions that fence in even the most disinterested assertion of authority" that faced the nation with the crisis of Watergate.

The strongest and weightiest opinion in the *Steel Seizure Case* was written by Justice Jackson.[15] Because of his experience as a member of the executive branch under President Roosevelt, he was given to weighing such experience more heavily than he would Black's commitment to the language of the Constitution, or Frankfurter's commitment to what Jackson termed "doctrine and legal fiction." But even he, who, when Attorney General, wrote a book in which he had chastised the Court for allowing the Constitution to interfere with the administration of government,[16] reached the same conclusion as Black and Frankfurter as to the necessity for confining each branch to its proper role. It was "checks and balances" more than "separation of powers" that guided his decision:[17]

> The actual art of governing under our Constitution does not and cannot conform to judicial definitions of the power of any of its branches based on isolated clauses or even single Articles torn from context. While the Constitution diffuses power the better to secure liberty, it also contemplates that practice will integrate the dispersed powers into a workable government. It enjoins upon its branches separateness but interdependence, autonomy but reciprocity. Presidential powers are not fixed but fluctuate, depending upon their disjunction or conjunction with those of Congress. We may well begin by a somewhat over-simplified grouping of practical situations in which a President may doubt, or others may challenge, his powers, and by distinguishing roughly the legal consequences of this factor of relativity.

> 1. When the President acts pursuant to an express or implied authorization of Congress, his authority is at its maximum, for it includes all that he possesses in his own right plus all that Congress can delegate. In these circumstances, and in these only, may he be said (for what it may be worth) to personify the federal sovereignty. If his act is held unconstitutional under these circumstances, it usually means that the Federal Government as an undivided whole lacks power. . . .
>
> 2. When the President acts in absence of either a congressional grant or denial of authority, he can only rely upon his own independent powers, but there is a zone of twilight in which he and Congress may have concurrent authority, or in which its distribution is uncertain. Therefore, congressional inertia, indifference or quiescence may sometimes, at least as a practical matter, enable, if not invite, measures on independent presidential responsibility. In this area, any actual test of power is likely to depend on the imperatives of events and contemporary imponderables rather than on abstract theories of law.
>
> 3. When the President takes measures incompatible with the expressed or implied will of Congress, his power is at its lowest ebb, for then he can rely only upon his own constitutional powers minus any constitutional powers of Congress over the matter. Courts can sustain exclusive presidential control in such a case only by disabling the Congress from acting upon the subject. Presidential claim to a power at once so conclusive and preclusive must be scrutinized with caution, for what is at stake is the equilibrium established by our constitutional system.

Jackson also met and rejected the argument of necessity, that emergency situations license the executive to meet them as he sees fit:[18]

> In view of the ease, expedition and safety with which Congress can grant and has granted large emergency powers, certainly ample to embrace this crisis, I am quite unimpressed with the argument that we should affirm possession of them without statute. Such power either has no beginning or it has no end. If it exists, it need submit to no legal restraint. I am not alarmed that it would plunge us straightway into dictatorship, but it is at least a step in that wrong direction.
>
> . . . The Constitution does not disclose the measure of the actual controls wielded by the modern presidential office. That instrument must be understood as an Eighteenth-Century sketch of a government hoped for, not as a blueprint of the Government that is. Vast accretions of federal power, eroded from that reserved by the States, have magnified the scope of presidential activity. Subtle shifts take place in the centers of real power that do not show on the face of the Constitution.

Executive power has the advantage of concentration in a single head in whose choice the whole Nation has a part, making him the focus of public hopes and expectations. In drama, magnitude and finality his decisions so far overshadow any others that almost alone he fills the public eye and ear. No other personality in public life can begin to compete with him in access to the public mind through modern methods of communications. By his prestige as head of state and his influence upon public opinion he exerts a leverage upon those who are supposed to check and balance his power which often cancels their effectiveness.

Moreover, rise of the party system has made a significant extra-constitutional supplement to real executive power. No appraisal of his necessities is realistic which overlooks that he heads a political system as well as a legal system. Party loyalties and interests, sometimes more binding than law, extend his effective control into branches of government other than his own and he often may win, as a political leader, what he cannot command under the Constitution. . . . I cannot be brought to believe that this country will suffer if the Court refuses further to aggrandize the presidential office, already so potent and so relatively immune from judicial review, at the expense of Congress.

But I have no illusion that any decision by this Court can keep power in the hands of Congress if it is not wise and timely in meeting its problems. A crisis that challenges the President equally, or perhaps primarily, challenges Congress. If not good law, there was worldly wisdom in the maxim attributed to Napoleon that "The tools belong to the man who can use them." We may say that power to legislate for emergencies belongs in the hands of Congress, but only Congress itself can prevent power from slipping through its fingers.

The essence of our free Government is "leave to live by no man's leave, underneath the law"—to be governed by those impersonal forces which we call law. Our Government is fashioned to fulfill this concept so far as humanly possible. The Executive, except for recommendation and veto, has no legislative power. . . . With all its defects, delays and inconveniences, men have discovered no technique for long preserving free government except that the Executive be under the law, and that the law be made by parliamentary deliberations.

Such institutions may be destined to pass away. But it is the duty of the Court to be last, not first, to give them up.

At least as of a quarter-century ago, it was clear that, whether on the premises of constitutional language, which were Black's, on the premises of constitutional doctrine, which were Frankfurter's, or on the premises of the realities of free government, which were Jackson's, the

Court rejected the concept of the "plebiscitary Presidency," the investment of the sovereignty of the nation in the chief executive.

Even if the validity of the '"plebiscitary Presidency" is rejected, however, there remains the question what actions taken by Nixon as charged by Schlesinger are innovations in presidential government to support the proposition that Nixon "was heading toward a new balance of constitutional powers, an audacious and imaginative reconstruction of the American Constitution." For it would seem that the catalog of usurpations stated by Schlesinger reveal no exercises of presidential authority not performed by Nixon's predecessors in office. A review of each of the charges would be too cumbersome for inclusion here. Examples suffice to show that Nixon was not an innovator but a follower in the untoward expansion of the presidential office.

Thus, with reference to Nixon's appropriation of the war-making power it is certainly most difficult to charge him with assuming authority not exercised by his predecessors. The Vietnam War was initiated by President Kennedy with full knowledge that it must expand if even a small military force were sent to aid the South Vietnamese.[19] And it was President Johnson who elevated the Vietnam expedition into a full-blown war, without congressional approval and, indeed, with misrepresentations to both the people and the Congress of what was going on, the most notorious of these incidents being that which called forth the Tonkin Bay Resolution.[20] President Truman brought the country into the Korean War without so much as a "by your leave" to Congress. Eisenhower invaded Lebanon. Abraham D. Sofaer has recently published a diligent, scholarly study of many similar presidential actions in our earliest history.[21]

At the time of the Korean "police action," a letter appeared in the *New York Times* defending it against attack by Senator Robert A. Taft:[22]

> Senator Taft in his speech on Jan. 5 made the flat statement that President Truman "had no authority whatever to commit American troops to Korea without consulting Congress and without Congressional approval"; and, further, that he "has no power to agree to send American troops to fight in Europe in a war between the members of the Atlantic Pact and Soviet Russia." When he sent troops to Korea, Senator Taft continued, "the President simply usurped authority, in violation of the laws and the Constitution."
>
> Senator Taft's statements are demonstrably irresponsible. The public is entitled to know what provisions of the law or of the Constitution have been violated by President Truman in sending troops overseas. From the day that President Jefferson ordered Commodore Dale and two-thirds of the American Navy into the Mediterranean to repel the Barbary pirates American Presidents have repeatedly

> committed American armed forces abroad without prior Congressional consultation or approval.
>
> . . . .
>
> Until Senator Taft and his friends succeed in rewriting American history according to their own specifications these facts must stand as obstacles to their efforts to foist off their current political prejudices as eternal American verities.

The author of that letter was Arthur Schlesinger. He did not stand alone in this position. For another, Henry Steele Commager argued the same point.[23]

None of this relieves Nixon of the fact that he, too, carried on a war —indeed, secretly extended it into Cambodia—as though Congress did not exist, often lying or telling half-truths both to Congress and to the people. And, perhaps, it should be noted that both Johnson and Truman surrendered their party's hold on the presidency because of the furor created by their warmaking activities. But it remains the fact that Nixon did not conceive or create this abuse of presidential power; he had a long line of precedents.

Nixon's pique at the rejection by the Senate of his Supreme Court nominations of Judges Carswell and Haynsworth, which resulted in his statement that the Senate confirmation should have been *pro forma*,[24] hardly rises to the action of a "plebiscitary Presidency." Nor did his efforts to secure a Supreme Court of his own persuasion, for which Franklin Roosevelt had set such an excellent example.[25]

Nixon's refusal to deliver data to the Congress at its demand was hardly an innovation,[26] although it was probably the first time data was denied to a House impeachment inquiry. But, then, it was the first time such a committee had made such a demand. And the Supreme Court did conclude, for the first time, that there was such a thing as a constitutionally derived executive privilege, albeit a conditional one, not assertable against a criminal court subpoena, however effective it may still prove to be against congressional demands.[27]

Nixon's calculated disparagement of the Cabinet is, again, hardly new. The Cabinet is not a constitutional office or body. The dismissal of cabinet officers who refused to do the President's bidding is of ancient vintage, never so clearly exercised as by President Jackson when he had to fire two secretaries of the Treasury, Louis McLane and William J. Duane, to get one, Roger B. Taney, who would remove the government's deposits from the Bank of the United States. The Cabinet has long since ceased to be an advisory body or one, like its namesake in Great Britain, where government policy is debated and resolved by the taking of opinions.

Of course, where the Cabinet is made up of individuals with independent political bases on which the President must rely, their powers in policy-making could be real. Even so, Roosevelt, for example, managed to go around, over, or through Cordell Hull and to rely on others, including the Under Secretary of State, for advice on foreign affairs. It was in 1948 that Edward Corwin wrote:[28]

> The truth is that the Cabinet has in our day become of negligible importance in the determination of national policy. Why is this? Doubtless the personal element has often operated to depress the Cabinet's role in the policy field. But when so variable a factor repeatedly produces the same result there must be an underlying constant factor at work.
>
> The Cabinet is of negligible influence in the shaping of broad governmental policies because it is composed of men whose principal business is that of administration and who, consequently, even when they are not administrative experts at the outset, are required to become such. Unfortunately, an expert in a particular area of governmental activity is not likely to possess the breadth of outlook which is most desirable in a political adviser, or the time or inclination to interest himself in the problems of other departments or of the country at large.
>
> So true is this, that Dr. Don K. Price, a competent critic, has recently expressed the opinion that even as an agency for the development of a unified executive policy among its own members, the Cabinet has today "become an administrative anachronism."

The Nixon Cabinet and his treatment of it is probably the least vulnerable to attack of any of the charges against his undue assertion of power. Harold Laski properly put the role of the American Cabinet in the same category of limited importance:[29]

> While it is true that it has attracted men of the first eminence, like Jefferson and Hamilton, into its ranks, it has rarely been an effective team, and its formal subordination to the president has meant that it has never been, in a really continuous way, a policy-making body. The president may or may not consult it, as he chooses; he may or may not compose it of men of national standing.

Nixon chose not to consult his Cabinet and chose, with few exceptions, not to "compose it of men of national standing." But the discretion was legitimately his, whichever way he chose to exercise it. Not within the memory of living Americans has the Cabinet played a substantial part in the governance of the nation, except through the administrative roles of heads of departments, for which constitutional provision exists.

Similarly with the charge that Nixon "carefully organized concentration of federal management in the White House." The Office of the

White House was not a Nixon creation; it derived from Franklin D. Roosevelt's reorganization plan.[30] In 1960, Louis Koenig described the advising process in the White House:[31]

> Modern-day Presidents normally surround themselves with sizable numbers of people endowed with skills, information and convictions, which will give purpose and substance to their administrations. Through counsel and action, these people provide assistance in all realms of the presidential office: in party and legislative affairs, in public relations, in dealings with the executive departments, in every conceivable sort of policy-making. Some of these assistants operate as free-ranging individualities; others function under the aegis of bureaus or committees, or out of positions whose duties and authority are officially designated. It is useful to visualize these various assistants who grace the modern-day White House scene as a series of concentric circles rotating around the President. This bit of symbolism is as meaningful nowadays as in Washington's time, only there are more people and more circles.
>
> At the center of the present-day circles is the White House staff, a modest corps of intimate personal assistants. Appointed without reference to the Senate, the staff are the President's own hired hands who help analyze and refine the problems injected unremittingly into the White House by the busy conveyor belts from the world outside. The staff also manage the considerable office routine of letter and memoranda writing, filing and record-keeping. . . .
>
> Over the years, the White House staff, which was not officially designated as such until 1939, grew slowly. Even as late as Herbert Hoover's day, it numbered only three secretaries, a military and naval aide, and two-score clerks. F.D.R. added six administrative assistants and . . . considerably expanded the clerical force. President Truman superimposed another layer on the growing structure by creating "The Assistant to the President." In Eisenhower's day, Sherman Adams, who bore and fully lived up to this title, managed a White House staff of approximately 250 employees, including the traditional press and appointments secretaries, the clerical force—many of whom date from the somnolent days of paper cuffs and roll-top desks—and a small galaxy of specialists in atomic energy, disarmament, foreign trade and aid, national security and the like.

Under the presidencies of Kennedy, Johnson, and Nixon, the White House staff more than doubled and President Carter has not seriously diminished this number, in spite of talk about reducing the size of the White House bureaucracy. At last count the Carter White House staff numbered 590. In the Roosevelt, Truman, Eisenhower, Kennedy, Johnson, Nixon, and Ford administrations, the assistants to the President and other members of the White House staff became assistant presidents, assuming control and disposition of matters submitted for presidential decision. They issued orders at their own discretion to departmental chiefs and even lesser bureaucrats in the executive branch. Under Nixon, this circle was not merely a source of advice and analysis, it became a force that closed off the President from access by all other government officials, and the President from access to others than the White House staff. The *sanctum sanctorum* of the Oval Office became a reality during the time of the Nixon presidency.

The concept of concentric circles quickly brings to mind Dante's imagery of hell. But, whatever its connotations, it is clear that it is a conception totally inconsistent with the expectations of the founders. As Alexander Bickel wrote:[32]

> Consent will not long be yielded to faceless officials, or to mere servants of one man, who themselves have no "connexion with the interest of the people." In opposing [George III's] cant of "not men, but measures," Burke therefore resisted rule by non-party ministers who lacked the confidence of the Commons. By the same token we may today oppose excessive White House staff-government by private men whom Congress never sees. It was not for nothing that the American Constitution provided for "executive Departments" and for Senate confirmation of the appointments of great officers of state.

We need not rely on Bickel's retrospective judgment on the intent of the framers. Heretofore, I have cited the revolutionists' abhorrence for the "corruption of the Constitution," the English constitution, that was reflected in the abandonment of the "balanced government" thought necessary to prevent tyrannic rule.[33] James Wilson also told us, contemporaneously with the adoption of the Constitution, of that document's rejection of government by executive counselors:[34]

> In one important particular—the unity of the executive power—the constitution of the United States stands on an equal footing with that of Great Britain. In one respect, the provision is much more efficacious.
>
> The British throne is surrounded by counsellors. With regard to their authority, a profound and mysterious silence is observed. One effect, we know, they produce; and we conceive it to be a very pernicious one. Between power and responsibility, they interpose an impenetrable barrier. Who possesses the executive power? The king. When its baneful emanations fly over the land; who are responsible for the mischief? His ministers. Amidst their multitude, and the secrecy, with which business, especially that of a perilous kind, is transacted, it will be often difficult to select the culprits; still more so, to punish them. The criminality will be diffused and blended with so much variety and intricacy, that it will be almost impossible to

ascertain to how many it extends, and what particular share should be assigned to each.

But let us trace this subject a little further. Though the power of the king's counsellors is not, as far as I can discover, defined or described in the British constitution; yet their seats are certainly provided for some purpose, and filled with some effect. What is wanting in authority may be supplied by intrigue; and, in the place of constitutional influence may be substituted that subtle ascendency, which is acquired and preserved by deeply dissembled obsequiousness. To so many arts, secret, unceasing, and well directed, can we suppose that a prince, in whose disposition is found any thing weak, indolent, or accommodating, will not be frequently induced to yield? Hence springs the evils of a partial, an indecisive, and a disjointed administration.

In the United States, our first executive magistrate is not obnubilated behind the mysterious obscurity of counsellors. Power is communicated to him with liberality, though with ascertained limitations. To him the provident or improvident use of it is to be ascribed. For the first, he will have and deserve undivided applause. For the last, he will be subjected to censure; if necessary, to punishment. He is the dignified, but accountable magistrate of a free and great people.

Once again, however, we do not have Nixon as the inventor of a device for the attainment of the "plebiscitary Presidency," but only its extrapolator. The opponents of the Roosevelt plan for the reorganization of the White House anticipated the evils of the present form of the White House Office. Their views were derided as a phantasm of imaginary evils. Those imaginary evils have turned out to be real ones. But they neither originated with Nixon, nor have they disappeared with his disappearance from office.

Surely, too, Nixon's relationships with the fourth estate were accurately described by Schlesinger as "calculated discrediting of the press." It was an enmity between the press and the presidency that has also had its precedents.

Writing of Thomas Jefferson, Leonard Levy said:[35]

By the time he left the presidency, a much wiser and embittered man, so convinced was he that the press was hopelessly abandoned to falsehoods and licentiousness—epithetical standards relinquished by libertarian theorists—that he professed to believe that it was doing more harm to the nation than would result from suppression. "I deplore, with you," he wrote to a correspondent, "the putrid state into which our newspapers have passed, and the malignity, the vulgarity, and mendacious spirit of those who write for them; and I enclose you a recent sample . . . as a proof of the abyss of degradation into which we have fallen. These ordures," he exclaimed—forgetting that the press mirrored American culture and the people whom he professed, in moments of intellectual isolation, to trust—"are rapidly depraving the public taste, and lessening its relish for sound food. As vehicles of information, and a curb on our functionaries, they have rendered themselves useless, by forfeiting all title to belief." The violence and malignity of party spirit, he thought, was the cause of the press's fall from grace.

The history of the New Deal is a history of conflict between Roosevelt and the press. While Kennedy like other Presidents had his media favorites, paid with presidential inside information, he too had a running battle with at least some of the media. If Johnson watched three television sets at one time, it was not out of affection for the newscasting, but to deplore its content. If there is presidential paranoia in this relationship, it is not without cause. While Roosevelt could go over the heads of the Congress to the people through the medium of radio, the medium of television has gone over the heads of the Congress and the President to the people.

Television has tended to destroy Congress by ignoring it, or by so selecting those aspects of its business for broadcast as to make it impotent in its conflict with the President, any President. Douglass Cater has written of all journalism:[36]

> Communications media have a vast power to shape government—both its policies and its leaders. This is not an editorial-page power. It is the power to select—out of the tens of thousands of words spoken in Washington each day and the tens of dozens of events—which words and events are projected for mankind to see. Equally powerful is the media's capacity to ignore; those words and events that fail to get projected might as well not have occurred.

Surely the case can be made out that there were Nixon administration threats to the freedom of the press. The defenders of the press "pointed to the administration's suggestions that public concern about media bias would lead to demands for antitrust action, its repeated complaints about news distortion, its wiretapping of journalists, the wave of subpoenas commanding journalists to testify about news sources, the thinly veiled threats to make political use of the FCC's power of licensing broadcasters, and the FBI investigation of CBS news correspondent Daniel Schorr."[37]

But it was not only the Nixon government that regarded the press as its adversary. The "new journalism" that eschewed objectivity in favor of "Truth" also came to regard the government as the enemy and fashioned their TV and newspaper stories accordingly:[38]

> Daniel Moynihan . . . decried in a widely read article what he regarded as the systematic hostility of journalists in the national media

to the institution of the presidency. He ascribed much of this hostility to the fact that the national media "thought to improve itself by recruiting more and more persons from middle- and upper-class backgrounds and trained at the universities associated with such groups." Moynihan contended that these recruits from the "adversary culture" infused their elitist, anti-Establishment attitudes into the national media. The muckraking heritage of American journalism, which in the past had been a small part of the overall tradition, has been inflated by dramatic instances of government deceit into a general attitude that exposing the seamy side of official acts is the optimum in successful reporting. Moynihan claimed that the result was a decline in journalistic objectivity, a harmful condition that is worsened by the absence of any tradition of self-correction in the American press.

Yes, Nixon abused the press and, implicitly or explicitly, threatened it with illegal sanctions. His stand was more forceful than Kennedy's cancellation of White House subscriptions to the now-defunct *Herald-Tribune*. But it must also be conceded that the press has abused a presidency that it always opposed. Its complaint that Nixon refused to confide in it can hardly be regarded as evidence of a failure to confine the presidency within appropriate bounds. Had he done otherwise, he would surely have been accused of attempting to manipulate the press.

The press regards itself as the governor of our government. So long as it insists on playing this role, it should be clear that we have almost as much to fear from an imperial press as we have to fear from an imperial presidency. Both have the capacity to reduce government to the agency of a single group, in a society with a government that was framed to respond to a multiplicity of organized and unorganized constituencies. It is, perhaps, unfortunate that it was Spiro Agnew who made the point that the spokesmen for the media were elected by none and represent none other than themselves. The fact remains that the voices of the Associated Press, and the United Press International, of A.B.C., N.B.C., and C.B.S., sound like but a single voice, not only in the editorial positions that they espouse but in the selection of news that they choose to publish and the way it is presented. And when the *New York Times*, the *Washington Post*, the *Los Angeles Times*, *Time* magazine, and *Newsweek* speak with that same voice—all in opposition to presidential government—as they certainly did during the Nixon era, his paranoia is understandable, even if his actions were indefensible.

Until the press returns to some concept of objectivity—the duty to tell the facts, all of the facts, and nothing but the facts—the First Amendment may continue to guarantee its freedom but not its responsibility. It may be hard for the viewer or reader or listener to distinguish fact from opinion, but that should be within the competence of a press with professional standards. The modern-day media, however, must be recognized as the inheritors of the partisan traditions of eighteenth- and nineteenth-century journalism, except that then each newspaper represented a different faction, whereas now they all seem to represent a single faction. The modern problem of the press lies primarily not in its editorializing but in its news reporting.

None of this affords a defense of Nixon's treatment of the press. An "imperial president," however, would not choose to destroy the press's freedom by threatening it, but rather by co-opting it, as the Kennedy administration almost succeeded in doing. Surely an approving press is a better ally for a "plebiscitary Presidency" than an adversary press. If Nixon failed to realize that and work toward it, however, it revealed only more bad judgment on his part and not an absence of cupidity for illegitimate power.

Schlesinger also complained of Nixon's arrogation of authority in "his unilateral determination of social priorities." Certainly this is an important element in the "plebiscitary Presidency." Equally certain is that this was not an innovation on the part of Nixon. Thus, for example, Richard Neustadt wrote of Eisenhower's "unilateral determination of social priorities" in approving terms:[39]

> Early in 1954, President Dwight D. Eisenhower presented to the Congress—and the country and his party—some 65 proposals for new legislation, over and above appropriations. . . .
>
> Throughout, one theme was emphasized: here was a comprehensive and coordinated inventory of the nation's current legislative needs, reflecting the President's own judgments, choices, and priorities in every major area of Federal action; in short, his "legislative program," an entity distinctive and defined, its coverage and its omissions, both, delimiting his stand across the board. . . .
>
> Thus, one year after his inaugural, Eisenhower espoused a sweeping concept of the President's initiative in legislation and an elaborate mechanism for its public expression; developments which no one seemed to take amiss. Both in governmental circles and in the press, the whole performance was regarded almost as a matter of course, a normal White House response to the opening of Congress. The pattern, after all, was quite familiar; the comprehensive program expressed in ordered sequence, with some sort of publicized preliminaries and detailed follow-up, had been an annual enterprise in Truman's time. Indeed, while Eisenhower had undoubtedly improved upon the earlier mechanics, his 1954 procedure seemed expressive less of innovation than of reversion to accustomed practice.
>
> . . . .
>
> Traditionally, there has been a tendency to distinguish "strong" Presidents from "weak," depending on their exercise of the initiative

in legislation. The personal appearances in the hall of the House, the special messages, the drafted bills, the public appeals, so characteristic of contemporary program presentation, have all been represented in the past—no farther back than Franklin Roosevelt's time—as signs of a President's intention or capacity to "dominate" the Congress. If these were once relevant criteria of domination, they are not so today. As things stand now they have become part of the regular routines of office, an accepted elaboration of the constitutional right to recommend; as such, no more indicative of presidential domination than the veto power, say, in Herbert Hoover's time.

Once again we see that the tools for the execution of the "plebiscitary Presidency" were not Nixon creations. Nixon revealed not a capacity for innovation but only a capacity for imitation. What he did do was to utilize devices created by predecessors, who used them sparingly, while he used them persistently; who used them in isolation, while he used them in combination; who used them unsuccessfully,[40] while he used them successfully, until they failed him in the end.

He was an innovator, however, in a way that showed less imitation of his presidential predecessors than of governors of less democratic nations. He created a presidential, political police force; he rejected the basic concept of Anglo-American political freedom, the rule of law. And he effected both these changes in American political tradition—deeply imbedded in the Constitution—through the device of the White House Office.

Voltaire recognized even before the American Revolution, that "Liberty consists of dependence on nothing but law."[41] "When he went to England, he tells us, it was in order to go 'to enjoy in a free country the greatest benefit I know, and humanity's most glorious right, which is to depend only on men's *laws and not on their whims.*' "[42] "This then is the foundation of Voltaire's political ideas: law, born of justice and reason, is the basis of a civilised society."[43] And here Voltaire was consistent with the constitutional jurisprudence that was emerging in his time in English political theory and American practice.

Nixon's creation of the White House political police and the perversion of the security agencies to his political needs did not derive from a desire to be perverse, or even from dreams of glory. They were evoked by fear, the fear of the marchers on Washington, of the despoilers of universities, of the burners of cities, of the bombers, many of whom he correctly regarded as the scions of the eastern establishment.[44] Revolution invokes suppression; force is met by force; conspiracy responds to conspiracy. Nixon did not act here, he reacted. And his reaction took the form of a lawlessness no less reprehensible—certainly more reprehensible because of his office—than the lawlessness he was seeking to put down. As Justice Jackson once told us: "Security is like liberty in that many are the crimes committed in its name."[45] Worse, in Nixon's case, he undertook to substitute himself and his personal staff for the police and the courts to determine what conduct he thought deserved sanction because he disapproved of it, not because it was illegal. "L'etat, c'est moi."

Nixon's primary Watergate evils consist of his violations of the rule of law as we and our common law brethren have come to know it. Dicey's classic statement of the English constitution summarizes the first two of the three essentials of the rule of law in this way:[46]

> It means, in the first place, the absolute supremacy or predominance of regular law as opposed to the influence of arbitrary power, and excludes the existence of arbitrariness, or prerogative, or even of wide discretionary authority on the part of the government. . . .
>
> It means, again, equality before the law, or the equal subjection of all classes to the ordinary law of the land administered by the ordinary law courts; the "rule of law" in this sense excludes the idea of any exemption of officials or others from the duty of obedience to the law which governs other citizens or from the jurisdiction of the ordinary tribunals.

Nixon violated the rule of law to make war on a large part of the presidential constituency. It will be remembered that King Charles was charged with subverting the "fundamental laws of the land" and confounding "the liberties and the property of England."[47] And as C. V. Wedgwood has said:[48]

> The King's friends might argue that the King had made war only in defence of his rights. But, rightly or wrongly, *he had made war on his subjects*, and in the crudest possible manner this was a violation of the fundamental bond between him and his people.

There are some who are concerned that Nixon's actions be recognized, not only as unconstitutional and illegal, but as immoral, and uniquely immoral:[49]

> There is something unresolved in our attitude toward him. A major source of this anxiety is that we have never been able to answer the question of the extent to which Nixon, elected by us, is made in our image. . . . This is why the term "Nixon-haters" still carries a sting; this is why allegations—no matter how clumsily put forth, or how righteously used as a justification—that Nixonian ethics have for a long time guided people in power are so unsettling. . . . [W]e have an imperative need to reach back into ourselves for some sense of principle by which to measure and judge him—by which to distinguish ourselves from him. We need to know whether such a sense of principle really exists. We are still not sure whether it is just Nixon

> who is morally bankrupt or the culture at large, and so we are compelled to test ourselves against Nixon in order to find out.

Theirs is essentially a plea for absolution by those who would themselves indulge illegalities and unconstitutionalities in the deep-seated belief that they, but not Nixon, are entitled to exemption from legal sanctions because of a call to respond to a higher law.

Surely there is a difference between law and ethics or morality. Again, Justice Jackson spoke to the point, if in a different context:[50]

> We should not forget that criminality is one thing—a matter of law—and that morality, ethics and religious teachings are another. Their relations have puzzled the best of men. Assassination, for example, whose criminality no one doubts, has been the subject of serious debate as to its morality. This does not make crime less criminal, but it shows on what treacherous grounds we tread when we undertake to translate ethical concepts into legal ones, case by case. We usually end up by condemning all that we personally disapprove and for no better reason than that we disapprove it. In fact, what better reason is there?

It should be recognized, however, that in an open society there is a moral duty to obey the law. Acts committed with political motivations are not the less criminal because of such motivations, but they cannot be made into crimes because of those motives. And certainly, whatever the moral justifications for civil disobedience, the narrow nature of the legitimacy of that concept must be kept in mind. Civil disobedience does not encompass the violation of law as a means of protest. At most it justifies disobedience of a particular law the validity of which it seeks to challenge and test both against legal norms and community standards. Civil disobedience cannot encompass violations of other laws as a form of protest against the law sought to be challenged.

Certainly civil disobedience affords no justification for violation of the laws by government officials. They cannot hold office under an oath to support the Constitution and laws of the United States and, at the same time, assert a right to violate the Constitution and the laws. As Professor Bickel put it:[51]

> There is a moral duty, and there ought to be, for those to whom it is applicable—most often officers of government—to obey the manifest constitution, unless and until it is altered by the amendment process it itself provides for, a duty analogous to the duty to obey final judicial decrees. No president may decide to stay in office for a term of six years rather than four, or, since the Twenty-second Amendment, to run for a third term. There is an absolute duty to obey; to disobey is to deny the idea of constitutionalism, that special

> kind of law which establishes a set of pre-existing rules within which society works out all its other rules from time to time. To deny this idea is in the most fundamental sense to deny the idea of law itself.

It was the denial of "the idea of law itself" that was Nixon's most egregious offense. And none need seek further than his own words to establish his guilt. His incapacity to understand the enormity of his proposition, "When the President does it, that means that it is not illegal," reflects immorality as well as paranoia. And it is this that none of his defenders can discount. It is this that justifies the removal of a president no less than of a king. It is the ultimate rejection of the validity of this rationale that will prevent the American president from becoming Louis Heren's twelfth-century English king or Orwell's "Big Brother."

Bickel, in imitation of Burke, said:[52]

> In order to survive, be coherent and stable, and answer to men's wants, a civil society had to rest on a foundation of moral values. Else it degenerated—if an oligarchy, into interest government, a government of jobbers enriching themselves and their friends, and ended in revolution; or if a full democracy, into a mindless, shameless thing, freely oppressing various minorities and ruining itself.

The Nixon administration partook of both dangers, tending toward a government of jobbers at the same time that it sought to create majority rule without minority rights. "Any true believer will want total power to achieve the true ends of government, and will be a democrat or an authoritarian depending, as Burke said, on which scheme or system he thinks will bring him nearer to total power."[53]

Nixon and his White House Office were guilty of reaching for "total power" in a constitutional state that recognized the need for dispersing and not concentrating governmental authority. Nixon and his White House Office were guilty of "corrupting the Constitution." And, if that is not a "high Crime and Misdemeanor," it should be. The lesson still to be learned, however, is that the Constitution abhors a benevolent despot no less than a malevolent one. As we continue to keep watch on our government, we should do well not to forget the equality of the rule of law that denies arbitrary power to those we like no less than those we dislike. We forget this—as we tended to forgive it in some of our earlier Presidents—at our peril. It remains true that "the price of liberty is eternal vigilance."

There are many possible inferences to be derived from the constitutional aspects of the Watergate affair. One attitude is that of the generation of the "counter-culture." It has been stated by Charles L. Mee in his recent book *A Visit to Haldeman and Other States of Mind*:[54]

> The ruins of our Republic lie about us, like shards of some other ancient dead civilization. . . .
>
> Dare we admit that we did not at first notice? That it died when no one was looking, and we scarcely missed it for days or, it may even be, for years? We only first noticed it, reluctantly, wishing not to see, when Nixon buggered the works, and then buggered those who went after him, a Bulgar holding out against the hordes until at last, unimpeachable, he was told he must step down—not by Congress and not by the courts but by four-star General Haig in a pinch play with Bad Kissinger, and then—oh, God, where is our sense of shame?—pardoned by his handpicked successor for crimes he protested he did not commit. We said it proved the Republic worked, but we knew that Republics are not saved when their constitutional usages are forgotten or avoided and salvation depends upon the accidents of a tape recording machine and the wits of a four-star general. Machiavelli could not do justice to this theme. Shakespeare's Richard II could not weep copiously enough. We watched it play itself out, with the nerves of dead men in a dead Republic.

Was Mee wrong in his judgment? An alternative is the reading long since given, years before the events of Watergate, by a scholar-historian, Charles H. McIlwain:[55]

> If the history of our constitutional past teaches anything, it seems to indicate that the mutual suspicions of reformers and constitutionalists . . . must be ended if we are to keep and enlarge the liberties for which our ancestors fought. Liberals must become more constitutional than some of them are, constitutionalists must become more liberal than most of them have been. We cannot get the needed redress of injustices and abuses without reform, and we can never make these reforms lasting and effective unless we reduce them to the orderly processes of law. . . .
>
> We live under a written constitution which classifies some things under *jurisdictio*, as legal fundamentals, . . . while it leaves other matters to the free discretion of the organs of positive government it has created. The distribution of these matters between *jurisdictio* and *gubernaculum*, made so many years ago, is of course in constant need of revision by interpretation or by amendment. . . . But the surest safeguard of a proper balance between the *jurisdictio* and the *gubernaculum*—and that even in a government *of* the people as well as *for* them—would seem to consist in some such constitution containing some such distribution. There is the problem of restriction and the problem of responsibility, and practical politics involves their interrelation. . . . The people have now replaced the king in these political matters of government; but even in a popular state, such as we trust ours is, the problem of law *versus* will remains the most

> important of all practical problems. . . . The two fundamental correlative elements of constitutionalism for which all lovers of liberty must yet fight are the legal limits to arbitrary power and a complete political responsibility of government to the governed.

Scholarly historians have seldom made good prophets. The prophecies of the counterculture of the sixties reveal only self-indulgence. Both share responsibility for the crisis of the imperial presidency. The former because of their advocacy of the desirability of presidential power; the latter because their nihilism and tactics contributed so largely to the reaction that was Watergate.

Surely there can be no return to the Jeffersonian idyll, but the Hamiltonian king has not yet been ensconced. The question is how many Americans are still, or may be persuaded to become, adherents of the "vital center" and of the rule of reason based on experience, both of which guided the Founding Fathers to the framing of a Constitution that we still purport to follow. It was the poet Yeats who warned us against the events certain to overtake us when "the centre cannot hold."[56] It was the artist Goya who graphically portrayed the consequences of the abandonment of reason in one of his etchings inscribed, "The sleep of reason brings forth monsters."[57]

There is yet hope. "And hope is brightest when it dawns from fears."[58] It is not fear of particular events, but fear of the corruption of the Constitution that should now provide us the motivating force for hope. "The greatest dangers to liberty lurk in insidious encroachment by men of zeal, well-meaning but without understanding."[59]

Notes

Chapter One. By Way of Introduction

1. "Out damned spot! out, I say! One; two, why, then, 'tis time to do't. Hell is murky! Fie, my lord, fie! a soldier, and afeard? What need we fear who knows it, when none can call our power to account? Yet who would have thought the old man to have had so much blood in him?" Shakespeare, Macbeth, act V, sc. i.
2. Kipnis, The Powerholders 169 (1976).
3. Roberts, Frankfurter, and Jackson, JJ., in Screws v. United States, 325 U.S. 91, 160 (1945).
4. Frankfurter, J., concurring in Youngstown Sheet & Tube Co. v. Sawyer, 343 U.S. 579, 594 (1952).
5. Radcliffe, The Problem of Power 100 (1952 ed.).
6. Myers v. United States, 272 U.S. 52, 293 (1926).
7. Commager, The Defeat of America 157–58 (1976 ed.).
8. Complete Poems of Keats and Shelley 817 (Mod. Lib. ed.).
9. Hazlitt, Political Essays 163 (1819).
10. Tolstoi, The Kingdom of God Is within You 250 (1894).
11. The Federalist 27 (John Harvard Library ed. 1961).
12. The Law School of The University of Chicago, Conference on Freedom and the Law 74 (1953).
13. The Federalist No. 43.
14. The Federalist No. 49.
15. *Ibid.*
16. *Ibid.*
17. See Hand, The Bill of Rights (1958).
18. 297 U.S. 1, 62–63 (1936).
19. 1 Cranch 137 (1803).
20. Black, A Constitutional Faith 8, 10 (1968).
21. McCulloch v. Maryland, 4 Wheat. 400, 421 (1819).
22. Black, note 20 *supra*, at 9–10.

23. KURLAND, ed., FELIX FRANKFURTER ON THE SUPREME COURT 336–37 (1970).
24. *Id.* at 504.
25. See Black, J., dissenting, in Adamson v. California, 332 U.S. 46, 70 (1947).
26. See POLANYI & PROSCH, MEANING (1975).
27. ADDRESSES AND PAPERS OF CHARLES EVANS HUGHES 139 (1908).
28. THE THREE FACES OF POWER vii–viii (1967).
29. *Id.* at 3.
30. Quoted in MASON, HARLAN FISKE STONE: PILLAR OF THE LAW 331 (1956).
31. *Id.* at 421.
32. Powell, *Commerce, Pensions, and Codes, II*, 49 HARV. L. REV. 193, 238 (1935).
33. PLATO, REPUBLIC, bk. 5, p. 458 (Jowett trans. 1908).

Chapter Two. THE CONGRESSIONAL POWER OF INQUIRY

1. BERGER, EXECUTIVE PRIVILEGE: A CONSTITUTIONAL MYTH (1974).
2. HAMILTON, THE POWER TO PROBE xii–xv (1976).
3. KEETON, TRIAL BY TRIBUNAL 12 (1960).
4. *Id.* at 21–22.
5. See BRYANT, SAMUEL PEPYS: THE YEARS OF PERIL (1935).
6. KEETON, note 3 *supra*, at 23–24.
7. See BOLINGBROKE, HISTORICAL WRITINGS xii (Kramnick ed. 1972); Kurland, *The Colonies, the Parliament, and the Crown: The Constitutional Issues*, in JONES, ed., POLITICAL SEPARATION AND LEGAL CONTINUITY 43, 69 n.13 (1976).
8. 1 PLUMB, SIR ROBERT WALPOLE 215 (1956).
9. 2 *id. passim.*
10. BERGER, note 1 *supra*, at 35.
11. 2 FARRAND, RECORDS OF THE FEDERAL CONVENTION OF 1787 154 (1937 ed.).
12. 2 ELLIOT, DEBATES IN THE SEVERAL STATE CONVENTIONS ON THE ADOPTION OF THE FEDERAL CONSTITUTION 11 (2d ed. 1836); 4 *id.* at 44.
13. 1 MCCLOSKEY, ed., WORKS OF JAMES WILSON 415 (1967).
14. *Id.* at 415–16.
15. See, *e.g.*, THE FEDERALIST No. 11.
16. NICHOLS, THE INVENTION OF THE AMERICAN POLITICAL PARTIES (1967).
17. WILSON, CONGRESSIONAL GOVERNMENT 198 (Meridian ed. 1956).
18. *Id.* at 179–80.
19. This quotation and much of the material on the St. Clair investigation reported here is taken from an invaluable source of information on congressional investigations, SCHLESINGER & BRUNS, eds., CONGRESS INVESTIGATES: A DOCUMENTED HISTORY 1792–1974 (5 vols. 1975). The quotation is reported 1 *id.* at 8.

20. *Id.* at 10.
21. *Id.* at 4.
22. Act of 3 May 1798, ch. 36, § 1, 1 Stat. 554.
23. 2 U.S.C. § 194.
24. Kilbourn v. Thompson, 103 U.S. 168 (1881).
25. See Landis, *Constitutional Limitations on the Congressional Power of Investigation*, 40 HARV. L. REV. 153 (1926); Potts, *Power of Legislative Bodies to Punish for Contempt*, 74 U. PA. L. REV. 691 (1926); Frankfurter, *Hands Off the Investigations*, 38 NEW REPUBLIC 329 (1924).
26. 103 U.S. at 195.
27. See 4 SCHLESINGER & BRUNS, note 19 *supra*, at 2385.
28. 273 U.S. 135 (1927).
29. 279 U.S. 263 (1929).
30. 273 U.S. at 174.
31. *Id.* at 178.
32. *Id.* at 179–80.
33. 279 U.S. at 291–92.
34. Kelly, *Clio and the Court: An Illicit Love Affair*, 1965 SUPREME COURT REVIEW 119; see also MILLER, THE SUPREME COURT AND THE USES OF HISTORY (1969).
35. 1 Wheat. 304 (1816). See HAINES, THE ROLE OF THE SUPREME COURT IN AMERICAN GOVERNMENT AND POLITICS, 1789–1835 340 (1944).
36. See also 9 HUNT, ed., WRITINGS OF JAMES MADISON 74 (1900–10).
37. Dred Scott v. Sanford, 19 How. 393, 536, 572 (1857).
38. 1 SCHLESINGER & BRUNS, note 19 *supra*, at 3.
39. *Id.* at 105.
40. *Id.* at 247.
41. *Id.* at 335.
42. *Id.* at 481.
43. *Id.* at 591.
44. *Id.* at 689.
45. 2 *id.* at 815.
46. *Id.* at 917.
47. *Id.* at 1071.
48. *Id.* at 1197.
49. *Id.* at 1361.
50. 3 *id.* at 1849.
51. *Id.* at 1983.
52. *Id.* at 2127.
53. *Id.* at 2251.
54. SHAPIRO, LAW AND POLITICS IN THE SUPREME COURT 59–61 (1964).
55. Hutcheson v. United States, 369 U.S. 599 (1962).
56. 354 U.S. 178, 187–88 (1957).
57. *Id.* at 201.
58. S. Res. 60, 93rd Cong., 1st Sess., was approved on 7 February 1973 by a unanimous vote of 77 to 0.
59. 5 SCHLESINGER & BRUNS, note 19 *supra*, at 3951, 3956.

60. See *In re* Chapman, 166 U.S. 661, 671 (1897); McGrain v. Daugherty, 273 U.S. 135, 174 (1927); United States v. Bryan, 339 U.S. 323, 331 (1950).
61. 354 U.S. at 187–88.
62. 2 U.S.C. § 190(b).
63. House Standing Rules XI 2(m)(2)(A).
64. See note 58 *supra.*
65. *Ibid.*
66. S. Res. 194, 93d Cong., 1st Sess. (7 Nov. 1973).
67. Nader v. Butz, 372 F. Supp. 175, 177 (D.D.C. 1974).
68. Hamilton, note 2 *supra,* at 97.
69. Anderson v. Dunn, 6 Wheat. 204 (1821); Marshall v. Gordon, 243 U.S. 521, 542 (1917).
70. See 2 U.S.C. §§ 192, 194.
71. See chap. 7 *infra.*
72. Quinn v. United States, 349 U.S. 155 (1955); Emspak v. United States, 349 U.S. 190 (1955); Bart v. United States, 349 U.S. 219 (1955); Hoffman v. United States, 341 U.S. 479 (1951); Rogers v. United States, 340 U.S. 367 (1951).
73. See 5 Schlesinger & Bruns, note 19 *supra,* at 3439, 3729.
74. Dash, Chief Counsel: Inside the Ervin Committee—The Untold Story of Watergate 191 (1976).
75. 11 Stat. 155 (1857).
76. 12 Stat. 333 (1862).
77. 142 U.S. 547, 586 (1892).
78. Murphy v. Waterfront Commission, 378 U.S. 52, 79 (1964).
79. 84 Stat. 927 (1970).
80. Kastigar v. United States, 406 U.S. 441 (1972).
81. See Dash, note 74 *supra,* at 97–98, 118–19.
82. Hamilton, note 2 *supra,* at 273.
83. *Id.* at 289–90.
84. *Id.* at 295.

Chapter Three. Executive Privilege to Deny Information to Congress

1. Berger, Executive Privilege: A Constitutional Myth (1974); Berger, Impeachment: The Constitutional Problems (1973).
2. Berger, Executive Privilege 1 (1974).
3. United States v. Nixon, 418 U.S. 683, 708 (1974).
4. *Id.* at 712, n.19. (Emphasis added.)
5. Reedy, The Twilight of the Presidency (1970).
6. See, *e.g.,* United States v. Brewster, 408 U.S. 501 (1972); United States v. Johnson, 383 U.S. 169 (1966).
7. 92d Cong., 1st Sess. (27, 28, and 29 July; 4 and 5 Aug. 1971). (Hereinafter "1971 Hearings.")
8. 1971 Hearings at 21–23.

9. *Id.* at 30, n.23.
10. *Id.* at 30.
11. *Id.* at 247.
12. *Id.* at 248–49.
13. *Id.* at 259–71.
14. *Id.* at 262.
15. *Id.* at 249.
16. *Id.* at 266.
17. *Nomination of L. Patrick Gray to be Director of the Federal Bureau of Investigation*, Hearings before the Committee on the Judiciary, United States Senate, 93d Cong., 1st Sess. (1973).
18. *Nomination of Elliot L. Richardson to be Attorney General*, Hearings before the Committee on the Judiciary, United States Senate, 93d Cong., 1st Sess. (1973).
19. *Freedom of Information; Executive Privilege; Secrecy in Government*, Hearings before the Subcommittees on Administrative Practice and Procedure and Separation of Powers of the Committee on the Judiciary, United States Senate and the Subcommittee on Intergovernmental Relations of the Committee on Government Operations, 93d Cong., 1st Sess. (10, 11, 12 April; 8, 9, 10, 16 May; 7, 8, 11, 26 June 1973). (3 vols.) (Hereinafter "1973 Hearings.")
20. 1973 Hearings at 31 (Vol. 1).
21. *Id.* at 35.
22. *Id.* at 36.
23. *Id.* at 19.
24. *Id.* at 39.
25. *Id.* at 45, 51–52.
26. *Id.* at 48–49.
27. See Jaworski, The Right and the Power 288 (1976).
28. 1973 Hearings at 209 (Vol. 2).
29. Richardson, The Creative Balance 52–53 (1976).
30. Isaiah 1:18.
31. Act III, sc. i.
32. 1973 Hearings at 41 (Vol. 1).
33. *Id.* at 52.
34. Dash, Chief Counsel 69–70 (1976).
35. See chap. 2 *supra.*
36. Dash, note 34 *supra*, at 107–08
37. Hamilton, The Power to Probe 275 (1976).
38. *Id.* at 289.

Chapter Four. Judicial Arbiter

1. 418 U.S. 683 (1974).
2. *Debate on Articles of Impeachment*, House of Representatives Committee on the Judiciary, 93d Cong., 2d Sess. (1974).

3. Ehrlichman v. United States, 97 S. Ct. 2641 (1977).
4. Hamilton, The Power to Probe 28–30 (1976).
5. *In re* Subpoena to Nixon, 360 F. Supp. 1 (D.D.C. 1973).
6. 1 Cranch 137 (1803).
7. Senate Select Committee on Presidential Campaign Activities v. Nixon, 366 F. Supp. 51 (D.D.C. 1973).
8. *Id.* at 55.
9. 28 U.S.C. § 1331.
10. 366 F. Supp. at 59.
11. See, *e.g.*, Spock v. David, 469 F.2d 1047 (3d Cir. 1972); see also Petroleum Exploration Co. v. Public Service Comm'n, 304 U.S. 209 (1938); Illinois v. Milwaukee, 406 U.S. 91 (1972); West End Neighborhood Corp. v. Stans, 312 F. Supp. 1066, 1068 (D.D.C. 1970).
12. Senate Select Committee on Presidential Campaign Activities v. Nixon, 370 F. Supp. 521 (D.D.C. 1974).
13. *Id.* at 522.
14. *Id.* at 524.
15. Senate Select Committee on Presidential Campaign Activities v. Nixon, 498 F.2d 725 (D.C. Cir. 1974).
16. *Id.* at 732.
17. *Ibid.*
18. 487 F.2d 700 (D.C. Cir. 1973).
19. Frank, *The Cult of the Robe*, in Courts on Trial 254 (1950); Jackson, The Struggle for Judicial Supremacy 178–79 (1941).
20. Jaworski, The Right and the Power 101–08 (1976).
21. *In re* Subpoena to Nixon, 360 F. Supp. 1 (D.D.C. 1973).
22. *Id.* at 5.
23. 345 U.S. 1 (1953).
24. 360 F. Supp. at 5.
25. *Ibid.*
26. *Ibid.*
27. *Id.* at 6.
28. *Ibid.*
29. *Id.* at 9–10.
30. See *Federal Grand Jury*, Hearings before the Subcommittee on Immigration, Citizenship and International Law of the Committee on the Judiciary, House of Representatives, 94th Cong., 2d Sess. (1976).
31. 360 F. Supp. at 11.
32. *Id.* at 13.
33. Nixon v. Sirica, 487 F.2d 700, 713 (D.C. Cir. 1973).
34. *Id.* at 708–16.
35. *Id.* at 717–18.
36. *Id.* at 719.
37. N.Y. Times, 20 Oct. 1973, p. 16, col. 4.
38. *Ibid.*
39. See Senator Ervin's statement on the facts of this phase of the Watergate affair, set out in Dash, Chief Counsel 267–72 (1976).

40. See RICHARDSON, THE CREATIVE BALANCE 44–45 (1976).
41. See chap. 5 *infra*.
42. RICHARDSON, note 40 *supra*.
43. N.Y. Times, 24 Oct. 1973, p. 1, col. 8, p. 32, col. 1.
44. *Id.* at 1, 32.
45. *Ibid.*
46. Youngstown Sheet & Tube Co. v. Sawyer, 343 U.S. 579 (1952).
47. 418 U.S. 683 (1974).
48. *Id.* at 703.
49. *Id.* at 703–04.
50. *Id.* at 705.
51. *Ibid.*
52. *Id.* at 707.
53. *Id.* at 708.
54. *Ibid.*
55. *Id.* at 710–11.
56. *Id.* at 713.
57. *Id.* at 712 n.20. The reference was to Clark v. United States, 289 U.S. 1 (1933).
58. 418 U.S. at 712 n.19.
59. Haldeman v. Sirica, 501 F.2d 714 (D.C. Cir. 1974).
60. United States v. Procter & Gamble, 356 U.S. 677, 682 (1958); United States v. Johnson, 319 U.S. 503, 513 (1943); Clark v. United States, note 57 *supra*.
61. 501 F.2d at 715.
62. United States v. Ehrlichman, 546 F.2d 910 (D.C. Cir. 1976).
63. *Id.* at 917 n.8.
64. *Ibid.*
65. United States v. Barker, 546 F.2d 940 (D.C.Cir. 1976); United States v. Mardian, 546 F.2d 973 (D.C.Cir. 1976).
66. 546 F.2d at 919–23.
67. 325 U.S. 91 (1945). *Cf.* United States v. Williams, 341 U.S. 70 (1951).
68. 546 F.2d at 926.
69. The words ascribed to Henry II by the court are: "Who will free me from this turbulent priest?" *Id.* at 926 n.68. The words ascribed to one of Becket's murderers by T. S. Eliot may be equally apposite: "We know perfectly well how things will turn out. King Henry—God bless him—will have to say, for reasons of state, that he never meant this to happen; and there is going to be an awful row; and at the best we shall have to spend the rest of our lives abroad." *Murder in Cathedral*, in ELIOT, COMPLETE POEMS AND PLAYS 215–16 (1952).
70. 546 F.2d at 951.
71. *Id.* at 951–52.
72. 408 U.S. 665 (1972).
73. *Id.* at 682, 692, 707–08.
74. N.Y. Times, 22 March 1973, p. 1, col. 2.
75. United States v. Liddy, 397 F. Supp. 947, 963 (D.D.C. 1975).

76. N.Y. Times, 24 March 1973, p. 12, col. 4.
77. Worcester v. Commissioner, 370 F.2d 713, 718 (1st Cir. 1966); *cf.* North Carolina v. Pearce, 395 U.S. 711, 724 (1969).
78. Scott v. United States, 419 F.2d 264 (D.C.Cir. 1969); *cf.* Machibroda v. United States, 368 U.S. 487, 493 (1962); Kercheval v. United States, 274 U.S. 220, 224 (1927).
79. The Courts of Appeals are in conflict on this question. *Compare* United States v. Vermuelen, 436 F.2d 72 (2d Cir. 1970); United States v. Sweig, 454 F.2d 181 (2d Cir. 1972); United States v. Hayward, 471 F.2d 388 (7th Cir. 1972); Mitchell v. Sirica, 502 F.2d 375, 384 n.17 (D.C.Cir. 1974), *with* United States v. Rogers, 504 F.2d 1079 (5th Cir. 1975); United States v. Acosta, 509 F.2d 539 (5th Cir. 1975); United States v. Garcia, 544 F.2d 681 (3d Cir. 1976).

Chapter Five. The Powers of Appointment and Removal

1. Jaworski, The Right and the Power 225–26 (1976).
2. 119 Cong. Rec. 13721–22 (1973).
3. *Id.* at 14086, 14704.
4. *Id.* at 13860.
5. Richardson, The Creative Balance 36–37 (1976).
6. 120 Cong. Rec. 15976 (1974).
7. For the extensive debates on questions of appointment and removal, see Farrand, Records of the Federal Convention of 1787 (1937 ed.) (4 vols.). It is unfortunate that all the recorded talk on the subject is not to the point on the constitutional questions that have arisen.
8. 1 Annals 607 (1st Cong., 1st Sess. 1789).
9. 5 Elliot, Debates on the Adoption of the Federal Constitution 329 (1845).
10. See chap. 8 *infra.* Pro-President historians, such as Clinton Rossiter, see his Constitutional Dictatorship (1948), thought Hamilton was embarrassed by the error of his position in *Federalist* No. 77. Rossiter, Alexander Hamilton and the Constitution 212 (1964). It is a conclusion without support in facts. Equally likely, it was Rossiter who was embarrassed rather than Hamilton by the hero's heterodoxy. See Corwin, *Tenure of Office and the Removal Power under the Constitution,* 27 Colum. L. Rev. 353, 370–71 (1927).
11. 1 Annals 516 (1789). A pro-executive reading of the debates may be found in Thach, The Creation of the Presidency 140 ff. (Storing ed. 1969).
12. See 5 Elliot, note 9 *supra,* at 328, 350.
13. 1 Stat. 50 (1789).
14. 1 Annals 635–36 (29 June 1789).
15. 1 Cranch 137, 162 (1803).
16. 42 Stat. 23, 24, § 303 (1921). The examples in this paragraph were taken from the brief of Senator George Wharton Pepper, Amicus Curiae,

in Myers v. United States, 272 U.S. 52 (1926). 24 KURLAND & CASPER, eds., LANDMARK BRIEFS AND ARGUMENTS OF THE SUPREME COURT OF THE UNITED STATES: CONSTITUTIONAL LAW 325–38 (1975). I am indebted to the materials published in this volume for much of the data reported here.

17. 11 CONG. DEB. 515–16 (1835).
18. 14 Stat. 430 (1867).
19. BENEDICT, THE IMPEACHMENT AND TRIAL OF ANDREW JOHNSON (1973).
20. Youngstown Sheet & Tube Co. v. Sawyer, 343 U.S. 579 (1952).
21. See *Ex parte* Hennen, 13 Pet. 230 (1839); United States v. Guthrie, 17 How. 284, 314 (1854); Blake v. United States, 103 U.S. 227, 236–37 (1881); United States v. Fisher, 109 U.S. 143 (1883); United States v. Perkins, 116 U.S. 483, 485 (1886); McAllister v. United States, 141 U.S. 174 (1891); United States v. Allred, 155 U.S. 591, 594 (1895); Parsons v. United States, 167 U.S. 324, 335, 343 (1897); Keim v. United States, 177 U.S. 290, 293–94 (1900); Reagan v. United States, 182 U.S. 419, 425 (1901); Shurtleff v. United States, 189 U.S. 311, 317 (1903).
22. 272 U.S. 52 (1926).
23. Burnap v. United States, 252 U.S. 512, 515 (1920).
24. 257 U.S. 541 (1922).
25. *Id.* at 544–45.
26. Eberlein v. United States, 257 U.S. 82 (1921).
27. Blake v. United States, 103 U.S. 227, 236–37 (1881); Wallace v. United States, 257 U.S. 541, 544–45 (1922).
28. *Ex parte* Hennen, 13 Pet. 230, 259, 260 (1839); United States v. Guthrie, 17 How. 284, 314 (1954); McAllister v. United States, 141 U.S. 174, 199–200 (1891); Burnap v. United States, 252 U.S. 512, 515 (1920).
29. Parsons v. United States, 167 U.S. 324, 335, 343 (1897).
30. Shurtleff v. United States, 189 U.S. 311, 317 (1903).
31. United States v. Perkins, 116 U.S. 483, 485 (1886); Reagan v. United States, 182 U.S. 419, 425 (1901).
32. Eberlein v. United States, note 26 *supra.*
33. The parallel between the Watergate investigation and the Ballinger-Pinchot investigation is well drawn by Charles Errico, in 3 SCHLESINGER & BRUNS, CONGRESS INVESTIGATES: A DOCUMENTED HISTORY 1792–1974 1983 (1975).
34. TODD, JUSTICE ON TRIAL 75–76 (1964). See also note 33 *supra.*
35. Daniel, 5:25.
36. The Brandeis confirmation battle is spelled out in TODD, note 34 *supra.*
37. *Id.* at 77–78.
38. THE NEW REPUBLIC, 18 March 1916, p. 165.
39. 19 Stat. 80 (1876).
40. MASON, HARLAN FISKE STONE: PILLAR OF THE LAW 222 (1956).
41. *Id.* at 231n.
42. 272 U.S. at 106.
43. *Id.* at 114.

44. *Id.* at 118.
45. *Id.* at 123.
46. *Id.* at 126.
47. *Id.* at 127.
48. Art. I, § 8, cl. 18.
49. 167 U.S. at 335, 343.
50. 272 U.S. at 143–44.
51. See chap. 3 *supra,* at notes 20–26, 29, 32.
52. 272 U.S. at 134–35.
53. See text *supra,* at note 41.
54. Professor Corwin was of the view that the broader reading of the opinion should be considered dicta, since all that was necessary to decision was the proposition that the President did not need the advice and consent of the Senate for the removal of officials in whose appointment they had concurred. The whole of Corwin's small book is given to analysis and refutation of the Taft opinion. See CORWIN, THE PRESIDENT'S REMOVAL POWER UNDER THE CONSTITUTION (1927).
55. 272 U.S. at 177.
56. 2 HOWE, ed., HOLMES-LASKI LETTERS 895–96 (1953).
57. 272 U.S. at 240–41.
58. *Id.* at 292–95.
59. MILLER, THE SUPREME COURT AND THE USES OF HISTORY 70 (1969).
60. LERNER, THE MIND AND FAITH OF JUSTICE HOLMES 286–87 (1943).
61. 189 U.S. 311, 317 (1903).
62. 295 U.S. 602 (1935).
63. *Id.* at 626.
64. *Id.* at 627–28.
65. *Id.* at 628.
66. *Id.* at 629, 631–32.
67. See JACKSON, THE STRUGGLE FOR JUDICIAL SUPREMACY 108–09 (1941).
68. 357 U.S. 349 (1958).
69. *Id.* at 352.
70. *Id.* at 356.
71. Nader v. Bork, 366 F. Supp. 104 (D.D.C. 1973).
72. 418 U.S. 683 (1974).
73. *Id.* at 694–96.
74. See text *supra,* at note 60.
75. 88 Stat. 1263.
76. 424 U.S. 1 (1976).
77. See chap. 9 *infra.* The Court's decision on the First Amendment questions is ably defended in Polsby, *Buckley v. Valeo: The Special Nature of Political Speech,* 1976 SUPREME COURT REVIEW 1.
78. 276 U.S. 394 (1928).
79. 99 U.S. 508 (1878).
80. 424 U.S. at 126.
81. *Id.* at 127.
82. *Id.* at 137.

83. *Id.* at 137–39.
84. 418 U.S at 697.
85. For examples of proposed legislation and opinions on its constitutionality, see *Special Prosecutor and Watergate Grand Jury Legislation*, Hearings before the Subcommittee on Criminal Justice of the Committee on the Judiciary of the House of Representatives, on H.J. Res. 784 and H.R. 10937, 93d Cong., 1st Sess. (29 and 31 Oct.; 1, 5, 7, and 8 Nov. 1973).
86. 100 U.S. 371, 397–98 (1879).
87. See United States v. Solomon, 216 F. Supp. 835 (S.D. N.Y. 1963); Hobson v. Hansen, 265 F. Supp. 902 (D.D.C. 1967).
88. See text *supra*, at note 41.
89. See United States v. Cox, 342 F.2d 167 (5th Cir. 1965).

Chapter Six. IMPEACHMENTS

1. Curtis, *A Better Theory of Legal Interpretation*, 3 VAND. L. REV. 407, 426 (1950).
2. See KURLAND, ed., FELIX FRANKFURTER ON THE SUPREME COURT 389 (1970).
3. Gompers v. United States, 233 U.S. 604, 610 (1914).
4. See, *e.g.*, CLARKSON & JETT, LUTHER MARTIN OF MARYLAND 206–28 (1970); 2 CURTIS, THE LIFE AND WRITINGS OF B. R. CURTIS 343–422 (1879).
5. HAND, THE SPIRIT OF LIBERTY 132 (Phoenix ed. 1976).
6. 4 MALONE, JEFFERSON THE PRESIDENT: FIRST TERM, 1801–1805 478 (1970).
7. *Debate on Articles of Impeachment*, Committee on the Judiciary of the House of Representatives, 93d Cong., 2d Sess. 133 (1974).
8. *Id.* at 7.
9. See chap. 1 *supra*, at note 18.
10. See FEILING, WARREN HASTINGS 343–71 (1954).
11. 1 THE WORKS OF EDMUND BURKE 495 (1889).
12. MAITLAND, THE CONSTITUTIONAL HISTORY OF ENGLAND 317–18, 322 (Fisher ed. 1961).
13. BERGER, IMPEACHMENT: THE CONSTITUTIONAL PROBLEMS 69–70 (1973).
14. 4 BLACKSTONE, COMMENTARIES *259.
15. *Id.* at *121.
16. MAITLAND, note 12 *supra*, at 477.
17. BLACKSTONE, note 14 *supra*, at *259.
18. MAITLAND, note 12 *supra*, at 477.
19. Trist v. Child, 21 Wall. 441, 450 (1875).
20. 1 FARRAND, THE RECORDS OF THE FEDERAL CONVENTION OF 1787 244 (1937 ed.) (hereinafter FARRAND).
21. 2 *id.* at 134.

22. 1 *id.* at 292–93.
23. *Id.* at 78.
24. *Id.* at 79.
25. *Id.* at 87.
26. *Id.* at 86.
27. 2 *id.* at 65–66.
28. *Id.* at 66.
29. *Id.* at 67.
30. *Id.* at 116.
31. *Id.* at 337.
32. *Id.* at 495.
33. *Id.* at 545.
34. *Id.* at 550.
35. *Ibid.*
36. *Ibid.*
37. 6 Wheat. 264, 417 (1821).
38. 5 Elliot, Debates on the Adoption of the Federal Constitution 341, 528 (1845).
39. 4 *id.* at 380. Compare his position on the removal power, chap. 5 *supra,* at notes 9–11.
40. 1 Annals of Congress 387 (1789).
41. 4 Elliot, note 38 *supra,* at 281.
42. 3 *id.* at 117, 201, 486.
43. 4 *id.* at 127.
44. *Id.* at 47.
45. 2 *id.* at 168–69.
46. 1 Works of James Wilson 426 (R. McCloskey ed. 1967).
47. *Ibid.*
48. 1 Story, Commentaries on the Constitution 559 (5th ed. 1891).
49. 1 Kent's Commentaries on American Law 288–89 (12th ed., Holmes ed. 1873).
50. The use of this word despite its deletion at the Convention because of Madison's objection, text at note 35 *supra,* is a reminder that Madison's notes of the Convention were not published until 1840, after Madison's demise. But the text clearly reveals that Kent was not construing the word the way that Madison feared it would be construed, but according to the interpretation of the state constitutions that had used that standard, and in keeping with Madison's remarks that were made after the Convention but published before the "Notes."
51. 1 Kent, note 49 *supra,* at 344 n.1.
52. 1 Tocqueville, Democracy in America 108 (Bradley ed. 1945).
53. *Id.* at 110.
54. 7 Annals of Congress 43–44 (1797).
55. 8 Annals of Congress 2319 (1799).
56. This construction was confirmed in Buckley v. Valeo, 424 U.S. 1, 131 (1976).
57. See Powell v. McCormack, 395 U.S. 486 (1969).

58. CONG. GLOBE, 40th Cong., 2d Sess. 1400 (1868); Act of 2 March 1867, 14 Stat. 430 (1867).
59. CONG. GLOBE, 40th Cong., 2d Sess. 1638–39 (1868).
60. KENNEDY, PROFILES IN COURAGE 146–71 (1956).
61. See, *e.g.*, BROCK, AN AMERICAN CRISIS: CONGRESS AND RECONSTRUCTION, 1865–67 (1963); FRANKLIN, RECONSTRUCTION AFTER THE CIVIL WAR (1960); STAMPP, THE ERA OF RECONSTRUCTION, 1865–77 (1965); TREFOUSSE, THE RADICAL REPUBLICANS: LINCOLN'S VANGUARD FOR RACIAL JUSTICE (1968).
62. BENEDICT, THE IMPEACHMENT AND TRIAL OF ANDREW JOHNSON (1973).
63. MCKITRICK, ANDREW JOHNSON AND RECONSTRUCTION 506–07 (1960).
64. BURNS, PRESIDENTIAL GOVERNMENT 52 (1966).
65. *Impeachment of Richard M. Nixon, President of the United States*, Report of the Committee on the Judiciary of the House of Representatives, Rep. No. 93–1305, 93d Cong., 2d Sess. pp. 1–2. (20 Aug. 1974).
66. *Id.* at 3.
67. *Ibid.*
68. 80 CONG. REC. 5607 (17 Apr. 1936).
69. 49 CONG. REC. 1447 (13 Jan. 1913).
70. 1 SCHWARTZ, A COMMENTARY ON THE CONSTITUTION OF THE UNITED STATES: THE POWERS OF GOVERNMENT 113 (1963).
71. BLACK, IMPEACHMENT: A HANDBOOK 53 (1974).
72. *Id.* at 54–55.
73. See HAND, THE BILL OF RIGHTS 4 (1958).
74. See BRANT, IMPEACHMENT: TRIALS AND ERRORS 178–200 (1972); BERGER, IMPEACHMENT: THE CONSTITUTIONAL PROBLEMS 103–21 (1973).
75. See Griffin v. Illinois, 351 U.S. 12 (1956).
76. Ritter v. United States, 84 Ct. Cl. 293, 296 (1936).
77. 4 Wall. 475, 501 (1867).
78. *Id.* at 500–01.
79. Ritter v. United States, 300 U.S. 668 (1937).
80. 2 FARRAND at 186.
81. *Id.* at 423.
82. *Id.* at 427.
83. *Id.* at 551.
84. *Ibid.*
85. *Ibid.*
86. *Ibid.*
87. *Id.* at 41–42.
88. *Id.* at 42.
89. *Id.* at 46.
90. 2 THE BILL OF RIGHTS: A DOCUMENTARY HISTORY 902 (Schwartz ed. 1971).
91. *Id.* at 917.
92. 1 BRYCE, AMERICAN COMMONWEALTH 107 (2d ed. rev. 1891).

93. Wechsler, *Toward Neutral Principles of Constitutional Law*, 73 HARV. L. REV. 1, 8 (1959).
94. 1 Cranch 137 (1803).
95. 395 U.S. 486 (1969).
96. 408 U.S. 606 (1972).
97. 328 U.S. 303 (1946).
98. Anderson v. Dunn, 6 Wheat. 204 (1821).
99. Kilbourn v. Thompson, 103 U.S. 168, 192–200 (1881).
100. 395 F.2d 577 (D.C.Cir. 1968).
101. 395 U.S. at 513–14.
102. *Id.* at 517–18.
103. *Id.* at 521 n.42.
104. 418 U.S. 683 (1974).
105. 395 U.S. at 549.
106. 369 U.S. 186 (1962).
107. 395 U.S. at 553.
108. SHAPIRO, LAW AND POLITICS IN THE SUPREME COURT 215 (1964).

Chapter Seven. PRESIDENTIAL PROSECUTIONS AND PRESIDENTIAL PARDONS

1. BEN-VENISTE & FRAMPTON, STONEWALL: THE REAL STORY OF THE WATERGATE PROSECUTION 211–12 (1977).
2. *Id.* at 226.
3. *Id.* at 227.
4. *Impeachment of Richard M. Nixon, President of the United States*, Report of the Committee on the Judiciary, of the House of Representatives, Rep. No. 93–1305, 93d Cong., 2d Sess., pp. 363–72 (20 Aug. 1974) (minority view of Congressmen Hutchinson, Smith, Sandman, Wiggins, Dennis, Mayne, Lott, Moorhead, Maraziti, and Latta).
5. 3 FARRAND, RECORDS OF THE FEDERAL CONVENTION OF 1787 617, 625 (1937 ed.) (hereinafter FARRAND).
6. 2 *id.* at 500.
7. The decision was rendered under the rubric, United States v. Isaacs, 493 F.2d 1124, 1142 (7th Cir. 1974).
8. 417 U.S. 976 (1974).
9. United States v. Nixon, 418 U.S. 683, 687 n.2 (1974).
10. Memorandum for the United States, Application of Spiro T. Agnew, Civ. No. 73–965 (D.Md., 5 Oct. 1973).
11. Bickel, *The Constitutional Tangle*, THE NEW REPUBLIC 14, 15 (6 Oct. 1973).
12. Note 10 *supra*, at 5.
13. 10 ANNALS OF CONGRESS 72 (1800).
14. 2 ELLIOT, DEBATES ON THE ADOPTION OF THE FEDERAL CONSTITUTION 480 (1836).
15. See chap. 4 *supra*.

16. See Bradley v. Fisher, 13 Wall. 335 (1872); Pierson v. Ray, 386 U.S. 547 (1967).
17. N.Y. Times, 12 March 1974, p. 24, col. 1.
18. JAWORSKI, THE RIGHT AND THE POWER 99–100 (1976).
19. See HAND, THE BILL OF RIGHTS (1958).
20. See 3 BEVERIDGE, JOHN MARSHALL 445 (1919).
21. 5 MALONE, JEFFERSON AND HIS TIMES: JEFFERSON THE PRESIDENT, SECOND TERM 1805–1809 324 (1974).
22. N.Y. Times, 29 Aug. 1974, p. 1, col. 8.
23. 39 Fed. Reg. 32601–02 (1974).
24. N.Y. Times, 9 Sept. 1974, p. 24, col. 1.
25. VI RICHARDSON, ed., MESSAGES AND PAPERS OF THE PRESIDENTS 276–77 (1897).
26. Art. II, § 1, cl. 8.
27. N.Y. Times, 11 Sept. 1974, p. 1, col. 3.
28. *Pardon of Richard M. Nixon, and Related Matters*, Hearings before the Subcommittee on Criminal Justice of the Committee on the Judiciary, House of Representatives, 93d Cong., 2d Sess. 96 (24 Sept., 1 and 17 Oct. 1974).
29. *Id.* at 97.
30. *Id.* at 96.
31. N.Y. Times, 11 Sept. 1974, p. 28, col. 6.
32. See note 1 *supra*. See also Hearings, note 28 *supra*, at 147–48.
33. 2 STUBBS, CONSTITUTIONAL HISTORY OF ENGLAND 583–84 (1880 ed.)
34. 31 Chas. II, c.2, 5 Statutes of the Realm 935; 12 & 13 Wm. III, c.2, 7 Statutes of the Realm 636.
35. See, *e.g.*, I POORE, UNITED STATES, FEDERAL AND STATE CONSTITUTIONS AND CHARTERS 380; 2 *id.* at 1335, 1312 (1878).
36. 1 FARRAND at 228–32, 242–45.
37. 3 *id.* at 599.
38. 1 *id.* at 292.
39. 2 *id.* at 185.
40. 2 *id.* at 419.
41. 2 *id.* at 426.
42. *Ibid.*
43. 2 *id.* at 426.
44. *Id.* at 626.
45. *Ibid.*
46. *Ibid.*
47. *Id.* at 626–27.
48. *Id.* at 627.
49. *Ibid.*
50. DORRIS, PARDON AND AMNESTY UNDER LINCOLN AND JOHNSON (1953).
51. 3 ELLIOT, note 14 *supra*, at 497.
52. 2 *id.* at 408.
53. 3 *id.* at 497.

54. See N.Y. Times, 26 April 1977, p. 18, col. 5: *Ex-Nixon Aides Continue to Meet as Informal Group.*
55. See text *supra*, at notes 28–30.
56. 4 Blackstone, Commentaries on the Law of England *400. See 32 Cong. Q. Weekly Report 2459 (1974).
57. Note 22 *supra.*
58. See chap. 5 *supra*, text at notes 72–73.
59. See text *supra*, at note 30.
60. 4 Blackstone, note 56 *supra*, at *397–*398.
61. 1 Montesquieu, The Spirit of the Laws bk. VI, c. 21 (1750).
62. 2 Farrand at 426.
63. *Ibid.*
64. 236 U.S. 79 (1915).
65. 4 Wall. 333, 380 (1867).
66. Lattin, *The Pardoning Power in Massachusetts*, 11 B.U.L. Rev. 505, 519 (1931).
67. 236 U.S. at 94.
68. Humbert, The Pardoning Power of the President 25 (1941).
69. Brown v. Walker, 161 U.S. 591 (1896).
70. See text *supra*, following note 53.
71. See 32 Cong. Q. Weekly Rep. 2458 (1974).
72. N.Y. Times, 13 Oct. 1974, p. 76, col. 2.
73. *E.g.*, Humbert, note 68 *supra*, at 63 n.42.
74. 32 Cong. Q. Weekly Rep. 2457–59 (1974).
75. Chap. 5 *supra*, text at notes 39–60.
76. 274 U.S. 480 (1927).
77. *Id.* at 486.
78. 7 Pet. 150 (1833).
79. *Id.* at 160.
80. Abington School District v. Schempp, 374 U.S. 203, 234 (1963).
81. Miller, The Supreme Court and the Uses of History 70 (1969).
82. Holmes, Collected Legal Papers 139 (1920).
83. Missouri v. Holland, 252 U.S. 416, 433 (1920). For a critique of that decision, see Lofgren, *Missouri v. Holland in Historical Perspective*, 1975 Supreme Court Review 77.
84. See, *e.g.*, Mass. Const., pt. 2, ch. 2, art. VIII, § 1; Calif. Const., art. V, § 8.
85. United States v. Cox, 342 F.2d 167 (5th Cir. 1965).
86. Confiscation Cases, 7 Wall. 454 (1869).
87. Downum v. United States, 372 U.S. 734 (1963); Illinois v. Somerville, 410 U.S. 458, 467 (1973).
88. See McNeal v. Hollowell, 481 F.2d 1145 (5th Cir. 1973).
89. Burdick v. United States, *supra*, text at notes 64 and 67.
90. 18 U.S.C. § 6002.
91. 419 U.S. 256 (1974).
92. *Id.* at 263.

93. *Ibid.*
94. See text *supra*, at note 48.
95. 2 POORE, note 35 *supra*, at 1335.
96. 419 U.S. at 262–63.
97. *Id.* at 260–61.
98. See CHITTY, PREROGATIVES OF THE CROWN 98 (1820 ed.).
99. 419 U.S. at 262.
100. CORWIN, THE TWILIGHT OF THE SUPREME COURT 147 (1934).
101. See 4 BLACKSTONE, note 56 *supra*, at *398–*399; COKE, THIRD INSTITUTE 238 (1644); 2 HAWKINS, PLEAS OF THE CROWN 543–46 (8th ed. 1824). But see CHITTY, note 98 *supra*, at 100.
102. 236 U.S. at 93.
103. 28 C.F.R. §§ 0.35–0.36, 1.1–1.9 (1976).
104. 38 Fed. Reg. 30738–39, 32805 (1973).
105. See chap. 5 *supra*, text at notes 76–88.
106. 418 U.S. 683, 696 (1974).
107. Hearings before the Senate Judiciary Committee on the Special Prosecutor, 93d Cong., 1st Sess., pt. 2, 513 (1973).
108. MAITLAND, THE CONSTITUTIONAL HISTORY OF ENGLAND 480 (1961 ed.).
109. *Ibid.*
110. See DREW, AMERICAN JOURNAL: THE EVENTS OF 1976 27, 235, 322, 367, 377 (1977).

Chapter Eight. SEPARATION OF POWERS AND CHECKS AND BALANCES

1. HARDIN, PRESIDENTIAL POWER & ACCOUNTABILITY: TOWARD A NEW CONSTITUTION (1974).
2. 1 FARRAND, RECORDS OF THE FEDERAL CONVENTION OF 1787 20 (1937 ed.) (hereinafter FARRAND).
3. For a description of the government under the Confederation, which suggested that it was less hapless than our political mythology has led us to believe, see JENSEN, THE NEW NATION: A HISTORY OF THE UNITED STATES DURING THE CONFEDERATION (1950).
4. Gladstone, *Kin Beyond Sea*, NORTH AM. REV. (Sept.–Oct. 1878).
5. WHEARE, FEDERAL GOVERNMENT 7 (4th ed. 1963).
6. *Id.* at 2.
7. ROCKEFELLER, THE FUTURE OF FEDERALISM (1962); and see ELAZAR, THE AMERICAN PARTNERSHIP (1962), which is concerned with nineteenth-century developments.
8. HEREN, THE NEW AMERICAN COMMONWEALTH 9 (1968).
9. *Id.* at 8.
10. 1 FARRAND at 65.
11. *Ibid.*

12. *Id.* at 65–66.
13. Madison inserted words later that made this phrase read: "not [appertaining to and] appointed by the Legislature." This would seem to have reflected Madison's own later notions more than Wilson's. See text and note 9, chap. 5 *supra.*
14. 1 FARRAND at 66. See also *id.* at 86 (Dickinson); *id.* at 88 (Randolph); *id.* at 113 (Mason).
15. *Id.* at 66.
16. *Id.* at 67.
17. These words were inserted as an amendment by Pinckney, lest "improper powers . . . be delegated." *Ibid.*
18. 1 FARRAND at 119, 125, 341; 2 *id.* at 638; 3 *id.* at 420.
19. 2 FARRAND at 73, 298–300; see notes 10, 15 *supra.*
20. *Id.* at 300–01.
21. *Ibid.*
22. *Id.* at 407.
23. *Id.* at 551.
24. 2 *id.* at 34.
25. See chap. 6 *supra.*
26. VILE, CONSTITUTIONALISM AND THE SEPARATION OF POWERS 98 (1967).
27. PAINE, COMMON SENSE 8 (1819 ed.).
28. See 8 JEFFERSON'S WORKS 361–63 (1861 ed.).
29. 2 FARRAND at 35, 74.
30. See THE FEDERALIST Nos. 49, 50, 51.
31. MAIN, THE ANTI-FEDERALISTS (1961).
32. 418 U.S. 683 (1974).
33. The phrase, commonly attributed to Washington, is in fact Jefferson's from his first inaugural, but the essence of the message was the same. See BOORSTIN, ed., AN AMERICAN PRIMER 208 (1966).
34. *Ibid.*
35. *Id.* at 201–02.
36. ARENDT, ON REVOLUTION 131 (1963).
37. FRANKFURTER, THE PUBLIC AND ITS GOVERNMENT 3–4 (1930).
38. *Id.* at 78. *Cf.* Frankfurter, J., concurring, in Youngstown Sheet & Tube Co. v. Sawyer, 343 U.S. 579, 593 (1952).
39. 430 U.S. 762 (1977).
40. Weinberger v. Wiesenfeld, 420 U.S. 636, 638 n.2 (1975).
41. 430 U.S. at 777–79.
42. 1 Cranch 137 (1803).
43. SCHLESINGER, THE IMPERIAL PRESIDENCY 212, 216 (1973).
44. SCHLESINGER, KENNEDY OR NIXON: DOES IT MAKE ANY DIFFERENCE? 10 (1960).
45. For another admiring description of the Nixon campaign techniques and strategy, see SAFIRE, BEFORE THE FALL (1975).
46. WHITE, BREACH OF FAITH: THE FALL OF RICHARD NIXON (1975).
47. MCCARTHY, THE MASK OF STATE: WATERGATE PORTRAITS (1974).

48. Bailyn, The Ideological Origins of the American Revolution 124–25 (1967).
49. *Id.* at 19.
50. *Id.* at 124.
51. Story, Miscellaneous Writings 150 (1835).
52. Guizot, Historical Essays and Lectures 412 (1972 ed.).
53. 299 U.S. 304, 315–17 (1936).
54. *Id.* at 320.
55. Rossiter, Constitutional Dictatorship 313–14 (1948).
56. 297 U.S. 1 (1936).
57. *Id.* at 67.
58. Steward Machine Co. v. Davis, 301 U.S. 548 (1937).
59. Wickard v. Filburn, 317 U.S. 111 (1942).
60. Katzenbach v. McClung, 379 U.S. 294 (1964).
61. 1 Farrand at 67.
62. Pub. L. 95–17, Reorganization Act of 1977.
63. 10 Wheat. 1 (1825).
64. *Id.* at 43.
65. United States v. Grimaud, 220 U.S. 506 (1911).
66. Interstate Commerce Commission v. Illinois Central R.R., 215 U.S. 452 (1910).
67. Federal Radio Commission v. Nelson Bros., 289 U.S. 266 (1933).
68. 276 U.S. 394 (1928).
69. *Id.* at 406.
70. See Panama Refining Co. v. Ryan, 293 U.S. 388 (1935); Schechter Corp. v. United States, 295 U.S. 495 (1935); Carter v. Carter Coal Co., 298 U.S. 238 (1936).
71. See, *e.g.*, Currin v. Wallace, 306 U.S. 1 (1939); United States v. Rock Royal Co-operative, 307 U.S. 533 (1939); H. P. Hood & Sons v. United States, 307 U.S. 588 (1939); Opp Cotton Mills v. Administrator of Wage and Hour Division, 312 U.S. 126 (1941); Yakus v. United States, 321 U.S. 414 (1944); Bowles v. Willingham, 321 U.S. 503 (1944); Lichter v. United States, 334 U.S. 742 (1948).
72. See Barber, The Constitution and the Delegation of Congressional Power (1975); Lowi, The End of Liberalism 128 *et seq.* (1969).
73. Congressional Budget and Impoundment Control Act of 1974, Pub. L. 93–344, 88 Stat. 297.
74. Art. I, § 9, reads in part: "No Money shall be drawn from the Treasury, not in Consequence of Appropriations made by Law; and a regular Statement and Account of the Receipts and Expenditures of all public Money shall be published from time to time." See Fisher, Presidential Spending Power 202–28 (1975). And see Hearings before Senate Select Committee on Intelligence, 95th Cong. 1st Sess. (28 April 1977), especially the testimony of Gerhard Casper, reprinted in 23 The Law School Record 19 (Fall 1977).

75. Anderson, The President's Men (1968).
76. *Id.* at 397.
77. *Id.* at 398.

Chapter Nine. Reforms

1. Halasz, Captain Dreyfus: The Story of a Mass Hysteria 233 (1955).
2. 1 Timothy 6:10.
3. Bacon, Essays XV (1625).
4. The Imperial Presidency 275 (1973).
5. N.Y. Times, 2 Oct. 1973, p. 43, col. 1.
6. *E.g.*, Jaworski, The Right and the Power 279 (1976).
7. *E.g.*, Commager, The Defeat of America 153 (1976 ed.).
8. See chap. 8 *supra.*
9. 26 U. Toronto L.J. 125 (1976).
10. *Id.* at 125–26.
11. See Minow, Martin, & Mitchell, Presidential Television (1973).
12. *Final Report of the Select Committee on Presidential Campaign Activities*, S. Rep. No. 93–981, 93d Cong., 2d Sess. (1974) (hereinafter "*Report*").
13. *Id.* at 564.
14. *Id.* at 567.
15. *Id.* at 568.
16. *Id.* at 570.
17. *Id.* at 569.
18. *Id.* at 572.
19. *Id.* at 573.
20. *Id.* at 575.
21. *Ibid.*
22. *Id.* at 1109–10.
23. *Id.* at 361–444.
24. Federal Election Campaign Act Amendments of 1974, 88 Stat. 1263.
25. See chap. 5 *supra.*
26. Buckley v. Valeo, 424 U.S. 1 (1976).
27. *Id.* at 13.
28. *Id.* at 19.
29. *Id.* at 21.
30. *Id.* at 23–35.
31. *Id.* at 35–36.
32. *Id.* at 36–37.
33. *Id.* at 38.
34. *Id.* at 39–51.
35. *Id.* at 51–58.
36. *Id.* at 68.
37. *Id.* at 74.

38. *Id.* at 74–84.
39. *Id.* at 86–90.
40. See *id.* at 90–91, 247–49.
41. *Id.* at 27.
42. *Ibid.*
43. *Report* at 579–867.
44. *Id.* at 127–29.
45. McCarthy, The Mask of State 162 (1974).
46. *Report* at 1127.
47. *Id.* at 1161.
48. *Id.* at 1162.
49. *Id.* at 1131–32.
50. The committee's minority counsel, Fred D. Thompson, addressed these questions in his book, At That Point in Time 145–82 (1975).
51. Report to the President by the Commission on CIA Activities within the United States 181–82 (1975).
52. *Id.* at 204.
53. *Report* at 101–02.
54. *Id.* at 1107.
55. See *Foreign and Military Intelligence*, Book I, S. Rep. No. 94–755, 94th Cong., 2d Sess. (1976); *Intelligence Activities and the Rights of Americans*, Book II, S. Rep. No. 94–755, 94th Cong., 2d Sess. (1976); *Supplementary Detailed Staff Reports on Intelligence Activities and the Rights of Americans*, Book III, S. Rep. No. 94–755, 94th Cong., 2d Sess. (1976); *Supplementary Detailed Staff Reports on Foreign and Military Intelligence*, Book IV, S. Rep. No. 94–755, 94th Cong., 2d Sess. (1976); *The Investigation of the Assassination of President John F. Kennedy: Performance of the Intelligence Agencies*, Book V, S. Rep. No. 94–755, 94th Cong., 2d Sess. (1976); *Supplementary Reports on Intelligence Activities*, Book VI, S. Rep. No. 94–755, 94th Cong., 2d Sess. (1976). There were many other legislative investigations. See, *e.g.*, *FBI Oversight*, Hearings before the Subcommittee on Civil and Constitutional Rights of the Committee on the Judiciary of the House of Representatives, 94th Cong., 1st & 2d Sess. (1975–76) (3 parts).
56. S. Rep. No. 94–755, note 55 *supra*, Book I, at pp. 4–5. See H.R. 6051, 95th Cong., 1st Sess. (1977), for one response.
57. N.Y. Times, 19 May 1977, p. 15, col. 6.
58. The Federalist 18–19 (Wright ed., 1961).
59. *Report* at 101.
60. *Ibid.*
61. See text *supra*, following note 56.
62. See *Removing Politics from the Administration of Justice*, Hearings before the Subcommittee on Separation of Powers of the Committee on the Judiciary, United States Senate on S.2803, To Insure the Separation of Constitutional Powers by Establishing the Department of Justice as an Independent Establishment of the United States, and S.2978, To Establish a Special Commission to Study the Establishment of an Inde-

pendent Permanent Mechanism for the Investigation and Prosecution of Official Misconduct and Other Offenses Committed by High Government Officials (93d Cong., 2d Sess. 1974).

63. *Report* at 1085.
64. *Watergate Reorganization and Reform Act of 1975*, Hearings before the Committee on Government Operations, United States Senate on S.495, To Establish Certain Federal Agencies, Effect Certain Reorganizations of the Federal Government, and to Implement Certain Reforms in the Operation of the Federal Government Recommended by the Senate Select Committee on Presidential Campaign Activities, and for Other Purposes; S.2036, To Promote Accountability in the Executive Branch of the Government, to Require the Disclosure of the Financial Status of Public Officials, to Establish an Office of Legal Counsel to the Congress, and for Other Purposes (94th Cong., 1st Sess., 1975–76) (2 parts).
65. See H.R. 2835, 95th Cong., 1st Sess. (1977).
66. Hearings, note 64 *supra*, at 256–58 (part I).
67. See H.R. Rep. No. 93–990 (93d Cong., 2d Sess. 1974).
68. 1974 CQ ALMANAC 663.
69. *Contempt Proceedings against Secretary of Commerce, Rogers C. B. Morton*, Hearings and Related Documents before the Subcommittee on Oversight and Investigations of the Committee on Interstate and Foreign Commerce, House of Representatives, 94th Cong., 1st Sess. (1975) (Ser. No. 94–45).
70. N.Y. Times, 6 Jan. 1973, p. 1, col. 8.
71. See H. Doc. No. 92–75 (25 March 1971); H. Doc. No. 92–273 (29 March 1972).
72. H.R. 14715, 93d Cong., 2d Sess. (1974).
73. 1974 CQ ALMANAC 658.
74. N.Y. Times, 31 March 1977, p. 20, col. 3.
75. *White House Green*, NEWSWEEK 19 (23 May 1977).
76. Pub. L. 95–17, Reorganization Act of 1977.
77. See TIME 16–24 (6 June 1977).

Chapter Ten. THE PLEBISCITARY PRESIDENCY

1. GASH, SIR ROBERT PEEL 721 (1972).
2. See, *e.g.*, PALMER, TWELVE WHO RULED: THE YEAR OF THE TERROR IN THE FRENCH REVOLUTION (1941); GOTTSCHALK, JEAN PAUL MARAT (1927); GOSSELIN, ROBESPIERRE'S RISE AND FALL (Eng. tr. 1927).
3. (1977).
4. SHAKESPEARE, JULIUS CAESAR, act III, sc. ii.
5. "But I am an 'idiot', an *idiōtēs*, as the Greeks originally defined the noun—'a person in a private station,' of whom Pericles declared that 'we do not say that the man who takes no interest in politics is a man who minds his own business; we say that he had no business here at all.' " QUENNELL, THE MARBLE FOOT 242 (1977).

6. *The Trial of Richard Nixon—and of America*, N.Y. Times, 6 May 1977, p. A28, col. 1.
7. BARBAULD, EIGHTEEN HUNDRED AND ELEVEN (1812).
8. SHAKESPEARE, HAMLET, act I, sc. iii.

"Mr. [Solicitor General] Beck was an industrious and doubtless learned Philadelphia lawyer, but how long-winded, and how by the yard he loved to quote Shakespeare at [the Court]. . . . The brethren didn't like it, all except perhaps the Chief Justice, Taft in those days, who would go to sleep, very gently, and wake up smiling. Beck liked to end his arguments with a good solid quotation. . . .

"But finally when Beck declaimed, looking rather angrily at the dozing Chief Justice—

> Force should be right; or, rather, right and wrong,
> (Between whose endless jar justice resides,)
> Should lose their names, and so should justice too.
> Then every thing includes itself in power,
> Power into will, will into appetite;
> And appetite, an universal wolf,
> [Beck seemed to be glowering at the Chief]
> So doubly seconded with will and power,
> Must make perforce an universal prey,
> And, last, eat up himself.

Holmes could stand it no longer, and leaning to the Chief, who sat next to him, whispered in his ear, not inaudibly: 'I hope to God Mrs. Beck likes Shakespeare!' " BIDDLE, MR. JUSTICE HOLMES 145–47 (1942).

9. SCHLESINGER, THE IMPERIAL PRESIDENCY 252–53 (1973).
10. *Id.* at 254.
11. N.Y. Times, 19 May 1977, p. 1, col. 1.
12. Hirschfield, *The Power of the Contemporary Presidency*, 14 PARLIAMENTARY AFFAIRS 353, 360, 362, 363 (1961).
13. Youngstown Sheet & Tube Co. v. Sawyer, 343 U.S. 579, 585, 587–89 (1952).
14. *Id.* at 593–94.
15. *Id.* at 634.
16. JACKSON, THE STRUGGLE FOR JUDICIAL SUPREMACY (1941).
17. 343 U.S. at 635–38.
18. *Id.* at 653–55.
19. See THE PENTAGON PAPERS (N.Y. Times ed. 1971); see also HALBERSTAM, THE BEST AND THE BRIGHTEST (1972).
20. Pub. L. 88–408, 78 Stat. 384 (1964).
21. SOFAER, WAR, FOREIGN AFFAIRS AND CONSTITUTIONAL POWER: THE ORIGINS (1976).
22. N.Y. Times, 9 Jan. 1951, p. 28, col. 6.
23. Commager, *Presidential Power: The Issue Analyzed*, N.Y. TIMES MAGAZINE 11 (14 Jan. 1951).
24. See ABRAHAM, JUSTICES & PRESIDENTS 8–9 (1974); and see Wilson's successful persistence in the nomination of Justice Brandeis, when Wil-

son wouldn't take no for an answer from the Senate. TODD, JUSTICE ON TRIAL (1964).

25. See BAKER, BACK TO BACK (1967); Leuchtenburg, *The Origins of Franklin D. Roosevelt's "Court-Packing" Plan*, 1966 SUPREME COURT REVIEW 347.
26. See chaps. 3 and 4 *supra.*
27. See chap. 4 *supra.*
28. Corwin, *Wanted: A New Type of Cabinet*, N.Y. TIMES MAGAZINE 14 (10 Oct. 1948).
29. LASKI, THE AMERICAN DEMOCRACY 92–93 (1948).
30. See KARL, EXECUTIVE REORGANIZATION AND REFORM IN THE NEW DEAL (1963).
31. KOENIG, THE INVISIBLE PRESIDENCY 15–16 (1960).
32. BICKEL, THE MORALITY OF CONSENT 18 (1975).
33. See chap. 8 *supra.*
34. 1 WORKS OF JAMES WILSON 318–19 (McCloskey ed. 1967).
35. LEVY, JEFFERSON AND CIVIL LIBERTIES 67 (1963).
36. Cater, *Toward a Public Philosophy of Government-Media Relations*, ASPEN NOTEBOOK ON GOVERNMENT AND THE MEDIA 6 (Rivers & Nyhan eds. 1973).
37. SCHMIDT, FREEDOM OF THE PRESS VS. PUBLIC ACCESS 56 (1976).
38. *Id.* at 60–61.
39. Neustadt, *Presidency and Legislation: Planning the President's Program*, 49 AM. POL. SCI. REV. 980, 981, 1014 (1955).
40. FAIRLIE, THE KENNEDY PROMISE (1973).
41. VOLTAIRE, PENSÉES SUR LE GOUVERNEMENT vii (1752), quoted in BESTERMAN, VOLTAIRE 311 (2d ed. 1976).
42. BESTERMAN, note 41 *supra*, at 311.
43. *Ibid.*
44. See, *e.g.*, WHITE, BREACH OF FAITH chap. 5 (1975).
45. United States *ex rel.* Knauff v. Shaughnessy, 338 U.S. 537, 551 (1950).
46. DICEY, LAW OF THE CONSTITUTION 202–03 (10th ed. 1959).
47. WEDGWOOD, A COFFIN FOR KING CHARLES 184 (1964).
48. *Id.* at 186.
49. *The Talk of the Town*, THE NEW YORKER 27 (23 May 1977).
50. Jordan v. De George, 341 U.S. 223, 241–42 (1951).
51. BICKEL, note 32 *supra*, at 30.
52. *Id.* at 23.
53. *Id.* at 18.
54. 18–19 (1977).
55. CONSTITUTIONALISM: ANCIENT AND MODERN 144–46 (rev. ed. 1947).
56. THE SECOND COMING, in THE COLLECTED POEMS OF W. B. YEATS (1956 ed.).
57. GOYA, CAPRICHOS.
58. SCOTT, THE LADY OF THE LAKE Canto IV, i (1810).
59. Olmstead v. United States, 277 U.S. 438, 479 (1928) (Brandeis, J., dissenting).

Index